Writing
Research Papers

A Complete Guide
Fifth Edition

Writing
Research Papers

A Complete Guide
Fifth Edition

James D. Lester
Austin Peay State University

Scott, Foresman and Company
Glenview, Illinois • London, England

Cover: Northbrook Public Library
1201 Cedar Lane, Northbrook, IL 60062

Also available:

Instructor's Manual to accompany *Writing Research Papers, Fifth Edition*

This may be obtained through a local Scott, Foresman representative or by writing to English Editor, College Division, Scott, Foresman and Company, 1900 E. Lake Avenue, Glenview, IL 60025.

Library of Congress Cataloging-in-Publication Data

Lester, James D.
   Writing research papers.

   Bibliography: p.
   Includes index.
   1. Report writing.   I. Title.
LB2369.L4   1986b   808'.02   86-24875
ISBN 0–673–18533–8 (pbk.)

        5 6—RRC—91 90 89 88

ACKNOWLEDGMENTS   P. 7,8   From Table of Contents and "Galaxies" index excerpt in *The Universe,* Revised Third Edition, by Isaac Asimov. Copyright © 1980 by Isaac Asimov. Reprinted by permission of Walker and Company. **P. 9**   "Flight, history of" from *The New Encyclopaedia Britannica, Micropaedia,* Volume IV, 1982. Copyright © 1982 by Encyclopaedia Britannica, Inc. Reprinted by permission. **P. 10**   From "Aerial Sports" from *The New Encyclopaedia Britannica, Macropaedia,* Volume 1, 1982. Copyright © 1982 by Encyclopaedia Britannica, Inc. Reprinted by permission. **P. 11,12**   Reproduced from Edition 18, *Dewey Decimal Classification and Relative Index* (1971), by permission of Forest Press Division, Lake Placid Education Foundation, owner of copyright. **P. 15**   Material from *Humanities Index,* April 1981–March 1982, p. 778. Copyright © 1981, 1982 by The H. W. Wilson Company. Reproduced by permission of the publisher.

Acknowledgments continued on page 280, which constitutes a legal extension of the copyright page.

PREFACE

No magic formulas exist for introducing students to the world of scholarly research—an enterprise many of them face with trepidation and bewilderment. What's more, the rules keep changing. The Modern Language Association, the American Psychological Association, and the Council of Biological Editors have all changed their documentation standards within the last few years. Nevertheless, *Writing Research Papers* has kept pace with these changes so you can be confident that your students are receiving up-to-date instruction and authentic guidelines on matters of form and style. This new edition of *Writing Research Papers* and its restructured Instructor's Manual provide you with numerous approaches, techniques, and exercises for teaching the research paper.

The Writing Process

This text follows a linear pattern: choosing a topic, conducting research, taking notes, writing a draft, and typing the finished paper. In general, that's the process most students follow. However, recent research in the writing process tells us new things about writing habits.

Not all students begin from a fixed point and work progressively in neat stages to a finished paper. Students in the same class start the project with different skills and abilities, and they progress in recursive stages that are full of starts and stops, new beginnings, dead ends, and other disruptive elements—such as books missing from the library and lost notes—until instructors eventually collect a set of uneven papers, some of excellent quality and others of mediocre quality and, perhaps, of mysterious origin.

This text addresses the writing process with constructive guidelines for the student writer. Despite the necessary tight boundaries on form and style, it encourages a student to be recursive in thinking through a problem, in researching the issues, and in writing the necessary notes and drafts. It also encourages students to synthesize information with their own ideas and to learn that writing has practical value for exploring an issue or problem. They learn that their own writing is an act of discovery, yet they can learn to base their opinions on a blend of evidence, not on one authority or on their personal feelings.

This new fifth edition of *Writing Research Papers* brings the idea of writing as a process to research paper writing. Prewriting activities receive detailed explanation to help students discover topics with which they have a connection and thus a commitment. An expanded Chapter 3, Taking Notes, describes a "writing situation" students can use to discover distinctive voices, purposes, and specific audiences so that ideas can be summarized and organized. They learn to paraphrase from sources and not merely to copy verbatim everything they find.

Writing Research Papers encourages students to write some sort of outline. Some instructors argue that outlining is passé, unnecessary, or limiting to the natural flow of writing, yet few writers can build well-organized research papers without some sort of map, whether it is a list of code words, a set of questions, or a formal outline.

The text encourages students to write personal note cards to express their opinions on a topic so that writing becomes one element of discovery. It suggests that they condense some sources with précis notes, yet encourages them to record information from other sources with paraphrased notes. Throughout, the text emphasizes a blending of the writer's thoughts with those of source materials so students can accomplish some of their writing in the note-taking stage.

Writing Research Papers does not abandon the student in the writing phase. It explains the long, recursive nature of drafting a paper and adapting content to meet the needs of an audience. It provides numerous guidelines for developing an introductory section, building the body of the paper, and ending with a real conclusion rather than merely summarizing or restating the thesis. A new section on revision explains the roles of revising a draft on a global basis, editing before typing the final manuscript, and proofreading the finished paper.

For courses that include shorter papers, two short sample research papers, which depend on a minimal number of sources, now supplement the full-length essay on child abuse. One is a literary paper in MLA style; the other is a short survey of social science literature in APA style. (*Note:* additional sample papers are provided in the new Instructor's Manual, discussed below.)

Writing Research Papers provides guidance to those students who now write with word processors. The storage and retrieval capacities of the computer change the way writers can work. Thus a new section of *WRP* develops ideas for entering notes and text, maintaining files, writing, merging, and revising the drafts, and printing the finished work.

In short, the text moves with the student from discovery of a topic to generating ideas and from note-taking to the writing and rewriting stages. It presents in-text citation of sources as a natural, ongoing process during note-taking and writing. The mechanical concerns of typing or organizing the Works Cited page are presented in Chapters 5 and 6 after the student has conquered the major problem of building a substantial paper.

A New List of Reference Sources

The appendix, which lists reference works by discipline, has been altered to direct students to four fundamental sources: general guides to research in the discipline, bibliographies, data bases, and indexes to journals. This arrangement enables students to dip first into encyclopedias, dictionaries, and general information books for their preliminary reading and then go to the list of bibliographies by discipline, plus the best indexes for their fields as they define their topics (e.g., a writer on an economics topic will be sent to *The Wall Street Journal Index,* but a political science student will be directed to *P.A.I.S.*). At those colleges where undergraduate students have access to data base sources, the appendix lists a few major ones for each discipline (e.g., BIOSIS PREVIEWS for biology or ENVIRONLINE for ecology).

A New Instructor's Manual

A new Instructor's Manual in 8½ by 11 format provides a set of in-class exercises for each chapter, plus several exercises for each chapter that you can photocopy and distribute to your students for independent work on special problems, and review exercises and posttests for each chapter. It also provides three additional sample papers, one on "Creative Marriages" in the new 1985 MLA style; one on "Creative Marriages" in APA style with an abstract and with a body adjusted to scientific reporting of introduction, method, results, and discussion; and a third paper on Hansberry's *A Raisin in the Sun* that uses the MLA footnote system for instructors who prefer that standard.

A Note on Research Manuals

The main body of the text, Chapters 1 through 6, conforms to standards approved by the Modern Language Association in their official text:

The MLA Style Manual. Ed. Walter W. Achtert and Joseph Gibaldi. New York: The Modern Language Association, 1985.

Basically, the Advisory Committee on Documentation Style of the MLA advocates in-text citation of source materials with no documentation footnotes. A "Works Cited" list provides full information on sources. This format conforms to standards in most other fields. Some historians and fine arts scholars still use the footnote style, yet many instructors in those fields have now adopted the format standards presented in *Writing Research Papers.*

Chapter 7 of the text explores several options in documentation style by describing the Name and Year System, the Number System, and the Footnote System. It explains the stipulations of several official style guides. The most widely used are:

Publication Manual of the American Psychological Association. 3rd ed. Washington, DC: APA, 1983.
Sets the standards for the popular APA style, used in the social sciences.

CBE Style Manual. 4th ed. Washington, DC: American Institute of Biological Sciences, 1983.

Sets standards for scientific papers.

A Manual of Style. 13th ed. revised. Chicago: U of Chicago P, 1982.

Sets standards for the traditional footnote style.

Chapter 7 also provides explanation of several other documentation methods, so students can write papers that conform to the official styles described in the *Handbook for Authors* for chemistry, *Style Manual* for physics, *A Manual for Authors of Mathematical Papers, Suggestions to Authors of the Reports of the United States Geological Survey,* and other specialized publications.

Acknowledgments

We celebrate the 20th anniversary of *Writing Research Papers* with this edition. About two million students have used the text since its publication in 1967. Hundreds of students, faculty, and editorial professionals have contributed to its success. Dick Welna and Verne Reaves of Scott, Foresman helped to launch the project years ago. Today editors Patricia Rossi and Carol Leon keep the tradition of excellence alive. My family, Martha, Jim, and Mark, has supported the project with unending enthusiasm and encouragement. Jim, now an English teacher in his own right, has actively participated by writing and proofreading various portions of the manuscript.

Several students deserve special mention: Pamela Howell, Glenda Durdin, Jon Ezell, Jo Walker, and Tommy Burchett. I also want to thank other students from different parts of the country who have sent me valuable tips and suggestions.

At Motlow State Community College Linda C. Rollins and Nancy G. Wright both provided valuable tips on revision of both the text and Instructor's Manual. The faculty of Austin Peay State University helped to revise the appendix's long list of reference sources. Other instructors around the country contributed valuable ideas and thoughts for this new edition: Edra Bogle, North Texas State University; Ronnie Lee Collins, Bowie State College; Keith W. Hamon, University of Houston; Shelby Lee, Broward Community College; and Nancy T. Zuercher, University of South Dakota.

James D. Lester

Contents

Introduction   xvii

1

Finding a Topic   1

DISCOVERING YOUR PURPOSE   *1*
An Argumentative Purpose   1
An Analytical Purpose   2
An Explanatory Purpose   2

GENERATING IDEAS AND
DISCOVERING A GENERAL SUBJECT   *3*
Using Personal Experience for Topic Discovery   3
Talking With Others to Find a Subject   4
Using Your Imagination to Develop a Topic   4
Using Source Materials for Topic Discovery   6
Search a Table of Contents to Find a Subject 7 • *Examine a Book's Index to Discover a
Subject 8* • *Scan an Encyclopedia Article When Searching for a Subject 8* • *Check the
Dewey Decimal Index 11* • *Examine the Library of Congress System 13* • *Search the
Headings in Periodical Indexes 15*

NARROWING THE GENERAL SUBJECT
TO A SPECIFIC TOPIC   *16*
Meeting the Needs of Your Audience   16
Determining Your Writing Situation   17
Developing a Preliminary Thesis   17
Narrowing and Focusing Comparison Topics   18
Restricting and Narrowing Disciplinary Topics   19
Narrowing the Topic to Match Source Materials   19

2

Gathering Data 20

GATHERING DATA IN THE LIBRARY   20
Library Organization   22
WORKING BIBLIOGRAPHY CARDS   23
Writing Basic Bibliography Cards   24
Recording Call Numbers at the Card Catalog   28
The Call Number   32
SEARCHING GENERAL BIBLIOGRAPHIES   33
Using the Bibliographies in General Reference Books   33
Using Bibliographic Index   33
Using Trade Bibliographies   34
SEARCHING GENERAL INDEXES   36
Indexes to Biographies, Dissertations, and Essays within Books   37
Indexes to the Literature in Periodicals   40
Newspaper Indexes   42
Searching the Pamphlet Indexes   43
USING THE SPECIALIZED INDEXES OF YOUR DISCIPLINE   44
SEARCHING GOVERNMENT DOCUMENTS   47
USING THE MICROFORMS   48
CONDUCTING A DATA BASE SEARCH   49
CITATION SEARCHING   50
SUPPLEMENTING LIBRARY MATERIALS AND COLLECTING DATA
OUTSIDE THE LIBRARY   54

3

Taking Notes 55

THE PRELIMINARY OUTLINE   55
Using Your Writing Situation   56
Roughing Out a Preliminary Outline   56
Using Questions to Outline Ideas   57
Outlining by Methods of Development   57
Ordering from General to Particular Items   57
Ordering from Particular to General Issues   58
Revising the Rough Outline During Research   58

EVALUATING YOUR SOURCE MATERIALS *59*
Use Recent Sources 59
Use Reliable Source Materials 59
Quote the Best Scholars 60
Use Relevant Source Materials 60
Examine the Book Reviews 61
Understanding What You Read 63
Getting the Author's Idea 64
Understanding the Difference between Primary and Secondary Sources 65

TECHNIQUE OF NOTE CARDS *66*

METHODS OF NOTE-TAKING *67*
Building a Set of Personal Note Cards 67
Writing Summary Notes 68
Writing Plot Summaries and Review Notes 69
Condensing Sources with Précis Notes 70
Rewriting Sources with Paraphrased Notes 72
Copying Sources with Quotation Notes 74
Writing Notes into a Computer 76

AVOIDING PLAGIARISM *77*
Purpose of Documentation of Source Materials 77
An Explanation of Plagiarism 78
Common Knowledge Exceptions 81

4

Writing the Paper 82

WRITING A FINAL THESIS SENTENCE *82*

WRITING A TITLE *84*

WRITING A FINAL OUTLINE *84*
Use Standard Outline Symbols 84
Use Balanced and Parallel Form 85
Use Content-Oriented Headings 86
List the Thesis Sentence Separately above the Outline 87
Use Dynamic Order with the Outline 87

CHOOSING A FINAL OUTLINE FORM *87*
Topic Outline 87
Sentence Outline 88
Paragraph Outline 89

REVIEWING YOUR NOTES AND PREPARING TO WRITE   *89*
Reviewing the Thesis Sentence and Outline   90
Reviewing Your Approach to the Topic   90
Using Basic Formulas as Paradigms for Papers in Special Fields   91

DRAFTING THE PAPER   *94*
Adjusting to the Long, Recursive Nature of Research Writing   94
Remembering Your Audience as You Write   95
Adapting Your Language to Your Purpose and Audience   95
Writing in Third Person and First Person Voice   96
Writing with Unity and Coherence   96
Writing in the Proper Tense   97

WRITING AN INTRODUCTION   *98*
Opening with Your Thesis Statement   99
Relating to the Well Known   99
Providing Background Information   100
Reviewing the Literature   100
Reviewing and Quoting the Literature   101
Taking Exception to Critical Views   101
Challenging an Assumption   102
Providing a Brief Summary   102
Supplying Data, Statistics, and Special Evidence   102
Defining Key Terms   103
Avoiding Certain Mistakes in the Opening   103

WRITING THE BODY OF YOUR PAPER   *103*
Strategies of Writing   104

WRITING THE CONCLUSION OF YOUR PAPER   *105*
Restate the Thesis and Reach Beyond It   105
Close With an Effective Quotation   105
Return the Focus of a Literary Study to the Author   106
Compare Past to Present   106
Offer a Directive or Solution   107
Discussion of Test Results   107
Avoiding Certain Mistakes in the Conclusion   108

BLENDING REFERENCE MATERIALS INTO YOUR WRITING   *108*
Provide Both Name of Authority and Page Number   108
Punctuate Quotations Accurately   111
Provide Extra Information within Citations If Necessary   113
Handling Frequent Page References to the Same Work   114
Omitting Parenthetical Citation for Nonprint Sources   115
Handling Long Quotations of Prose and Poetry   115
Alter Initial Capitals in Some Quoted Matter   117
Use Ellipsis Points to Omit Portions of Quoted Matter   118
Use Brackets to Insert Your Words Inside Quoted Matter   120

REVISING, EDITING, AND PROOFREADING   *121*

Revising Your First Draft   121

Editing Before You Type the Final Manuscript   122

Editing to Avoid Discriminatory Language   123

Proofreading the Final Typed Manuscript before Submitting It   124

WRITING WITH WORD PROCESSORS   *125*

Storing and Retrieving Notes, Documents, and Bibliography Sources   125

Entering Your Text into a Computer   125

Revising Your First Draft   126

Proofreading the Final Printout   127

5

Handling the Format and Mechanics of Your Paper   128

PREPARING THE FINAL MANUSCRIPT   *128*

Title Page or Opening Page   128

Outline   130

Abstract   130

The Text of the Paper   131

Content Endnotes Pages   131

Appendix   131

Works Cited Page   131

HANDLING GENERAL TECHNICALITIES OF PREPARING THE MANUSCRIPT   *132*

Abbreviations 132 • Acknowledgments 133 • Ampersand 133 • Annotated Bibliography 133 • Apostrophe 134 • Arabic Numerals 134 • Asterisks 135 • Bible 135 • Capitalization 136 • Content Endnotes 138 • Copyright law 141 • Definitions 141 • Endnotes for Documentation of Sources 141 • Enumeration of Items 141 • Etc. 142 • Footnotes for Documentation 142 • Foreign Cities 142 • Foreign Languages 142 • Headings 143 • Illustrations and Tables 143 • Indention 147 • Italics 147 • Length of the Research Paper 147 • Margins 147 • Monetary Units 148 • Names of Persons 148 • Numbering (Pagination) 148 • Paper 148 • Percentages 149 • Postal Abbreviations 149 • Punctuation 150 • Roman Numerals 152 • Running Heads 152 • Shakespearean Plays 152 • Short Titles in the Text 153 • Slang 153 • Spacing 153 • Spelling 153 • Statistical and Mathematical Copy 153 • Superscript Numerals in the Text 154 • Table of Contents 154 • Typing 154 • Underlining Titles 154 • Underlining for Emphasis 155 • Word Division 155

SAMPLE PAPER: A SHORT ESSAY WITH DOCUMENTATION   *155*

SAMPLE PAPER: THE FORMAL RESEARCH PAPER WITH OUTLINE AND CONTENT NOTES   *160*

6

Works Cited 183

FORMAT FOR "WORKS CITED" PAGE *184*

BIBLIOGRAPHY FORM—BOOKS *185*

SAMPLE BIBLIOGRAPHY ENTRIES—BOOKS *189*

BIBLIOGRAPHY FORM—PERIODICALS *198*

SAMPLE BIBLIOGRAPHY ENTRIES—PERIODICALS *199*

BIBLIOGRAPHY FORM—NEWSPAPERS *202*

BIBLIOGRAPHY FORM—GOVERNMENT DOCUMENTS *203*

BIBLIOGRAPHY FORM—OTHER SOURCES *204*

7

Form and Style for Other Disciplines 210

GUIDE TO DOCUMENTATION SYSTEMS *211*

THE NAME AND YEAR SYSTEM *211*

SAMPLE PAPER IN APA STYLE *214*

Social Sciences *220*

Psychology 220 • *Sociology and Political Science 221* • *Education 222* • *Home Economics 223* • *Linguistics 223* • *Physical Education 224*

Biological and Earth Sciences *224*

Agriculture 224 • *Anthropology/Archaeology 225* • *Astronomy 226* • *Biology/Botany/Zoology 226* • *Geology 228*

Business and Economics *229*

THE NUMBER SYSTEM *231*

Applied Sciences *232*

Chemistry 232 • *Computer Science 233* • *Mathematics 234* • *Physics 235*

Medical Sciences *236*

Health/Medicine/Nursing 236

THE FOOTNOTE SYSTEM *237*

Humanities *240*

History/Philosophy/Religion/Theology 240

Fine Arts *242*

Art/Dance/Music/Theater 242

Appendix

List of Reference Sources by Discipline   245

Art   245
Biological Sciences   246
Business   247
Chemistry and Chemical Engineering   247
Computer Science   248
Economics   249
Ecology   249
Education   250
Electronics   250
Ethnic Studies   251
Geography   252
Geology   253
Health and Physical Education   253
History   254
Journalism/Mass Communications   255
Language and Literature   255
Foreign Languages   259
Mathematics   260
Medical Studies   261
Music   262
Philosophy   262
Political Science   263
Physics   264
Psychology   264
Religion   265
Sociology and Social Work   266
Speech   266
Women's Studies   267

Index   269

INTRODUCTION

RATIONALE FOR RESEARCH WRITING

As you begin this important task of writing a research paper, you may feel inadequate, even overwhelmed, about dealing with the assignment—ten or more typewritten pages with all sorts of documentation rules! This writing manual will help you with its step-by-step explanation of the writing process—from selecting a significant topic all the way down to typing the final draft.

Keep in mind that the process of creating a long, scholarly paper is not always neat and logical but can be chaotic and disorganized. In general, it is best to follow the order of this text—choose a topic, gather data, plan and write a draft, revise and polish the manuscript, and develop a final bibliography. However, in actual practice this order will disappear at times as you work backwards and forwards in starts and stops. This text will help you stay on track by providing guidelines, formulas, and examples.

Approach the research paper assignment one step at a time. You will develop confidence as you complete each step. Confidence lets you write essays that do more than merely repeat lecture notes or duplicate paragraphs from books and articles. You will discover your own ideas and generate new ones. You will be able to defend your position with the weight of your arguments and the strength of the evidence you have gathered from sources.

You will become adept at the following:

1. Narrowing your focus on an issue to a manageable topic that addresses the problem for your special audience,
2. Locating source materials and taking notes,
3. Analyzing, evaluating, and interpreting materials,
4. Arranging and classifying materials,
5. Writing the paper with a sense of purpose as well as with clarity and accuracy,
6. Handling problems of quoting and properly documenting your sources according to MLA (Modern Language Association) style.

This text will carry you through all these stages beginning with the first step in Chapter 1—finding a suitable topic that has merit as a scholarly issue or research question. Take your time in selecting a topic because a poor one will cause untold anguish for weeks and weeks, while a good one will pave the way to significant research and quality writing.

Chapters 2 and 3 carry you into library research and note card gathering. Included is a section about plagiarism, which is not a disease but a curse that afflicts many students who think proper scholarly credit is unnecessary, or who become confused about proper placement of references.

Chapter 4 will train you to handle quoted and paraphrased materials, a task which often baffles even experienced writers. How do you distinguish comments drawn from the source materials from your own ideas and thoughts? *Writing Research Papers* will provide guidelines and plenty of examples.

Matters of format and the technicalities of numbers, margins, spacing, and so on are treated in Chapter 5. This text offers answers and models for all your questions—from design of the title page to the minor issues of entering dates, underlining titles, and numbering the pages.

Chapter 6 introduces you to the format of bibliography entries. It explains the form of individual entries for your list of references so that you can fully document the sources used in writing the paper. Chapter 7 introduces the APA (American Psychological Association) style along with styles for other disciplines. The chapter correlates the similarities of the MLA style with that used in other disciplines such as psychology, biology, or geology. Your training in the MLA style of this text is not dissimilar to the APA style or the CBE (Council of Biological Editors) style.

Finally, the appendix contains an exhaustive list of reference works and journals (by subject) to be consulted as you begin research in a particular discipline, be it psychology, home economics, or drama. These reference works will trigger your exploration of issues in numerous fields of study.

1

Finding a Topic

DISCOVERING YOUR PURPOSE

The first step in writing a research paper is to determine the purpose of your research for a specific field. An instructor may assign a topic and relieve you of worries about topic discovery, but most instructors expect you to participate in the search for a narrowed and worthy topic. You will need to discover, with the instructor's input, whether the study will interpret a piece of literature, analyze a sociological issue, or generate technical and statistical data for a scientific report.

Simply needing to fill up ten pages is not a purpose that leads to good research. You cannot copy copiously from sources without developing your own position. You must develop a *purpose* for your research if you want to end up with an effective and satisfying paper. Your purpose should be defined by your own interests, the needs of your reader (who is not just your instructor), or the demands of an employer or a business associate.

An Argumentative Purpose

Write an argumentative paper to convince a specific audience of your point. More so than other modes, this one demands your careful identification of the audience, who might be, for example, the city officials who have failed to provide sufficient parks and playgrounds, or perhaps the feminists who endorse equal pay, or even critics of Shakespearean drama who would portray Hamlet as a wimpy, romantic weakling. In effect, your purpose extends beyond investigation to making judgments about the issue at hand.

Of course, you must arrive at these judgments after careful research into primary and secondary materials. For example, condemning child abuse is inadequate because you have only a universal audience that agrees with you. Instead, you will need to reach into the issues and cite evidence to argue perhaps for broad powers to police and social workers so that they can enter homes to prevent abuse before it occurs. Now you would have an argument on your hands with pro/con issues and a divided audience, because some readers will not want the sanctity of the family unit invaded by public officials.

Argumentative papers are controversial to various degrees and therefore require careful research into all sides of the issues and fair presentation of the fruits of that research. Bias and prejudice will be your enemies here, not your allies, for the scholarly research paper should be reasonable, not strident, cautious in assertions, not rash, and full of careful assimilation and presentation of evidence. The reader of a research paper is an intellectual who asks for sound reasoning and documented evidence. Your voice will need the ring of quiet authority if it is to be convincing.

An Analytical Purpose

Instructors often require papers that ask you to draw general conclusions from facts and basic evidence. Your purpose in this case becomes one of analysis: you must separate the issues, comment on each one, and arrive, finally, at a synthesis. For example, you might classify and examine the stages of hypnosis as a treatment for nail biting or smoking.

In brief, your purpose is to analyze component parts so that you arrive at meanings, causes, or consequences. Thus, your analysis of incidents of child abuse during times of high unemployment could lead to conclusions about the unfortunate effects of an economic depression upon children. Similarly, you might examine the vocabulary of native speakers in one isolated geographical area in order to arrive at general conclusions about dialects or speech patterns.

An Explanatory Purpose

The explanatory purpose serves those who review books or articles. The *article précis* and book review summarize and briefly discuss one work in order to explain its contribution to a particular field of knowledge. The *literature review paper* surveys available source materials on a narrowed topic by providing (1) an annotated bibliography that lists works with brief commentaries on each, or (2) a formal essay which compares published works on the topic, examines prevailing theories, and explains the contributions of various writers in the field. A review paper is not a full-blown research paper, but it does serve researchers during preliminary stages.

The report of *empirical research* is a general term to describe papers based on experience and experiment. For example, a psychological researcher might *test* human behavior or an educator might *observe* human behavior. The explanatory report introduces a hypothetical problem, explains methods for conducting the test, gives results, and discusses the findings. The purpose of *applied research* is the discovery of new uses or new applications of a product or idea. An applied researcher starts with somebody else's work and applies it to a new area. For example, the isolation of a germ cell may be useless until somebody connects the germ cell with cancer growth. The purpose of *market research* is to develop information about products and services to customers. For example, market research has produced a vast array of soap products—from bar soap to soap flakes to liquid soap—all to satisfy the demands of soap users. *Technical research* produces information to serve as the basis for executive decisions about production, personnel needs, or space requirements. In particular, one economics student studied the traffic patterns at one intersection to determine its feasibility as the location for a fast-food outlet. The purpose of a *computer-generated research paper* is to control data. The computer lets you store, sort, and retrieve vast amounts of data and thus has value for statistical research.

GENERATING IDEAS AND DISCOVERING A GENERAL SUBJECT

To locate a good research subject, writers often use four exercises: they reflect on personal experience, they talk with other people, they stretch their imaginations, and they read source materials. These four activities can stimulate your thinking for all stages of research. Above all, you need to avoid unimaginative approaches, such as copying a statement from an encyclopedia and calling it a topic, or using an expert's quotation as a thesis without understanding the issues of the subject.

Using Personal Experience for Topic Discovery

Writers' special interests can help them narrow a general subject to a paper-topic size. Assume, for instance, that three writers all select the same general subject—latchkey children. The first writer combines an interest in crime to focus on dangers for latchkey children who must return from school to empty houses and apartments. Another student combines an interest in television to investigate programming during after-school hours for the lonely child. The third writer combines a major in economics with a study of latchkey children and conducts a cost/benefit analysis of different child-care options for schoolchildren. The three writers use personal concerns to guide them through discussions of the same topic.

Talking With Others to Find a Subject

Research often starts with talking to fellow investigators, instructors, friends, and even relatives. Ask people in your school and community for ideas and leads to topics needing investigation. One writer, for example, decided to argue for more liberal arts courses in high school curriculums. Before spending hours reading in the library, however, she talked with her former high school teachers. She discovered that a liberal arts curriculum was in place; the problem was something different—how to motivate students toward liberal arts courses in a marketplace which demands utilitarian skills such as typing, auto mechanics, or computer programming. To that end, the writer developed a different sort of paper, all because she took time to communicate with others. Researchers sometimes need to start their research on a park bench rather than at the card catalog.

Using Your Imagination
to Develop a Topic

The research paper requires mental exercise in search of answers. Source materials and conversations with others can help you find and narrow a topic, but you also need to sit back, relax, and speculate on issues. Out of that meditation may come topic possibilities. One writer speculated on Ernest Hemingway's novel *The Old Man and the Sea,* especially the author's portrayal of Santiago as a long-suffering man. He connected Santiago with the biblical Job and also considered Santiago as a Christ figure. These thoughts, in combination with ideas gained by reading source materials, eventually narrowed the issues to a workable topic, "The Suffering Man: Christ, Job, and Santiago."

Another writer chose the topic "Taxation." After brief critical reading and speculation she discovered the severance tax, which is levied on timber, oil, and minerals when they are taken from the earth. She considered both the benefits of taxation and problems of environmental damage before advancing a thesis: eliminating or reducing the severance tax could cause environmental abuse.

Here are some other ways to generate ideas:

Free Write. To free write, merely focus on a topic and write whatever comes to mind. Keep writing with your mind on the topic. Do not worry about style or penmanship. The result? Writing has started! The exercise requires non-stop writing for a page or so to develop valuable phrases, comparisons, episodes, and specific thoughts that help focus issues of concern. Note this brief example:

> Child abuse? Does that mean abuse of children by adults or children who abuse others? I have abused my folks on occasion. Oh, I didn't hit them or anything like that, but I took advantage of Mom's love and Dad's generosity. I can recall getting my way by crying, sulking, and--yes--even lying. Maybe I could write about children who abuse their parents--at least that's a different look at the subject of child abuse.

This rough paragraph focuses the student's topic for library reading and note-taking.

List Key Words. During preliminary reading keep a sharp eye out for fundamental terms and concepts that might focus the direction of your research. For instance, the subject "Roads and Highways" might produce the preliminary words *interstate system, primary highway, local road, intersection, bypass, toll road,* or *bridge.* Such words flag items of interest so that "toll roads" might become your primary subject.

Outline Issues. Connect a topic's subissues with an outline, that, like a tree, has developing branches of ideas, issues, and topics:

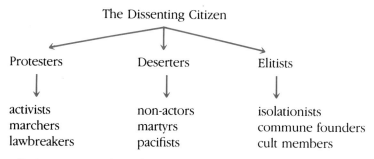

The Dissenting Citizen

Protesters	Deserters	Elitists
activists	non-actors	isolationists
marchers	martyrs	commune founders
lawbreakers	pacifists	cult members

This preliminary, incomplete plan generates ideas by testing connections and relationships. It exposes weaknesses in major and minor divisions of the initial plan. In all likelihood, this writer would narrow to one division—perhaps elitists who withdraw from society into their own private circle.

Ask Questions.   Stretch your imagination with questions. Some may have ready answers and others may need investigation:

How is dissent defined?
Who benefits?
Is dissent legal? Is it moral? Is it patriotic?
Should dissent be encouraged by the government? Stifled?
Is dissent a liberal activity? Conservative?
What is "civil disobedience"?

The list (which could continue) stimulates thinking. Some questions will never be answered; others will lead to a central issue and a thesis statement to govern the entire project.

Another method frames questions by rhetorical modes, as illustrated:

Comparison:	How does a state lottery compare with horse racing?
Definition:	What is a lottery in legal terms? In religious terms?
Cause/Effect:	What are the consequences of a state lottery on funding for education, highways, prisons, and social programs?
Process:	What are one's chances of winning?
Classification:	What types of lotteries exist and which are available in this state?
Evaluation:	What is the value of lotteries to the average citizen? What are the disadvantages?

Any one question can define a key research issue or prompt an issue outline.

Using Source Materials for Topic Discovery

Critical reading of sources will help you reach beyond your experience and dip into the knowledge of others. A history text, reference book, biography, journal article—all can contribute to your understanding of background issues and fundamental problems. Preliminary reading opens the door to a special topic, such as *childhood trauma* for a psychological study, *automobile emissions control* for an environmental paper, or *character development* in Robert Browning's dramatic poems for a literature study.

This early reading may include primary sources of direct evidence, such as novels, letters, interviews, and case studies, but most of it will consist of essays in books and journals by experts in the field, called secondary sources. This preliminary investigation precedes serious note-taking, but keeping a record of good information would certainly be in order.

SEARCH A TABLE OF CONTENTS TO FIND A SUBJECT

A book's table of contents should itemize the many subject areas of your topic. Note below "Herschel's Lens" under Chapter 4, "The Galaxy," in this table of contents:

Fig. 1: Table of Contents from *The Universe* by Isaac Asimov

Table of Contents:

CHAPTER 1 — *The Earth*

Introduction	1
The Flat Earth	2
The Spherical Earth	4
The Size of the Earth	7

CHAPTER 2 — *The Solar System*

The Moon	11
The Sun	14
Parallax	17
The Size of the Solar System	21

CHAPTER 3 — *The Stars*

The Vault of the Sky	27
A Multiplicity of Suns	33
The Search for Stellar Parallax	35
The Distance of the Nearer Stars	39

CHAPTER 4 — *The Galaxy*

Olbers' Paradox	43
Herschel's Lens	46
The Moving Sun	49
Star Clusters	52
Variable Stars	54

Major areas stand out boldly with subtopics. Investigation of page 46, "Herschel's Lens," could excite your curiosity about Sir William Herschel (1738–1822) who, it turns out, was a pioneer in astronomy. He developed a lens that enabled him to discover the planet Uranus. Focusing on some aspect of Herschel and his career would be one method of narrowing the scope of research to a specific, manageable topic.

EXAMINE A BOOK'S INDEX TO DISCOVER A SUBJECT

Most books contain an index which lists alphabetically the book's contents. Such listings have investigative possibilities, as with "colliding" or "exploding" galaxies found in the index below:

Fig. 2: Index from *The Universe* by Isaac Asimov

```
Galaxies
    antimatter and, 257
    classes of, 176-178
    clusters of, 194-195, 284, 300-301
    colliding, 288
    continuous formation of, 224-225
    distances of, 188, 201-203
    electric charge on, 224
    expanding Universe and, 193
    exploding, 288-293
    gravitation and, 193-194
    microwave energies of, 288-298
    number of, 93, 198 199
    peculiar, 290
    radio, 288-298
    recession of, 185-188, 209, 224-229
    red shift of, 185-188
    spectral class of, 178-179
    structure of, 93-94
    x-ray, 250
```

A logical follow-up involves reading the designated pages to consider issues and to find a general subject. Also, feel free to shift topics during this stage; for example, investigation of "microwave energies" or "X-ray" might change your focus from galaxies and astronomy to microwave and X-ray technology in homes and factories.

SCAN AN ENCYCLOPEDIA ARTICLE WHEN SEARCHING FOR A SUBJECT

Encyclopedia articles point to specific topics because they list numerous details on the subject in summary fashion. Ten minutes or so spent reading an encyclopedia article might easily produce two or three possible topics. Note especially the index entry for "aerial sport development and form, **1**:123h":

flight, history of 7:380.   Transportation above the Earth's surface in any form of craft, though first realized by 18th-century balloonists, has had its entire main development in the form of powered, heavier-than-air machines, in the 20th century.

The text article is divided into seven sections: (1) flight in man's imagination; (2) the development of balloons, airships, gliders, models, and kites through the 19th century; (3) the momentous developments from 1900 to 1914; the introduction of the gasoline engine; the contributions of the Wright brothers and others; and helicopter, balloon, airship, and parachute developments; (4) the rapid advances brought by World War I; (5) developments from 1918 to 1930; (6) developments from 1930 to 1945, including those in commercial aviation; private flying and air racing; military aviation; and research; (7) developments since 1945; commercial aviation including development of jet propulsion; general aviation, including private and special uses; military aviation; flight research; and the forseeable future.

REFERENCES in other text articles:
*aerial sport development and form **1**:123h
*aeronautical engineering development **1**:129e
*aerospace industry history **1**:132g
*aircraft design and aerodynamics **1**:370d
*air transport history and development **18**:633a
*Antarctic explorations **1**:962h
*automatic pilot invention **8**:525e
*aviation and space medicine origins **1**:144h
*Goddard's space flight experiments **8**:222g
*hurricane structure and flight patterns **9**:64a
*jet plane development and engine
     design **10**:156b
*life-support system development **10**:918d
*Lindbergh nonstop New York–Paris
     flight **10**:991g
*military aircraft technical development **1**:383b
*military engineering history **6**:864f
*modern aircraft development
     influences **18**:657b
*Montgolfier brothers' balloons **12**:409g
*natural prototypes of aircraft ideas **2**:1032g
*navigational methods and
     instruments **12**:903d
*radio installation in aircraft **15**:427a
*Sikorsky's helicopter development **16**:750e
*technological developments in the
     1900s **18**:48h
*warfare and tactical use of aircraft 19:585e
*Wright brothers' experiments and
     impact **19**:1032b

RELATED ENTRIES in the *Ready Reference and Index:*
aeronautical engineering; aircraft; airship;
autogiro; biplane; glider; ornithopter; Spirit of
Saint Louis

The entry above from the *Micropaedia* of *Encyclopaedia Britannica* suggests numerous subtopics on "flight" with specific directions, "1:123h," for finding a full article in the *Macropaedia,* as follows:

Fig. 4: Entry
from the
Macropaedia of
*Encyclopaedia
Britannica*

Aerial Sports

Aerial sports have a fundamental position in aviation and encompass the true origins of aviation. Individuals in the 1800s and early 1900s imagined, contrived, and developed contraptions that would enable them to experience the unique sensation of being airborne. The development of aircraft for commercial and military purposes came much later. Flight was founded in sport, and sport flying still thrives.

The Fédération Aéronautique Internationale was founded in Paris in 1905 to encourage the progress of world aeronautics. It has long exercised general supervision over most phases of aerial sport, certifying world records and sanctioning international competition. It includes national federations from more than 50 countries in its membership.

This article is intended for the general reader who may have no knowledge of the activities described. It deals chiefly with the four most popular varieties of aerial sport—power-plane sports, soaring (or gliding), sport parachuting (skydiving), and sport ballooning—sketching the history and present status of each. For more detailed information on specific activities, the reader should consult the works listed in the bibliography.

BIBLIOGRAPHY. LINN EMRICH, *The Complete Book of Sky Sports* (1970), an instructional text on the fundamentals of flight in five categories: soaring, parachuting, hot-air ballooning, gyrocopters, and power planes; CARL CONWAY, *Joy of Soaring* (1969), a complete modern training manual on sailplane flying; P.M. BOWERS, *Guide to Homebuilts* (1962), a guide to the history, design, construction, testing, costs, and material sources for homebuilt aircraft, *Antique Plane Guide* (1962), a comprehensive study on the identification, restoration, costs, material and data sources for antique planes; DON VORDERMAN, *The Great Air Races* (1969), a fascinating resume of prominent planes, pilots, and air races since 1909; DUANE COLE, *Roll Around a Point* (1965), an instructional text on how to perform aerobatics by a world authority.

Periodicals: Sailplane and Gliding (bimonthly), official organ of the British Gliding Association; *Soaring* (monthly), a publication of the Soaring Society of America; *Parachutist* (monthly), publication of the U.S. Parachute Association; *National Aeronautics* (quarterly), official publication of the U.S. National Aeronautic Association. See also *Popular Rotorcraft Flying* (bimonthly), *Sport Flying* (monthly), *Motorgliding* (monthly), *Antique Airplane News* (monthly), *Sport Aviation* (monthly), and *Ballooning* (quarterly).

(L.E.)

The brief article suggests possible topics and its bibliography provides references. You can have a narrowed topic and a list of several books on the subject rather quickly.

CHECK THE DEWEY DECIMAL INDEX

If your s is a free-choice topic, the basic 100 divisions of the *Dewey Decimal Classification and Relative Index* will suggest several broad areas for topic selection:

Fig. 5: From the Dewey Decimal Classification and Relative Index

Second Summary *
The 100 Divisions

000	**Generalities**	500	**Pure sciences**
010	Bibliographies & catalogs	510	Mathematics
020	Library & information sciences	520	Astronomy & allied sciences
030	General encyclopedic works	530	Physics
040		540	Chemistry & allied sciences
050	General serial publications	550	Sciences of earth & other worlds
060	General organizations & museology	560	Paleontology
070	Journalism, publishing, newspapers	570	Life sciences
080	General collections	580	Botanical sciences
090	Manuscripts & book rarities	590	Zoological sciences
100	**Philosophy & related disciplines**	600	**Technology (Applied sciences)**
110	Metaphysics	610	Medical sciences
120	Knowledge, cause, purpose, man	620	Engineering & allied operations
130	Popular & parapsychology, occultism	630	Agriculture & related
140	Specific philosophical viewpoints	640	Domestic arts & sciences
150	Psychology	650	Managerial services
160	Logic	660	Chemical & related technologies
170	Ethics (Moral philosophy)	670	Manufactures
180	Ancient, medieval, Oriental	680	Miscellaneous manufactures
190	Modern Western philosophy	690	Buildings
200	**Religion**	700	**The arts**
210	Natural religion	710	Civic & landscape art
220	Bible	720	Architecture
230	Christian doctrinal theology	730	Plastic arts Sculpture
240	Christian moral & devotional	740	Drawing, decorative & minor arts
250	Local church & religious orders	750	Painting & paintings
260	Social & ecclesiastical theology	760	Graphic arts Prints
270	History & geography of church	770	Photography & photographs
280	Christian denominations & sects	780	Music
290	Other religions & comparative	790	Recreational & performing arts
300	**The social sciences**	800	**Literature (Belles-lettres)**
310	Statistics	810	American literature in English
320	Political science	820	English & Anglo-Saxon literatures
330	Economics	830	Literatures of Germanic languages
340	Law	840	Literatures of Romance languages
350	Public administration	850	Italian, Romanian, Rhaeto-Romanic
360	Social pathology & services	860	Spanish & Portuguese literatures
370	Education	870	Italic languages literatures Latin
380	Commerce	880	Hellenic languages literatures
390	Customs & folklore	890	Literatures of other languages
400	**Language**	900	**General geography & history**
410	Linguistics	910	General geography Travel
420	English & Anglo-Saxon languages	920	General biography & genealogy
430	Germanic languages German	930	General history of ancient world
440	Romance languages French	940	General history of Europe
450	Italian, Romanian, Rhaeto-Romanic	950	General history of Asia
460	Spanish & Portuguese languages	960	General history of Africa
470	Italic languages Latin	970	General history of North America
480	Hellenic Classical Greek	980	General history of South America
490	Other languages	990	General history of other areas

* Consult schedules for complete and exact headings

If item 500, "Pure Sciences," looks interesting, then look to the "520" category on "Astronomy and allied sciences."

**Fig. 6: Broad
Subject Areas**

> **520 Astronomy & allied sciences**
> 521   Theoretical astronomy
> 522   Practical & spherical astronomy
> 523   Descriptive astronomy
> 524
> 525   Earth (Astronomical geography)
> 526   Mathematical geography
> 527   Celestial navigation
> 528   Ephemerides (Nautical almanacs)
> 529   Chronology (Time)

These broad subject areas will require further narrowing toward a topic. You must move to a specific numbered item, such as "523 Descriptive Astronomy":

**Fig. 7:
Numbered Items**

> 523   **Descriptive astronomy**
>
> Including quasars, pulsars, zodiac
>
> Class here comprehensive works on specific celestial bodies, groupings, phenomena
>
> Use 523.001–523.009 for standard subdivisions, classing planetariums [*formerly* 523.28] in 523.0074
>
> Class "earth" sciences of other worlds in 550
>
> *For theoretical astronomy, see 521.5–521.8*
>
> .01   Astrophysics
>
> Physics and chemistry of celestial bodies and phenomena
>
> .013   Heat
>
> Add to 523.013 the numbers following 536 in 536.1–536.7, e.g., heat transfer 523.0132
>
> .015   Visible light and paraphotic phenomena
>
> Add to 523.015 the numbers following 535 in 535.01–535.89, e.g., ultraviolet radiation 523.015014
>
> [.016–.017]   Radio and radar astronomy
>
> Class in 522.68
>
> .018   Electricity and magnetism
>
> Add to 523.018 the numbers following 53 in 537–538, e.g., magnetism 523 0188
>
> .019   Molecular, atomic, nuclear physics
>
> Add to 523.019 the numbers following 539 in 539.1–539.7, e.g., cosmic rays 523.0197223

EXAMINE THE LIBRARY OF CONGRESS SYSTEM

Major categories of this system follow (in particular, note "Q Science"):

LIBRARY OF CONGRESS CLASSIFICATION SCHEDULES

For sale by the Cataloging Distribution Service, Library of Congress, Building 159, Navy Yard Annex, Washington, D.C. 20541, to which inquiries on current availability and price should be addressed.

A	General Works
B-BJ	Philosophy. Psychology
BL-BX	Religion
C	Auxiliary Sciences of History
D	History: General and Old World (Eastern Hemisphere)
E-F	History: America (Western Hemisphere)
G	Geography. Maps. Anthropology. Recreation
H	Social Sciences
J	Political Science
K	Law (General)
KD	Law of the United Kingdom and Ireland
KE	Law of Canada
KF	Law of the United States
L	Education
M	Music
N	Fine Arts
P-PA	General Philology and Linguistics. Classical Languages and Literatures
PA Supplement	Byzantine and Modern Greek Literature. Medieval and Modern Latin Literature
PB-PH	Modern European Languages
PG	Russian Literature
PJ-PM	Languages and Literatures of Asia, Africa, Oceania. American Indian Languages. Artifical Languages
P-PM Supplement	Index to Languages and Dialects
PN, PR, PS, PZ	General Literature. English and American Literature. Fiction in English. Juvenile Belles Lettres
PQ Part 1	French Literature
PQ Part 2	Italian, Spanish, and Portuguese Literatures
PT Part 1	German Literature
PT Part 2	Dutch and Scandinavian Literatures
Q	Science
R	Medicine
S	Agriculture
T	Technology
U	Military Science
V	Naval Science
Z	Bibliography. Library Science

These general categories, subdivided into specific areas, provide numerous topic suggestions, especially when you explore further into the "Q Science" category:

Fig. 9: Specific Areas

QB		Astronomy
	140-237	Practical and spherical astronomy
	275-343	Geodesy
	349-421	Theoretical astronomy and celestial mechanics
		Including perturbations, tides
	460-465	Astrophysics
	468-479	Non-optical methods of astronomy
	500-991	Descriptive astronomy
		Including stellar spectroscopy, cosmogony

Another entry narrows further:

Fig. 10: Narrowed Topic

```
                              .                                    QB
                        ASTRONOMY

                 Popular works
      44             Through 1969
       .2            1970-
      45         Elementary textbooks
      46         Juvenile works
                     Cf. QB63, Stargazers' guides
      47         Special aspects of the subject as a whole
      51         Addresses, essays, lectures
       .5        Astronomy as a profession
      52         Miscellany and curiosa
      54         Extraterrestrial life
     (55)        Astronomical myths, legends, and superstitions, see GR625
      61         Study and teaching.  Research
      62             Outlines, syllabi
       .5            Problems, exercises, examinations
       .7            Laboratory manuals
      63         Stargazers' guides
      64         Observers' handbooks
                     Cf. TL796.8, Artificial satellites
      65         Atlases and charts
      66         Astronomical globes
                     Cf. GA12, Manual for globes
      67         Miscellaneous models
      68         Pictorial works and atlases
      70         Planetaria
                     Including orreries
                     Subarranged like Q105
                 Observatories
      81             General works
      82             By region or country, A-Z
                         Under each country:
                         .x   General works
                         .x2  Individual observatories.  By name, A-Z
                                  Including description, history, annual
                                  reports, etc.
      84             Observatory buildings
                         Including domes, piers, rising floors, chairs
```

Another classification, *Library of Congress: Subject Headings,* categorizes subtopics; note a portion of the entry for "flight":

Fig. 11: From the *Library of Congress: Subject Headings*

Flight   *(Bird flight. QL698; Mechanics of
              flight. TL570-578)*
     sa Aeronautics
          Animal flight
          Flying-machines
          Stability of airplanes
          Wings
      x Flying
     xx Aeronautics
          Locomotion
          Wings
     — Medical aspects
          See Aviation medicine
     — Physiological aspects   *(RC1075)*
       x Aviation physiology
          Physiological aspects of flight
      xx Aviation medicine
          Aviation toxicology
     — — Age factors
     — Psychological aspects
          See Aeronautics—Psychology
  Flight, Unpowered
     See Gliding and soaring
  Flight attendants
     See Air lines—Flight attendants

SEARCH THE HEADINGS IN PERIODICAL INDEXES

Any index to periodicals, such as the *Readers' Guide, Bibliographic Index,* or *Humanities Index* categorizes and subdivides topics. A key word or phrase will often trigger your interest. A portion of the *Humanities Index* is shown here:

Fig. 12: From *Humanities Index*

WOMEN and men
   Communication and helping behavior: the effects
   of information, reinforcement, and sex on help-
   ing responses. R. N. Bostrom and others. bibl
   Comm Q 29:147-55 Summ '81
   How to do things without words: the taken-for-
   granted as speech-action. R. Hopper. bibl
   Comm Q 29:228-36 Summ '81
   Interruption in conversational interaction, and
   its relation to the sex and status of the
   interactants. G. W. Beattie. bibl Linguistics
   19 no 1/2:15-35 '81
   Partnership in marriage and family: problems
   and possibilities. C. Frühauf. Ecum R 32:410-15
   O '80
   Presence and absence: joy and sorrow. Ecum R
   32:427-9 O '80

A close look at the titles of such journal articles, as shown, might suggest *communication, reinforcement,* or *interaction* as possible subjects.

NARROWING THE GENERAL SUBJECT TO A SPECIFIC TOPIC

Research writing requires accurate facts and evidence to support your proposition, which should focus on a specific issue, such as "The Role of the Narrator in 'The Raven' " or "The Symbolic Blackness of Poe's Raven," not a broad subject such as "Edgar Allan Poe: His Poetic Genius." Vague, indefinite statements about a too extensive, too generalized subject will lead to an ineffective paper. Your judgments and opinions will persuade your audience effectively if supported by a clear focus, specific detail, and pertinent reference material as discovered by use of the following techniques.

Meeting the Needs of Your Audience

At college, instructors serve as a primary audience. Other potential readers would be supervisors, managers, professionals in the field, peers, and associates. In general, you will address intelligent, critical readers who expect your writing to display a certain depth of understanding. These are readers who will be familiar with the subject, yet they wish to know more about it. After all, even a college instructor may know little about certain topics. Therefore, during planning stages, ask: Who is my audience? What does my audience know? What do I need to tell these readers?

A sense of audience blends with topic selection and overall purpose. For instance, the nature of a paper—review, thesis proposal, interpretation of literature, or report of investigative research—determines whether you want to give the reader summary, analysis, or explanation. Readers of a paper on social issues (child abuse, death penalty, working mothers) expect analysis that points toward a social theory or answer. Readers of an interpretation of a novel expect to read literary theories on the novel's symbolism, narrative structure, and characterization. Readers of an empirical study on the behavior of mice would expect a scientifically documented explanation featuring hypotheses, methods, results, and discussion.

With this in mind, establish your topic development strategies on the basis of your purpose and your assumed audience. This effort will give you a better feel for who your readers are. You will know that they want a discussion of issues on a child abuse topic, that they expect interpretation, not plot summary, with a novel, and that they demand accurate findings and data in a technical study.

If you have a problem with imagining your audience, a bit of prewriting may help. For example, one writer planned a paper on scoliosis, which is curvature of the spine. Her research notes reflected an abundance of medical terminology and the makings of a mere medical report, not an analytical research paper. After developing her writing situation, she identified her audience as those persons who have recently been diagnosed as having scoliosis. She then played the role of interpreter for the purpose of educating and perhaps lessening the trauma of the victims.

Determining Your Writing Situation

To understand your purpose and the audience's needs, try writing a paragraph that includes as many of these items as possible:

1. The purpose of the paper (see above, 1–3)
2. The intended audience (see immediately above)
3. Your persona as writer (see below)
4. The thesis or hypothesis (see below)

For example, one writer developed this paragraph:

> I'm going to investigate the Illinois lottery to determine the contribution of the average ticket buyer to the state's funding of education, highways, prisons, and social programs. Perhaps I can argue that the portion which helps the state should be tax exempt. I'm not sure, but my target audience might be state legislators and even the governor.

As demonstrated above, identify your writing persona, which is your role as a research writer for the purposes of the study. You might be an investigator into social behavior, an interpreter of artwork, a reviewer of music lyrics, or a laboratory scientist. Say to yourself, "My job is to advance a thesis about women in three Shakespeare plays." Note another example:

> My role is to interpret this short story by John Updike for fellow literature students who have read "A & P." My purpose is to explore the A & P store as the setting for social conflict between a teenager and his perceptions of the stuffy, conservative establishment.

You may need to wait until research is well underway before developing a complete writing situation, which will surely change as research proceeds. Feel free to alter your plans at any point.

Developing a Preliminary Thesis

A thesis statement is a scholarly proposal that you will prove or maintain against argument. It controls the paper's direction. (Note: A thesis statement is similar to a hypothesis, which is an unverified assumption advanced in empirical research as probable but one that needs investigative, first-hand research.)

For example, let's suppose that you restrict your preliminary speculation on "Demands for Energy Production in the U.S." to the effects of the energy shortage upon the environment. Research questions will surface: Does the energy crisis require that we sacrifice the environment? Should we allow utility companies to pollute air and water in order to heat our homes? Can we have a safe, clean environment and also drive our automobiles at will? Asking such questions might uncover a preliminary thesis: "The demands for energy production in the United States will increase environmental pollution and delay, perhaps forever, our chances for clean air and water." The thesis would then control investigation of source materials and note-taking. However, it could later need narrowing to: "Acid rain, although harmful, is not the apocalyptical annihilation that some scientists would have us believe."

Your preliminary thesis can be general at first, then after note-taking, defined to a clear proposition. For example, the role of a pediatric nurse prompted these questions: "Whom does the pediatric nurse serve—the child, the family, or the medical community? How does the nurse serve? What functions are important? Does a nurse answer to doctor or patient?" The questions narrowed the writer's topic toward the relationship of the nurse to the child, to the medical community, and to the child's family: "The pediatric nurse satisfies several needs of the community—the health needs of the child, the personnel demands of the medical community, and the medical education of the family." Later, after note-taking, the writer narrowed it to an issue-oriented thesis on the nurse's medical education of child and family in addition to and in lieu of the doctor's advice.

Formulating a thesis sentence early sets satisfactory limits on note-taking, but the writer should remain flexible. Researchers often change directions as evidence pulls first one way, then another. Be open to changes.

Narrowing and Focusing Comparison Topics

Historians compare Lee and Grant or Hamilton and Jefferson. Political scientists often compare one president with another. Literary scholars compare one poet with another or one short story to another. Any two works, any two authors, any two groupings may serve as the basis for a comparative study. However, the study should focus on issues. Note how the following plan assures the examination of the differences between Hamilton and Jefferson on fiscal issues, not on biography:

National Bank	Currency	Tariffs
Jefferson	Jefferson	Jefferson
Hamilton	Hamilton	Hamilton

Restrict investigations to your comparison of specific issues in order to avoid wandering aimlessly in the voluminous details of historical and biographical facts. You can, of course, discuss Hamilton and then Jefferson if you itemize issues carefully:

Hamilton	Jefferson
National Bank	National Bank
Currency	Currency
Tariffs	Tariffs

Restricting and Narrowing Disciplinary Topics

Every discipline, whether sociology, geology, or literature, has its analytical categories, which are those areas requiring detailed study, such as the *behavior* of mice, the *interpretation* of a poem, or the *function* of computer loops. Literature students soon learn the importance of these terms:

language	imagery	symbolism
theme	character	setting
narration	structure	irony

The list could continue. In particular, writers on literature learn concepts as analytical categories for writing symbolic studies, image studies, or thematic studies. In similar manner, the psychological writer becomes familiar with other terms:

systematic sampling	experimenting	observing
interviewing	measuring	correlating

Knowledge of the terminology helps you to limit your study to one category so that research will proceed with *interview* questions, *observation* of a group of subjects, *reading* in the library, or *experimentation* in a laboratory. Of course, you cannot afford to get so infatuated with the jargon of the discipline that you forget to write clearly, yet do use the terms of the field to help narrow the subject.

Narrowing the Topic to Match Source Materials

Finally, restricting a subject will require you to study the available sources. For example, if you select the general subject area of the U.S. presidency, your first step in restriction should limit the topic to one president, let's say Ronald Reagan. The overwhelming amount of written data about Reagan would soon force you to limit the paper to one aspect of Reagan's administration, perhaps his Israeli policies. Next, speculation while scanning available source materials in the library might indicate that Reagan's proposals were ineffective, negative, and stultifying (or effective, positive, and innovative). Either way, specific evidence for a manageable topic appears available, so you can then proceed with your study.

2

Gathering Data

GATHERING DATA IN THE LIBRARY

This text assumes that you will enter the library to research a specific subject, perhaps *child abuse, world banking networks,* or *perfectionism as a neurosis.* Consequently, it shows how to search out the most timely and authoritative materials on a topic, beginning not only at the card catalog but also with indexing and abstracting services. Instructors expect more than a quick dip into an encyclopedia; they demand a search of indexes and the subsequent review of scholarly research on a topic.

In addition to printed catalogs, new techniques of document retrieval ease one's way, such as computer catalogs, citation indexes, and data base searches. Because of the new technology, libraries now undergo periods of growing pains as new methods of storage and retrieval are introduced. Printed periodicals are being discarded in favor of microfilm. Printed card catalogs are giving way to computerized catalogs. Abstracts may now appear as computer printouts from a data base that is located across the country.

During this revolution in library storage and retrieval techniques, there is one easily accessible source of library information—the librarian, who can recommend the best or most productive indexes to search. Approach the librarian after you have tried a few preliminary steps by saying, "I'm doing a research paper for my freshman English class on the possibilities of computers replacing assembly-line workers. I've used the card catalog without much success. Can you help me?" In addition, you ought to use the "List of Reference Sources by Discipline" at the end of this book, 245–69, which provides sources by discipline (e.g., Psychology, Art, Black literature, Myths and Folklore, and many others). It suggests general guides to research in your field, a few book bibliographies, the data bases for your field, and the best journal article indexes.

If you are experienced in library research, you might want to leapfrog various preliminary steps by going directly to specialized indexes of your discipline, as explained on pages 44–47. For example, if yours is a social issue, you can often go directly to *Sociological Abstracts.* Likewise, a literature student might begin the search with the *MLA Bibliography.* However, you need to know your way around the library before making such bold, advanced moves.

In general, this text moves from the general to the specific with the flow of the library, tracing issues from general reference sources to indexes and abstracts, and then to specific articles and books. After narrowing a topic by preliminary reading (see Chapter 1), a researcher's strategy might conform to this chart with adjustments for individual needs:

Preliminary search of:	*Narrowing by:*	*Reading from:*
indexes	reading abstracts	articles
abstracts	skimming articles	essays
bibliographies	collating sources	books
data base sources	researching citations	reviews
reference books	skimming books	government
card catalogs	browsing	documents
		bulletins

Preliminary reading serves several purposes: it gives you an overview of the subject, provides a beginning set of bibliography cards (see 23–31). restricts the subject, and suggests the availability of sufficient source materials with diverse opinions and real disagreements. As a starting point, begin with a book or journal article recommended by an instructor, supervisor, or librarian. Or begin with an encyclopedia, especially *The Encyclopaedia Britannica,* a biographical dictionary, such as *Webster's Biographical Dictionary,* or other general reference works, such as *Encyclopedia of Psychology* or *Mythology of All Races.* Also valuable are guides to the literature on a subject, such as Stevenson's *Guide to Victorian Fiction* or Stovall's *Eight American Authors.* See "List of Reference Sources by Discipline" (245–69).

Narrowing the subject is a step-by-step process. With topic in hand you search the indexes, build a set of bibliography cards, skim material to limit bibliography cards to the most authoritative sources, then begin serious reading and note-taking. Some leads will turn out to be dead ends; others will provide only trivial information. Some research will be duplicated, and a recursive pattern may develop that takes you back and forth from reading to searching indexes, and back again to reading. In every case, try to adjust research to your experience, moving from general reference works to the more specific sources (following the order of this book) or moving immediately to specialized indexes and abstracts in your field if your narrowed topic and experience so warrant.

Orderly reference searching helps you (1) avoid shallow plot summary, (2) avoid switching your topic every other day, (3) avoid working backward rather than forward, and best of all (4) avoid a paper with no focus, no thesis, and with too many paraphrases or instances of plagiarism.

Library Organization

Because of the sheer number of books and magazines, plus the vast array of retrieval systems, it will be to your advantage to tour the library and learn its arrangement—from the circulation desk to the reference room, and on to the stacks.

Circulation Desk.   This counter is usually located at the front of the library where personnel can point you in the right direction and later check out your books for withdrawal. Many libraries now have computerized machines for book checkout and electronic security devices to prevent theft. Whenever you cannot find a book on your own, check with the circulation desk to determine whether it is checked out, on reserve, or lost. If the book is checked out, you may place a hold order and librarians will contact you when it is returned. The circulation desk also handles most general business, such as renewing books, collecting fines, and handling keys and change for video and photocopying machines.

Reference Room.   Here you will find encyclopedias, biographical dictionaries, and other general works to help refine your topic. After your subject is set, the reference room provides the bibliographies and indexes for your search of the sources (see "Searching General Bibliographies," 33–36, and "Searching General Indexes," 36–54). Here in the reference area you should develop a set of bibliography cards that will direct your search in books and articles.

Reserve Desk.   Instructors often place books and articles on reserve with short loan periods—two hours or one day—so that large numbers of students will have access to them. This system prevents one student keeping an important, even crucial, book for two weeks while others suffer its absence. Your library may also place on reserve other valuable items that might otherwise be subject to theft, such as recordings, videotapes, statistical information, or unbound pamphlets and papers.

Card Catalog.   Your library places its holdings in the card catalog by call numbers that will locate all books, listing them by author, title, and subject—all interfiled in one alphabetical catalog. Many libraries are updating the card catalog system with microfilm systems or computer terminals (see "The Call Number," page 32.)

Stacks.   The numerous shelves of the library hold books where, armed with proper call numbers, you can locate specific works and perhaps browse for others that interest you. However, libraries with closed stacks will not permit you into the stacks at all. Rather, you provide the call number(s) to an attendant who goes into the stacks for you.

Computer Facilities.   Over the past decade libraries have increased use of on-line data base computer facilities. A new type of librarian now helps you tap into computerized networks that dispatch information nationwide on almost any topic. See "Conducting a Data Base Search" 49–51, for additional information.

Interlibrary Loans.   One library may borrow from another. The interlibrary loan service thereby supplements a library's resources by making materials available from other libraries. Understand, however, that receiving a book or article through interlibrary loan may take seven to ten days.

Photocopiers.   Photocopying services provide a real convenience, enabling you to carry home articles from journals and reserve books that cannot be withdrawn from the library. However, copyright laws protect authors and place certain restrictions on the library. You may use the copying machines and services for your own individual purposes, but be sure that you credit sources correctly (see "Avoiding Plagiarism," 77–81, and also "Copyright Law," 141).

Nonprint Materials.   Libraries serve as a storehouse for recordings, videotapes, film, microfilm, and many other items. These nonprint materials are usually listed in the general catalog or in a special catalog. If you know how to search this overlooked area of scholarly holdings, you may uncover a valuable lecture on cassette tape or a significant microfiche collection of manuscripts.

WORKING BIBLIOGRAPHY CARDS

A working bibliography is a set of reference cards that lists sources about your research subject. Index cards, not a notebook or slips of paper, work well for three reasons:

1. They locate articles and books on the subject for note-taking purposes.
2. They provide information for citing the work correctly in the paper, as in the following example in MLA style:

> The numerous instances of child abuse among step
>
> fathers has been noted by Stephens (31-32) and McCormick
>
> (419), which leads Austin to declare, "A mother who
>
> brings a non-father male into her home has statistics
>
> stacked against her and her children" (14).

3. They provide information for the final "Works Cited" page (see Chapter 6, 183–209). Therefore, detailed bibliography cards in alphabetical order will serve your best interests.

Your stack of bibliography cards will grow rapidly in the beginning but will diminish in size as you toss out various cards from sources that prove unfulfilling. Note: If you seem to be accumulating too many cards, your topic is probably too broad; if your stack of cards is pitifully small, you probably have narrowed the subject too much, at least for preliminary work.

Write bibliography cards for all references that show promise about the topic as drawn from various bibliographies and indexes, including the card catalog. In general, a *bibliography* is a list of works on a subject, and an *index* is a similar list with the addition of page citations. In particular, look for recent bibliographies because they suggest the best of the old books and articles in addition to the newest works. Such citations, recorded on cards and collated, reveal recent, reliable authorities on a subject.

Writing Basic Bibliography Cards

For each new reference, record the data onto *individual,* three- by five-inch index cards. The card system enables you to collate items easily into alphabetical order. But if you have another efficient system, by all means use it.

Each working bibliography card should contain the following information:

1. Author's Name
2. Title of the Work
3. Publication Information
4. Other Publication Items (i.e., editor, edition, issue)
5. Library Call Number
6. A Personal Note About the Contents of the Source

The following cards display the correct MLA form of basic entries. Other samples appear throughout this chapter. For special bibliography forms (e.g., lecture, letter, or map), consult the index which will direct you to appropriate pages of Chapter 6 for examples of almost every imaginable type of citation. If needed, consult Chapter 7 for the bibliography form for citations in other fields of study.

Fig. 13: Card for a book cited in the card catalog, in MLA style

HV/741/F65

Fontana, Vincent J. *Somewhere a Child Is Crying: Maltreatment — Causes and Prevention.* New York: Macmillan, 1973.

HV
741
.F65
1973

Fontana, Vincent J
    Somewhere a child is crying; maltreatment—causes and preven-
tion ₍by₎ Vincent J. Fontana. New York, Macmillan ₍1973₎
    xx, 268 p. 22 cm. $6.95

      1. Cruelty to children—United States. 2. Child welfare—United States. I.
Title.

HV741.F65 1973   364.1'5   73-10566
                                       MARC
Library of Congress   73

Fig. 14: Card for a magazine article cited in *Readers' Guide to Periodical Literature*, in MLA style (Note: see front of *Readers' Guide* for explanations of abbreviations)

Beezer, B. "Reporting Child abuse and Neglect: Your Responsibility and Your Protections." *Phi Delta Kappan* 66 (1985): 434-36.

Child abuse
    See also
    Child molesting
  Emotional child abuse: the invisible plague. S. Jacoby. il *Read
    Dig* 126:86-90 F '85
  A father's monstrous crime against his son has caused Kirk
    Crocker a life of pain [radiation poisoning] J. Calio. il pors
    People Wkly 23:44-6 Ap 8 '85
  Reporting child abuse and neglect: your responsibility and your
    protections [teachers] B. Beezer. bibl f il *Phi Delta Kappan*
    66:434-6 F '85

Fig. 15: Card for a journal article cited in *Social Sciences Index*, in MLA style

Giles-Sims, Jr., and D. Finkelhor.
"Child Abuse in Stepfamilies."
<u>*Family Relations*</u> *33 (1984):*
407-13.

Child abuse
   See also
   Child Abuse Prevention and Treatment Act (1974)
   Child molesting
   Incest
Abstract perceptual information for age level: a risk factor for maltreatment? V. McCabe. bibl *Child Dev* 55:267-76 F '84.
Abused, neglected, and nonmaltreated children's conceptions of moral and social-conventional transgressions. J. G. Smetana and others. bibl *Child Dev* 55:277-87 F /84
Child abuse in stepfamilies. J. Giles-Sims and D. Finkelhor. bibl *Fam Relat* 33:407-13 Jl /84
Home safety: development and validation of one component of an ecobehavioral treatment program for abused and neglected children. D. A. Tertinger and others. bibl *J Appl Behav Anal* 17:159-74 Summ /84
The relationship between affect and cognition in maltreated infants' quality of attachment and the development of visual self-recognition. K. Schneider-Rosen and D. Cicchetti. bibl *Child Dev* 55:648-58 Ap '84
Time-limited, goal-focused parent aide service. K. Miller and others. *Soc Casework* 65:472-7 O '84

Fig. 16: Card for a government document cited in the *Monthly Catalog of United States Government Publications*, in MLA style

Chest—Radiography.
   Are routine chest X rays really necessary?,
   85-14864

Child abuse—United States.
   Child sexual abuse prevention : tips to parents.,   85-14899

Child development.
   A guide for operating a homebased child development program.,   85-14902

85-14899
              HE23.1002:Se 9
Child sexual abuse prevention : tips to parents. — [Bethesda, MD.?] : U.S. Dept. of Health and Human Services, Office of Human Development Services, Administration for Children, Youth and Families, National Center on Child Abuse and Neglect, 1984.
   1 folded sheet (6 p.) : ill. ; 22 x 10 cm Item 530-B-1
   1. Child molesting—United States. 2. Child abuse—United States. I. National Center on Child Abuse and Neglect. OCLC 11806726

**Fig. 16:
Continued**

> U.S. Dept of Health and Human
> Services. <u>Child Sexual Abuse
> Prevention: Tips to Parents.</u>
> Bethesda: GPO, 1984.

**Fig. 17: Card for
a newspaper
article cited in
*New York Times
Index 1984,* in
MLA style (Note:
be sure to
record the year
because it does
not appear in
the entries.)**

> Editorial. <u>New York Times</u>
> 4 Jan. 1984: I18, col.1.

CHILD Abuse. See also Educ, F 22, Je 3. Families, Ap 3,
15,17, My 20, S 29. Foster Care, N 11. Handicapped, F 3, Jl
4, S 14,27. Manslaughter, Je 24, D 13, D 18,19. Mental
Health, Ja 24. Murders, Ja 3, Ja 25,27,30, F 5,9, Ap 24, S 8,
29, O 7,11,13, O 17,19, O 30, N 25, D 1,15,18.
Pornography, My 16,22. Religious Cults, Ja 13,14,21, F 10,
Mr 17, Jl 14,15. Sex Crimes, Ja 8,9,10,15,21,31, F 8,28,
Mr 18,23,24,25,28,31, Ap 1,4,7,9,10,19,21,23,25,27,30, My 5,
6,7,8,12,13,19,214,26, Je 3,20, Jl 12,18,20,27, Ag 9, Ag 12,21,
24,25,26,30, S 3,4, S 5,6,7,8, S 9,11,17, S 20,22, S 28,29,30,
O 3,4,5,7,8,11, O 16,25,29,30, N 13,15,21,23,29, D 5,13,27
Major increase in child abuse in Maine and Vermont
discussed (S), Ja 2,1,8:1
Editorial praises New York City Major Koch for
responding to results of study by Mayor's Task Force on
Child Abuse with new programs to help spot cases of child
abuse and to fund social service groups to work in high-risk
neighborhoods with parents prone to abusing children: Says
work of task force should continue, Ja 4,1,18:1
Letter from NYC Council Pres Carol Bellamy, NYS
Assemblyman Angelo Del Toro and NYC Councilwoman
Ruth Messinger deplores Koch Administration's record in
combating child abuse, Ja 10,1,22:4
Letter from Assemblyman William B. Hoyt, chairman of
New York State Assembly Subcommittee on Child Abuse,
lauds Jan 4 editorial supporting New York City Mayor
Edward Koch's proposed action on behalf of abused
children in city: holds what is needed is broader-based
effort throughout state: comments on legislation he has
proposed, Ja 21,2,20:3

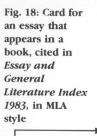

**Fig. 18: Card for
an essay that
appears in a
book, cited in
*Essay and
General
Literature Index
1983*, in MLA
style**

*Feinberg, J. "The Child's Right
to an Open Future." Ethical
Principles for Social Policy.
Ed. John Howie. n.p.:
Southern Illinois UP, 1983,
97-122.*

Ethical principles for social policy. Ed. by John Howie. Southern Ill.
  Univ. Press 1983 155p ISBN 0-8093-1063-5 LC 82-5801

History and criticism
Cushman, K. Hughes' poetry for children. *In* The
Achievement of Ted Hughes, ed. by K. Sagar p239-
56
Children's rights
  Feinberg, J. The child's right to an open future.
In Ethical principles for social policy, ed. by J.
Howie p97-122

Recording Call Numbers
at the Card Catalog

Your bibliography cards will need call numbers for locating each book
but not for journal articles. Most libraries maintain journals in alphabetical
order, a plan which eliminates the need for call numbers. The library's card
catalog may exist as (1) a massive card bank in file cabinets or as (2) a computerized data base. In either case, you should consult subject index cards
which, in theory, provide every book available in the library on one topic.
Divergent thinking will produce several possible headings; for example,
"cloning" may not appear as a subject head, but "reproduction" will. Thus,
searching under the heading "CHILD" might produce a collection of sources,
on a computer screen or cards, as shown next:

Fig. 19:
Subject cards

CHILD MOLESTING.

HQ
71   Rush, Florence, 1918-
.R87   The best kept secret : sexual abuse
of children / Florence Rush. --
Englewood Cliffs, N.J. : Prentice-Hall,
c1980.

CHILD MENTAL HEALTH--ADDRESSES,
ESSAYS, LECTURES.

RJ
504   Prescriptions for child mental health
.P7   and education / Arnold P. Goldstein,
1978   editor. New York : Pergamon Press,
c1978.

CHILD DEVELOPMENT--ADDRESSES, ESSAYS,
HQ   LECTURES.
758   Father and child : developmental and
.F368   clinical perspectives / edited by
1982   Stanley H. Cath, Alan R. Gurwitt,
John Munder Ross. --1st ed. --

CHILD DEVELOPMENT.
LB
1033   Best, Raphaela, 1925-
.B48   We've all got scars : what boys and
1983   girls learn in elementary school /
Raphaela Best. -- Bloomington : Indiana
University Press, c1983.
x, 181 p. ; 24 cm.
ISBN 0-253-36420-5

1. Interaction analysis in education.
2. Child development.   3. Sex
differences in education.   4. School
environment.   5. Age groups.   I. Title

TC1A   18 OCT 83   9393311 TPAAdc   82-49198

The next procedure is to record call numbers onto appropriate cards:

Fig. 20: Sample Bibliography Card

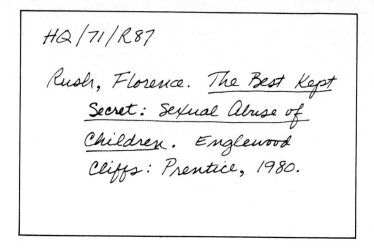

HQ/71/R87

Rush, Florence. The Best Kept
Secret: Sexual Abuse of
Children. Englewood
Cliffs: Prentice, 1980.

If any previously written cards remain without call numbers, you can examine other subject heading cards or consult the author card or the title card. Both types are displayed below:

Fig. 21: Main Entry Card (Author Card)

1. Classification number 2. Author number 3. Author 4. Life span of author 5. Title 6. Editor 7. Place of publication 8. Publisher 9. Date of publication 10. Technical description 11. Note on contents of the book 12. Separate card filed under editor's name 13. Publisher of this card 14. Order number 15. Library of Congress Call Number

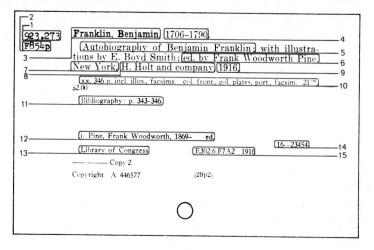

A sample bibliography card developed from this source follows:

**Fig. 22: Sample
Bibliography
Card**

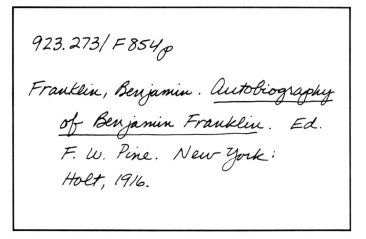

923.273/ F854p

Franklin, Benjamin. <u>Autobiography</u>
<u>of</u> Benjamin Franklin. Ed.
F. W. Pine. New York:
Holt, 1916.

Record the *complete* call number—in this case, 923.273 / F854p (see also "Call
Numbers," below). This information may provide other leads. Finding the
book in the stacks, you will discover many books with like numbers that you
will find helpful. In addition to the number, record any bibliographical notations, such as "Bibliography: p. 27–28," which signals another list of
sources.

**Fig. 23:
Title Card**
1. Title, usually
typed in black ink
2. Main entry card
filed under
"Newcomb,
Benjamin H."
3. Subject headings
under which you
will find this same
card

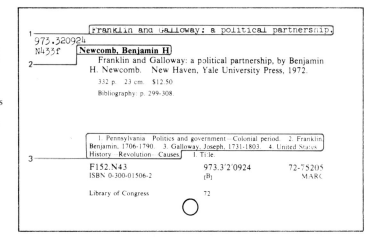

1 ———
973.320924
N433f

[Franklin and Galloway: a political partnership.]

[Newcomb, Benjamin H]

2 ———
     Franklin and Galloway: a political partnership, by Benjamin
H. Newcomb. New Haven, Yale University Press, 1972.

     332 p.   23 cm. $12.50

     Bibliography: p. 299-308.

     1. Pennsylvania—Politics and government—Colonial period.   2. Franklin,
Benjamin, 1706-1790.   3. Galloway, Joseph, 1731-1803.   4. United States—
History—Revolution—Causes.   I. Title.

3 ———
F152.N43
ISBN 0-300-01506-2

973.3'2'0924
[B]

72-75205
MARC

Library of Congress   72

The Call Number

Your library will classify its books by one of two systems, the Dewey Decimal System or the Library of Congress system. The Dewey system lists Franklin's *Autobiography* (see Figure 21) with "923.273/F854p," but the LC system uses "E / 302.6 / F7A2." Understanding the system of your library will prove helpful.

The Dewey Decimal System. Figure 5 on page 11 shows the complete 100 divisions of the Dewey system. The 900 category is labeled "General geography & history," and it lists in part these two subdivisions:

920 General biography & genealogy
970 General history of North America

The Benjamin Franklin book shown in Figure 22 belongs to the 920 category and is designated 923.273. The Newcomb book about Franklin, shown in Figure 23, belongs to the 970 category and is numbered 973.320924.

Immediately below the Dewey classification numbers you will see a second line of letters and numerals based on the Cutter Three-Figure Author Table. For example, "N433f" is the author number for Newcomb's *Franklin and Galloway.* The letter "N" is the initial of the author's last name; next, the Cutter table subclassifies with the Arabic numerals "433"; and the lowercase "f" designates the first important letter in the title to distinguish this entry from similar books by Newcomb. Thus, the complete call number for Newcomb's book is 973.320924 / N433f. You must use both to locate the book.

Library of Congress Classification System. The LC system also uses a combination of letters and numerals. The major divisions are shown in Figure 8 on page 13, which, in part, lists:

E–F   History: American (Western Hemisphere).

Accordingly, Franklin's book is assigned "E" with subnumbers "302.6." Then, like the Cutter system, LC uses the first letter of the author's name and subnumbers for the second line, "F7A2."

An example of these systems might be as follows:

Library of Congress:	Dewey Decimal:
TD [Environmental Technology]	628.53 [Engineering &
833 [Air Pollution]	allied operations]
.H48 [Author Number]	H461u [Author Number]

By using either set of numbers, depending upon your library, you would find this book: Howard E. Hesketh, *Understanding and Controlling Air Pollution,* 2nd ed. (Ann Arbor, Michigan: Ann Arbor Science, 1974).

SEARCHING GENERAL BIBLIOGRAPHIES

General bibliographies guide you to other, more specific indexes. Some, like *Bibliography of American Literature,* list sources in existence for some time. Others, like *Bibliographic Index* (see below), are current bibliographies kept up-to-date by supplements.

Bibliographies appear within most encyclopedias at the ends of articles, in critical and biographical studies at the backs of the books, and in most scholarly journals at the back of articles (for example, history students depend upon specific bibliographies in issues of *English Historical Review* but biology students consult *Biological Abstracts*).

Using the Bibliographies in General Reference Books

When starting out, you should consult one or two of the following general reference works, which contain bibliographies that direct you to sources on a wide range of subjects:

> Besterman, Theodore. *A World Bibliography of Bibliographies.* 4th ed. 5 vols. Lausanne: Societas Bibliographica, 1963.
>
> Hillard, James. *Where to Find What: A Handbook to Reference Service.* Rev. ed. Metuchen, NJ: Scarecrow, 1984.
>
> McCormick, Mona. *The New York Times Guide to Reference Materials.* Rev. ed. New York: Times Books, 1985.
>
> Sheehy, Eugene P., ed. *Guide to Reference Books.* 9th ed. Chicago: ALA, 1976. Supplements 1980, 1982.

These books serve as bibliographies to other indexes and bibliographies by subject. They narrow your search to topic-oriented lists.

Using Bibliographic Index

One of the best general bibliographies is:

> *Bibliographic Index: A Cumulative Bibliography of Bibliographies.* New York: H. W. Wilson, 1938–date.

An annually updated list of books and journals, it provides page numbers to many different books that contain bibliographies on numerous subjects. Although *Bibliographic Index* originally covered only the years 1937–42, it is kept current by supplements. A sample entry from *Bibliographic Index* of 1981 uncovers these sources:

Fig. 24: From
Bibliographic
***Index*, 1981.**

1. Subject heading
2. Entry of a book
that contains a
bibliography on
aggressiveness
3. Specific pages on
which bibliography
is located

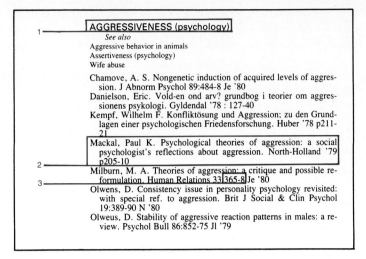

1 — [AGGRESSIVENESS (psychology)]
See also
Aggressive behavior in animals
Assertiveness (psychology)
Wife abuse

Chamove, A. S. Nongenetic induction of acquired levels of aggression. J Abnorm Psychol 89:484-8 Je '80
Danielson, Eric. Vold-en ond arv? grundbog i teorier om aggressionens psykologi. Gyldendal '78 : 127-40
Kempf, Wilhelm F. Konflitösung und Aggression; zu den Grundlagen einer psychologischen Friedensforschung. Huber '78 p211-21
Mackal, Paul K. Psychological theories of aggression: a social psychologist's reflections about aggression. North-Holland '79 p205-10
2 — Milburn, M. A. Theories of aggression: a critique and possible re-
3 — formulation. Human Relations 33 365-8 Je '80
Olwens, D. Consistency issue in personality psychology revisited: with special ref. to aggression. Brit J Social & Clin Psychol 19:389-90 N '80
Olweus, D. Stability of aggressive reaction patterns in males: a review. Psychol Bull 86:852-75 Jl '79

Each entry above cites a specific bibliographic section within a critical study. It displays 12 books about "aggressiveness" that have bibliographic lists. For example, a bibliography on aggression can be found in Tieger, pages 959–63 and 978–80, which is then noted on a card in MLA style:

Fig. 25:
Card Listing a
Bibliographic
Source

> Tieger, T. "On the Biological Basis of Sex Differences in Aggression." *Child Development* 51 (1980): 959-63, 978-80.

Using Trade Bibliographies

Trade bibliographies, intended primarily for use by booksellers and librarians, can help you in three ways: to discover sources not listed in other bibliographies or in the card catalog; to locate facts of publication, such as place and date; and to learn if a book is in print.

Subject Guide to Books in Print (New York: Bowker, 1957–date) supplies good subject indexes. The 1985–86 issue contains these entries under "Child Psychology—Bibliography" and "Child Psychology—Collections":

Fig. 26: From
Subject Guide to
Books in Print,
1985–86

1. Subject 2. Author
3. Title 4. Date of
publication 5. Price
6. Publisher
7. International
Standard Book
Number (used
when ordering)
8. Paperback book

CHILD PSYCHOLOGY-BIBLIOGRAPHY

Akins, F. R. et al. Parent-Child Separation: Psychosocial Effects on Development. 368p. 1981. 85.00x (ISBN 0-306-65196-3, IFI Plenum). Plenum Pub.

Bernstein, Joanne E. Books to Help Children Cope with Separation & Loss. 2nd ed. 439p. 1983. 34.95 (ISBN 0-8352-1484-2). Bowker.

Slobin, Dan I., ed. Leopold's Bibliography of Child Language. LC 79-184526. (Indiana University Studies in the History & Theory of Linguistics). Repr. of 1972 ed. 41.80 (ISBN 0-8357-9222-6, 2015833). Bks Demand UMI.

Supplement to Recommended Reading About Children & Family Life, 1970. 1974. 1.00 (ISBN 0-685-41670-40. Child Study.

Wilson, Louis N. Bibliography of Child Study. LC 74-21433. (Classics in Child Development Ser). 360p. 1975. Repr. 29.00x (ISBN 0-405-06482-9). Ayer Co Pubs

CHILD PSYCHOLOGY-COLLECTIONS

Apter, Steven J., ed. Troubled Children - Troubled Systems. rev. ed. (Pergamon General Psychology Ser.: No. 104). 285p. 1982. 31.00 (ISBN 0-08-027167-7); pap. 13.95 (ISBN 0-08-027166-9). Pergamon.

Articles of Supplementary Reading for Parents. pap. 2.00x (ISBN 0-918560-14-4). A Adler Inst.

Articles of Supplementary Reading for Teachers & Counselors. pap. 2.00x (ISBN 0-918560-15-20. A Adler Inst.

Make a note for any promising source (publishers' addresses are located separately):

Fig. 27: Sample
Bibliography
Card for Source
Found in
Subject Guide to
Books in Print
The publisher's
city will be
listed in a
separate section
of Books in
Print

Akins, F. R., et al. Parent-Child Separation: Psychosocial Effects on Development. n.p.: Plenum, 1981

Use also the following trade bibliographies:

> *Books in Print.* New York: Bowker, 1948–date.
>
> This work provides an author-title index to the *Publisher's Trade List Annual* (New York: Bowker, 1874–date), which lists all books currently in print.

> *Publishers Weekly.* New York: Bowker, 1872–date.
>
> This journal offers the most current publication data on new books and new editions.

> *Paperbound Books in Print.* New York: Bowker, 1955–date.
>
> Use this work to locate paperback books on one topic, especially books available at local bookstores rather than the library.

> *Cumulative Book Index.* New York: H. W. Wilson, 1900–date.
>
> Use this index to find complete publication data on one book or to locate *all* material in English on a particular subject.

> *The National Union Catalog: A Cumulative Author List.* Ann Arbor: Edwards, 1953–date.
>
> Basically, this work is a card catalog in book form, but use it to find titles reported by other libraries.

> *Library of Congress Catalog: Books, Subjects.* Washington, D.C.: Library of Congress, 1950–date.
>
> Use this work for its subject classification which provides a ready-made bibliography of books on hundreds of subjects. Separate volumes are available for the years 1950–54, 1955–59, 1960–64, and annually thereafter.

> *Union List of Serials in Libraries of the United States and Canada.* 3rd ed. New York: H. W. Wilson, 1965. Supplements, *New Serial Titles,* Washington, D.C.: Library of Congress, 1953–date.
>
> Consult this work to determine if a nearby library has a magazine or journal that is unavailable in a local library.

> *Ulrich's International Periodicals Directory.* Ed. Merle Rohinsky. 15th ed. New York: Bowker, 1973.
>
> Use this work to locate current periodicals, both domestic and foreign, and to order reprints of articles.

SEARCHING GENERAL INDEXES

A general index furnishes the exact page number(s) in specific sections of books or articles in magazines, journals, and newspapers. Fundamentally, there are four types: (1) indexes to materials in books and collections, (2) indexes to literature in periodicals, (3) indexes to materials in newspapers, and (4) indexes to pamphlets.

Indexes to Biographies, Dissertations, and Essays within Books

First, you should recall *Bibliographic Index* (see above, 33), which locates bibliographies in books and collections. Three others are:

Essay and General Literature Index, 1900–1933. New York: H. W. Wilson, 1934. Supplements, 1934–date.

Biography Index: A Quarterly Index to Biographical Material in Books and Magazines. New York: H. W. Wilson, 1946/47–date.

Dissertation Abstracts International (Ann Arbor: Univ. Microfilms, 1970–date; formerly *Microfilm Abstracts,* 1938–51, and *Dissertation Abstracts,* 1952–69).

The first work indexes material within books and collections of both a biographical and a critical nature. Note the following entry from a supplement of *Essay and General Literature Index:*

Fig. 28:
From *Essay*
and General
Literature Index
1. Subject 2. Article
by Franklin 3. Book
in which Franklin's
essay appears
4. Designates that
following essays are
about Franklin,
rather than essays
written *by* him
5. Author of essay
about Franklin
6. Title of the essay
7. Book in which
the essay appears

Franklin, Benjamin
1 — Benjamin Franklin calls for a volunteer militia
In Millis, W. ed. American military thought p 1-9
Experiments and ideas; excerpt from "The ingenious Dr Franklin"
In Shapley, H.; Rapport, S. B. and Wright, H. eds. The new Treasury of science p273-79
'On modern innovations in the English language and in printing'
2 —
In Bolton, W. F. ed. The English language p174-79
3 —
4 — About
Cawelti, J. G. Natural aristocracy and the new republic: the idea of mobility in the thought of Franklin and Jefferson
In Cawelti, J. G. Apostles of the self-made man p9-36
5 — Conkin, P. K. Benjamin Franklin: science and morals
In Conkin, P. K. Puritans and pragmatists p73-108
6 — Rossiter, C. L. Benjamin Franklin
In Rossiter, C. L. Six characters in search of a Republic p206-59
Sainte-Beuve, C. A. Franklin
In Sainte-Beuve, C. A. Portraits of the eighteenth century v 1 p309-75
7 — Stourzh, G. Sober philosophe: Benjamin Franklin
In Intellectual history in America v 1 p64-93
About individual works
Autobiography
Aldridge, A. O. Form and substance in Franklin's Autobiography
In Essays on American literature, in honor of Jay B. Hubbell p47-62

This index sends you to essays *within* books that you might otherwise over-look; for example, J. G. Cawelti's essay appears in *Apostles of the Self-Made Man* and P. K. Conkin's essay appears in a book with the title *Puritans and Pragmatists*. Neither title mentions Franklin, yet buried within each book is a good essay on the subject. The publishers and dates for these entries are found in a "List of Books Indexed" at the end of each volume of *Essay and General Literature Index.*

   Biography Index is a starting point for studies of famous persons. It gives clues to biographical information for people of all lands. Note the following short excerpt from *Biography Index:*

Fig. 29: From
Biography Index
1. Subject 2. Dates
of subject's birth
and death
3. Subject's
profession
4. Author of the
biography 5. Title
of the biography
6. Publisher 7. Date
of publication
8. Number of pages
9. Contains a
bibliography
10. Contains
portraits and a map
11. Illustrated
12. Publication data
for a periodical

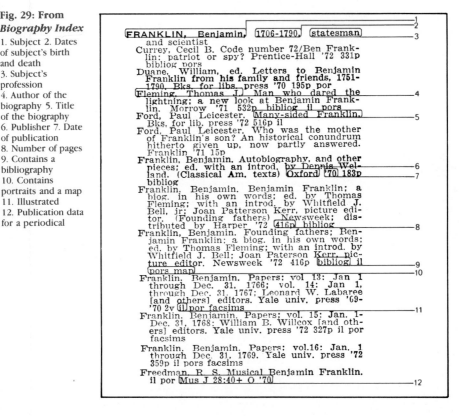

Most indexes published by the H. W. Wilson Company use this same code system. Specifically, note the code for journal volumes and page numbers—"23:81–91 D'71." To conform to the suggestions of this manual, you will want to record the data differently on your bibliography card:

Fig. 30: Sample Bibliography Card

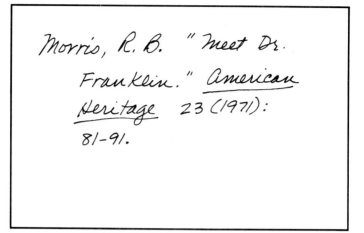

Dissertation Abstracts International supplies abstracts of graduate student research. Issue No. 12, Part II, of each volume contains the cumulated subject and author indexes for Issues 1–12 of the volume's two sections—A: Humanities and Social Sciences, and B: Sciences and Engineering. The index of *Dissertation Abstracts International* for 1985 lists the following entries under the heading "CHILD":

Fig. 31: From the Index to Vol. 46, *Dissertation Abstracts International*

1. Title of Dissertation 2. Page number where abstract can be found

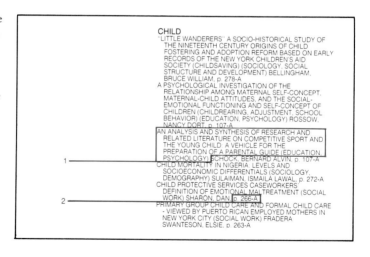

The abstract of one entry by B. A. Schock is to be found on page 107-A. It appears as follows:

Fig. 32: From
*Dissertation
Abstracts
International*
1. Title of
dissertation
2. Order number if
you desire to buy a
copy of the
complete work
3. Author, school,
and date 4. Total
number of pages of
the dissertation
5. Faculty chairman
of the dissertation
committee

1 ___ AN ANALYSIS AND SYNTHESIS OF RESEARCH AND RELATED
LITERATURE ON COMPETITIVE SPORT AND THE YOUNG CHILD:
A VEHICLE FOR THE PREPARATION OF A PARENTAL GUIDE
Order No. DA8505167 ___ 2

3 ___ SCHOCK, BERNARD ALVIN, ED.D *University of South Dakota, 1984.*
4 ___ 169pp Dr. John F. Byrde ___ 5

    Problem Statement. The purpose of this study was to establish a
body of analyzed and synthesized research related to the effects of
adult-organized, competitive sport on young children. The data was
organized in such a way that it can be used later in preparing a guide
for parents which will help them understand: (a) the strengths and
weaknesses of competitive sport, and (b) the role they play in: (1)
organizing their child's competitive sport, (2) guiding their child's
selection of a sport, (3) participating in their child's sport, and (4)
coaching children's sport.
    Procedures. There was no specific sample chosen for this study
since the purpose of the study was to analyze, synthesize and apply
research that had already been done relating to the effects of
competitive sport on young children. Thus the sample varied
according to the individual studies that were used.
    Findings and Implications of the Study. Though there has been a
great deal of research done on the effects of competition on young
children, very little of this information has been made available to
those who guide children in sport. One researcher has said that there
is a "myriad of data and a dearth of understanding." This study will
not be complete until the information has been effectively transmitted
to parents and other adults involved in youth sport. In addition to this
study, there will be a continuing need for researchers to look at the
whole rather than the parts when analyzing the impact of competitive
sport on young children.

An abstract, of course, only briefly summarizes the entire work. If you need
the full dissertation and have enough time, you can order a copy of the complete work from University Microfilms, Inc., Ann Arbor, MI 48106.

Indexes to the Literature in Periodicals

Some writers begin their research with general magazines indexed in:

Readers' Guide to Periodical Literature. New York: H. W. Wilson, 1900–date.

Although it indexes many non-scholarly publications, such as *Teen, Needle
and Craft,* and *Southern Living, Readers' Guide* also indexes important reading for the early stages of research in magazines such as:

Aging	*Foreign Affairs*	*Psychology Today*
American Scholar	*Foreign Policy*	*Scientific Review*
Astronomy	*Health*	*Science Digest*
Bioscience	*Negro History Bulletin*	*Science*
Business Week	*Oceans*	*SciQuest*
Earth Science	*Physics Today*	*Technology Review*

An entry from *Readers' Guide to Periodical Literature* follows:

Fig. 33: From Readers' Guide to Periodical Literature
1. Subject 2. A piece by Franklin himself 3. Designates that the following articles are *about* Franklin 4. Title of article 5. Author 6. Illustrated with portraits 7. Indicates a review: Van Doren's book *Benjamin Franklin* was reviewed in *Commonweal* by J. Cournos 8. Name of periodical and publication data

FRANKLIN, Benjamin ——————————————————1
Benjamin Franklin meets the press; excerpts
from his writings. por facsim Scholastic
67:14-15 Ja 12 '56
Benjamin Franklin on his religious faith;
letter to Ezra Stiles. Am Heritage 7:106
D '56 ——————————————————2
Excerpts from his voluminous writings. por
N Y Times Mag p76 Ja 15 '56
Farther experiments and observations in elec-
tricity; excerpt from Experiments and ob-
servations on electricity. bibliog Science
123:47-50 Ja 13 '56
From Ben's letters. Time 67:90 Ja 30 '56
Mr Franklin, self-revealed. facsim Life 40:
74-7+ Ja 9 '56
about ——————————————————3
Americana page. Hobbies 61:100 Jl '56
Ben Franklin: an affectionate portrait, by
N. B. Keyes. Review
Sat R 39:16 Ja 21 '56. W. M. Wallace
Ben Franklin, trail blazer for inventors. P. ————4
Lee. il pors map Pop Mech 105:99-102+ Ja
'56
Benjamin and the bell. M. Alkus. Ladies ————5
Home J 72:180 Ap '55
Benjamin Franklin and the French alliance;
adapted from Secret war of independence.
H. Augur. il por Am Heritage 7:65-88 Ap '56 ————6
Benjamin Franklin, by C. Van Doren. Re-
view
Commonweal 63:497 F 10 '56. J. Cournos ————7
Benjamin Franklin in modern life and educa-
tion. T. Woody. Sch & Soc 84:102-7 S 29 '56
Benjamin Franklin the diplomat. por U S
Dept State Bul 34:50-1 Ja 9 '56
Benjamin Franklin's grand design; Albany
plan of union. R. B. Morris. il por map
Am Heritage 7:4-7+ F '56 ——————————8

Bibliography cards would be made for any entries that looked promising. See Figure 22, page 31, for an example.

Next, consult the following index if your study involves a social science:

Social Sciences Index. Vols. 1—. New York: H. W. Wilson, 1974–date.

This work indexes journal articles for 263 periodicals in these fields:

anthropology
economics
environmental science
geography
law and criminology

medical science
political science
psychology
sociology

See Figure 15, page 26, for a sample entry from *Social Sciences Index.* Researchers in the humanities should consult:

Humanities Index. Vols. 1—. New York: H. W. Wilson, 1974–date.

This work catalogs 260 publications in several fields:

archaeology
classical studies
language and literature
area studies
folklore
history
performing arts
philosophy
religion
theology

See Figure 12, page 15, for a sample entry from *Humanities Index.*

For sources prior to 1974, consult two works that preceded *Humanities Index* and *Social Sciences Index:*

International Index. Vols. 1–18. New York: H. W. Wilson, 1907–65.

Social Sciences and Humanities Index. Vols. 19–61. New York: H. W. Wilson, 1965–1974.

Other general indexes of importance are the following:

Applied Science and Technology Index. New York: Wilson, 1958–date.
An index for chemistry, engineering, computer science, electronics, geology, mathematics, photography, physics, and other related fields.

Biological and Agricultural Index. New York: Wilson, 1947–date.
An index for biology, zoology, botany, agriculture, and related fields.

Education Index. New York: Wilson, 1929–date.
An index for education, physical education, and related fields.

In addition to these major indexes, you should examine especially the index for your discipline as listed in the appendix, 245–69.

Newspaper Indexes

Newspaper indexes provide contemporary information. One is especially helpful: *The New York Times Index* (New York: New York Times, 1913–date). It indexes the *New York Times* and thereby indirectly indexes most newspapers by revealing the date on which the same news probably appeared in other newspapers. Many libraries have the *New York Times* on microfilm. A search of "Child Abuse" produced this list:

Fig. 34: From
New York Times
***Index*, 1984**

1. Subject 2. Cross
references 3. Date,
section number,
and page number
(January 2, section
1, page 18, column
1) 4. Description of
the article

CHILD Abuse. See also Educ. F 22, Je 3. Families. Ap 3,
15,17, My 20, S 29. Foster Care, N 11. Handicapped, F 3, Jl
4, S 14,27. Manslaughter, Je 24, D 13, D 18,19. Mental
Health, Ja 24. Murders, Ja 3, Ja 25,27,30, F 5,9, Ap 24, S 8,
29, O 7,11,13, O 17,19, O 30, N 25, D 1,15,18.
Pornography, My 16,22. Religious Cults, Ja 13,14,21, F 10,
Mr 17, Jl 14,15. Sex Crimes, Ja 8,9,10,15,21,31, F 8,28,
Mr 18,23,24,25,28,31, Ap 1,4,7,9,10,19,21,23,25,27,30, My 5,
6,7,8,12,13,19,214,26, Je 3,20, Jl 12,18,20,27, Ag 9, Ag 12,21,
24,25,26,30, S 3,4, S 5,6,7,8, S 9,11,17, S 20,22, S 28,29,30,
O 3,4,5,7,8,11, O 16,25,29,30, N 13,15,21,23,29, D 5,13,27
Major increase in child abuse in Maine and Vermont
discussed (S), Ja 2,1,8:1
  Editorial praises New York City Major Koch for
responding to results of study by Mayor's Task Force on
Child Abuse with new programs to help spot cases of child
abuse and to fund social service groups to work in high-risk
neighborhoods with parents prone to abusing children: Says
work of task force should continue, Ja 4,1,18:1
  Letter from NYC Council Pres Carol Bellamy, NYS
Assemblyman Angelo Del Toro and NYC Councilwoman
Ruth Messinger deplores Koch Administration's record in
combating child abuse, Ja 10,1,22:4
  Letter from Assemblyman William B. Hoyt, chairman of
New York State Assembly Subcommittee on Child Abuse,
lauds Jan 4 editorial supporting New York City Mayor
Edward Koch's proposed action on behalf of abused
children in city; holds what is needed is broader-based
effort throughout state; comments on legislation he has
proposed, Ja 21,2,20:3

Note: The year is not given in the entries, so get it from the front of the volume you use, in this case 1984. For a sample bibliography card, see Figure 17, page 27.

Other important newspaper indexes are:

Wall Street Journal Index. New York: Dow Jones, annually.

Bell and Howell's Index to the Christian Science Monitor. Christian Science Publishing Society, annually.

Official Index [to *The London Times*] (London: *Times*, 1907–date).

Searching the Pamphlet Indexes

The principal index to most pamphlet material is:

Vertical File Index: A Subject and Title Index to Selected Pamphlet Material. New York: H. W. Wilson, 1932/35–date.

Your library may not own many of the items listed by this index, but it gives a description of each entry, the price, and information for ordering the pamphlets. Remember, too, that the federal government publishes many pamphlets and booklets on a vast array of topics. Look especially for the following:

U.S. Superintendent of Documents. *Monthly Catalog of United States Government Publications*. Washington, DC: Government Printing Office, 1895–present. Monthly.

Using the Specialized Indexes
of Your Discipline

You should resist any temptation to depend entirely on sources from the card catalog and *Readers' Guide to Periodical Literature*. Those sources serve well during preliminary reading and topic restriction, but not so well for serious note-taking for two reasons: first, since magazines are published without documentation and without professional review, they are suspect in their validity and authoritative voice; second, books found through the card catalog are, by the very nature of publication, often out-of-date quickly, especially for some scientific topics.

Therefore, after consultation with a supervisor or librarian, who can offer valuable tips about reference sources, search primary indexes in the field. These are found in the lists of reference sources arranged by disciplines in the appendix, 245–69. These lists are alphabetized by subject and will direct you to scholarly literature in your special field. Searching these bibliographies and indexes requires a detective's aptitude for finding clues and new leads to information. In all cases, of course, keep accurate records to prevent retracing a wasted step. For example, in the field of psychology, primary sources are:

Psychological Abstracts
Annual Reviews of Psychology
PSYCINFO, the data base for the behavioral sciences that includes
   Psychological Abstracts back to about 1967, but no farther

In some cases, indexes to the abstracts are available, as with the *Subject Index to Psychological Abstracts,* which searches the older files, but new issues must be examined right off the shelf. For example, you might discover this entry:

Fig. 35: From
Subject Index to
Psychological
Abstracts
1. Subject 2. Title and brief description
3. Abstract number

1 — **Child Abuse**
    abuse vs rescue environment, change in IQ, 2.3–16.1 yr olds with
       abuse dwarfism, 20746
    adolescent abuse, implications for family & school & individual &
2 —   group counseling & support services, 17976
    age & alcoholism & level of testosterone, aggressive behavior, 19–40
       yr old incarcerated rapists vs 19–55 yr old child molesters vs hospital
3 —   staff members, 12523
    age & sex & race & relationship to assailant, 6 mo through 16 yr old
       victims of sexual abuse, 15232
    analysis of social problems & identification of at-risk populations in so-
       cial epidemiology, child abuse, primary prevention implications,
       31586
    analytical hypnotherapy, victims of family violence & child sexual
       abuse, 4724

You would then search the appropriate issue of *Psychological Abstracts* for abstract number 17976:

Fig. 36: From
Psychological
Abstracts
1. Abstract number
2. Authors 3. Title
of the article
4. Citation that tells
you where to find
the full article
5. Abstract of the
article 6. Indication
that the article
features 15
references on the
subject 7. Author of
the abstract

1 —— 17976. **Foreman, Susan & Seligman, Linda.** (Georgetown Visita-
tion Preparatory School. Washington, DC) **Adolescent abuse.** —2
4 —— *School Counselor*, 1983(Sep), Vol 31(1), 17–25. —Contends that few —3
states have legal definitions of abuse that include standards of emotional abuse appropriate to adolescent victims (AVs). AVs are often
perceived of as provokers and sometimes engage in retaliatory behavior. The judicial system may treat AVs as offenders. Potential for
abuse is increased when parents are experiencing a stressful middle age
at the time the AV is facing the developmental taks of separation, indi-
viduation, and struggle for control. Four categories of abuse are discussed: (1) where AVs were initially abused as children; (2) where the
5 —— AV's move toward independence leads to anger or frustration in the
parents; (3) where the parents of the AV have been rigid and controlling; (4) where abuse begins in adolescence because the AV has disrupted the family system. It is suggested that many cases go unrecog-
nized and that removing the recognized AV from the home is difficult.
Family counseling is the treatment of choice, and support services
(e.g., for poverty, medical problems, and/or poor communications
skills) may be needed. The role of the school counselor and individual
or group counseling, including peer help, are discussed. (15 ref) —6
7 —— —*P. D. Burke.*

The complete article, if needed, is located in volume 31 of *School Counselor.* Make an appropriate bibliography card if the source appears useful, and then quote from the original journal, if at all possible, not the abstract. If you *do* quote from the abstract, note that fact in your bibliography entry (see 206).

Literature students should also consult such works as *McGill's Bibliography of Literary Criticism,* which lists critical materials by author and work:

Fig. 37:
From *McGill's*
Bibliography of
Literary
Criticism
1. Author and dates
2. Title of work
3. Citation of a
critical work on the
poem

1 —— **ROBERT FROST**
(1874-1963)

2 —— **"After Apple Picking"**

Brooks, Cleanth. *Modern Poetry and the Tradition.* Chapel Hill: University of North Carolina Press, 1939, pp. 114–116. Reprinted in *Robert Frost: An Introduction.* Edited by Robert A. Greenberg and James G. Hepburn. New York: Holt, Rinehart, 1961, pp. 3–5.

Brooks, Cleanth and Robert Penn Warren. *understanding Poetry.* New York: Holt, 1950, pp. 389–397.

3 —— **Brower, Reuben A.** *The Poetry of Robert Frost: Constellations of Intention.* New York: Oxford University Press, 1963, pp. 23–27.

Conder, John J. "'After Apple Picking': Frost's Troubled Sleep," in *Frost: Centennial Essays.* Edited by the Committee on the Frost Centennial of the University of Southern Mississippi. Jackson: University Press of Mississippi. 1974, pp. 171–181.

Works similar to McGill's bibliography are *Poetry Explication* and *Twentieth Century Short Story Explicator.* Language and literature students should also examine the *MLA International Bibliography,* which lists major works annually, as demonstrated by the following entry:

Fig. 38:
From *MLA*
International
Bibliography
1. Author and dates
2. General articles about Frost's poetry
3. An article about a specific poem

---

1 ⎯ **FROST, ROBERT (1874-1963)**

[8762] Iwayama, Tajiro. "Robert Frost." 439-475 in Ogata, Toshihiko, ed. *America Bungaku no Jikotenkai: 20-seiki no America Bungaku II.* Kyoto: Yamaguchi; 1982. ii, 638 pp.
[8763] Monteiro, George. "'A Way *Out* of Something': Robert Frost's Emily Dickinson." *CentR.* 1983 Summer; 27(3): 192-203. [†Relationship to Dickinson, Emily; includes comment on Bogan, Louise; MacLeish, Archibald; Wilbur, Richard.]

Poetry

[8764] Daniel, Charles L. "Tonal Contrasts in the Imagery of Robert Frost." *WGCR.* 1982 May; 14:12-15. [†Light imagery; dark imagery.]
[8765] Gage, John T. "Humour en Garde: Comic Saying in Robert Frost's Poetic." *Thalia.* 1981 Spring-Summer; 4(1): 54-61. [†Role of humor.]
[8766] Gonzàlez Martín, Jerónimo P. "Aproximación a la poesía de Robert Frost." *CHA.* 1983 Apr.; 394: 101-153. [†Includes biographical information.]
[8767] Greenhut, D. S. "Colder Pastoral: Keats, Frost, and the Transformation of Lyric." *MHLS.* 1983; 6: 49-55. [†Lyric poetry. Use of pastoral. Treatment of landscape compared to Keats, John.]
[8768] Marks, Herbert. "The Counter-Intelligence of Robert Frost." *YR.* 1982 Summer; 72(4): 554-578. [†Treatment of revelation, concealment. Sources in Bible; Milton, John: *Paradise Lost.*]
[8769] Slights, William W. E. "The Sense of Frost's Humor." *CP.* 1983 Spring; 16(1): 29-42. [†Humor; comedy; relationship to reader.]
[8770] Sutton, William A. "Some Robert Frost 'Fooling'." *MTJ.* 1983 Spring; 21(3): 61-62. [†Relationship to Clemens, Samuel.]
[8771] Trikha, Manoramma B. *Robert Frost: Poetry of Clarifications.* Atlantic Highlands, NJ: Humanities; 1983. 259 pp. [†Use of metaphor; symbolism. Sources in Emerson, Ralph Waldo; James, William.]

2 ⎯

Poetry/"Away"

[8772] Kau, Joseph. "Frost's 'Away!': Illusions and Allusions." *NMAL.* 1983 Winter; 7(3): Item 17.

3 ⎯

Poetry/"Beech"

[8773] Will, Norman P. "Robert Frost's 'Beech': Faith Regained." *NMAL.* 1982 Spring-Summer; 6(1): Item 2.

Poetry/A Boy's Will (1913)

[8774] Wordell, Charles B. "Robert Frost from *A Boy's Will* to *North of Boston.*" *SALit.* 1983 June; 19: 1-13. [†*North of Boston.*]

Skipping back and forth from indexes to periodicals and back to indexes is a normal procedure. In addition, the journals themselves often augment the indexes. For example, faced with the subject "Childhood Aggression," one researcher noticed that a majority of sources was located in a few key journals. In that instance, going straight to a journal was a short-cut that produced a good index:

Fig. 39:
From *Index to*
Child Welfare
1. Subject 2. Title
of article 3. Author
4. Month and page
number to volume
55

Administration
The Director of Professional Services: A Dilemma (Felitto) . . . . D 725

1 — **Adoption**
Tayari: Black Homes for Black Children (Neilson) . . . . J 41
2 — Another Road to Older Child Adoption (Rooney) . . . . N 665
The Sealed Adoption Record Controversy and Social
3 — Agency Response (Smith) . . . . F 73
4 — Adoption Trends: 1971–1875 (Haring) . . . . Jy 501

Behavior Modification
Collaboration in Behavior Modification
in a Day Care Center (Smith, Newcombe) . . . . .My 357
Behavior Modification in a Residence and School for Adolescent
Boys: A Team Approach (Scallon, Vitale, Eschenauer) . . . . . O 561

Searching Government Documents

All branches of the government publish massive amounts of material. Many documents have great value for researchers, but locating the material can be difficult and frustrating.

The first check point should be the *Monthly Catalog of United States Government Publications* (Washington, DC: GPO, monthly). An example can be found above on page 26.

A second place to look is *Public Affairs Information Service Bulletin* (New York: P.A.I.S., semimonthly). A sample entry from this work, known as *PAIS* is shown below:

Fig. 40: From
Public Affairs
Information
Service Bulletin
1. Subject
2. Citation to an
article on the
subject 3. Notes
that the article
contains a
bibliography
4. Annotation that
describes contents
of the article

1 — **CHILD ABUSE**
Abrams, Elliott. Child pornography: a worldwide problem.
Dept State Bul 85:55-6 Ap '85
Statement before the Subcommittee on Investigations,
Committee on Government Affairs, U.S. Senate, Feb.
21, 1985.
Report of a federal interagency group visit to the
Netherlands, Denmark, and Sweden.

Green, William. Children and pornography: an interest
analysis in system perspective [statutes to protect
children from abuse in the production of pornography
and from harm in the sale of obscene materials; issues
of free speech, privacy and due process]. charts
Valparaiso Univ Law R 19:441-70 Winter '85

2 — McMurtry, Steven L. Secondary prevention of child
maltreatment: a review. bibl Social Work *(Nat Assn
Social Workers)* 30:42-8 Ja/F '85
Reviews research on attempts to screen parents to
identify those who are at risk of maltreating their
children.

Pagelow, Mildred Daley. Family violence. '84 xiii + 592p
3 — bibl il tables indexes (Praeger special studies/Praeger
sci.) (LC 84-8244) (ISBN 0-03-070187-2) $47.95
(ISBN 0-03-070188-0) pa—*Praeger Pub*
Partial contents: Theoretical viewpoints; Child abuse
and neglect; Spouse abuse; Sexual abuse in the family:
the power game.

4 — Schwartz, Dari R. Child abuse and parental rights [New
York State]. *N Y State Bar J 57:16-22 + Ap '85*

If the article in the *Department of State Bulletin* looks promising, record it on a card. If your library does not house that special bulletin, you can write your request to:

> Superintendent of Documents
> Government Printing Office
> Washington, DC 20402

Most materials are free and will be shipped immediately.

Third, search out other indexes in the government documents section of your local library and learn the section's resources. In many libraries, a separate card catalog lists governmental holdings.

Finally, remember that various branches of government produce different types of documents. The key publication of Congress is the *Congressional Record,* published daily with regular indexes. Senate and House bills, documents, and committee reports are available at some libraries. If they are not, write either the Senate Documents Room or the House Documents Room for free copies of specific legislation. The publications of the Executive Branch, the President, and all members of the President's Cabinet, contain enormous amounts of vital information. Again, your best source for information and documents is the *Monthly Catalog of United States Government Publications.* *The U.S. Code and the Constitution* are the primary publications of the legal branch. The Supreme Court regularly publishes decisions, codes, and other rulings, as do appellate and district courts. State courts also publish rulings and court results on a regular basis.

Consult pages 203–204 for correct methods of writing bibliography citations to government documents of all three branches.

Using the Microforms

Libraries have a choice when ordering periodicals: they can buy expensive printed volumes or purchase inexpensive microfilm versions of the same material. Most libraries have a mixture of the two. Your library will specify how journals and magazines are housed.

Most libraries now store national newspapers and dissertation abstracts on microfilm. Therefore, after consulting *The New York Times Index,* look for microfilm files, not actual bound newspapers. Should you need a copy of a microfilmed article, the library will have the means to copy the microfilm.

In addition, watch for other special indexes or guides to microfilm holdings at your library. These guides carry such titles as *American Culture 1493–1806: A Guide to the Microfilm Collection* or perhaps *American Periodicals 1800–1850: A Guide to the Microfilm Collection.* Remember that every library has its own peculiar holdings of microfilm and microfiche materials.

Conducting a Data Base Search

Data base searches for source materials are now available at many libraries. Generally, librarians discourage undergraduate use of computer searches for small research papers, eight pages or less, for one reason: the computer is cost-effective on *large* retrospective searches, not on narrow research-paper subjects. After all, the data base vendors charge the library about $75 per hour when logged on. You may be required to pay a fee from $1.00 up to $60.00 or more. Fee schedules vary from university to university because some libraries absorb the cost while others charge for computer time. Determine these charges *in advance*.

If you use a computer search, several steps are involved. For example, one researcher began a bibliographic search on "Aggressive Behavior" with a focus on children who participate in athletics, such as Little League baseball. Investigation in this case began with a "Search Request," although each library uses different names and employs a different form. For example, a librarian will ask such questions as:

1. What title would best describe your paper's content?
2. List specific topics, synonyms, closely related phrases, and alternate spellings of your subject—using scientific, technical, and common names.
3. List related topics that can be excluded in order to narrow the search.
4. Do you desire any foreign language entries? Which languages?
5. Do you wish to limit citations to a publication year(s)?

The purpose of this questionnaire should be fairly obvious: the computer operator needs terminology to feed into the data base file.

Next, the computer librarian will interview you to formulate terminology for the computer search of specific files. A file contains a collection of records created by a data base producer, such as ERIC (Education Resources Information Center), which produes two files: *Research in Education* and *Current Index to Journals in Education*. Your library's computer will be connected by phone to a national data base vendor who will transmit by telephone hookup various files, such as the ERIC files.

Before that time you must select proper terminology for the data base search. The key words, known as descriptors, can be found in a computer dictionary and/or thesaurus, such as *Thesaurus of ERIC Descriptors* or *Thesaurus of Psychological Index Terms*. Your three key terms will control a search of citations:

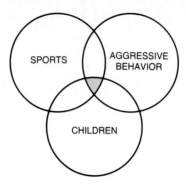

The computer will browse through records to select only those that match the
darkened area, which will be books and articles that feature the three key
terms. The librarian, having selected file PSYCINFO, now dials up by telephone

> the appropriate data base ⟶
>   logs on ⟶
>   enters subject profile ⟶
>   begins computer search ⟶

until the printout of a report is produced. (See Figure 41.) The file contains
only seven entries, a fact which suggests two things. First, the field appears
open to additional investigation; it is not glutted with articles. Also, additional
sources, if required, must be sought in another data base or in books and
magazines not listed in PSYCINFO. Caution: data bases feature contemporary
files and seldom list information from sources before 1965.

The day rapidly approaches when printed indexes will disappear, to be
replaced by floppy disks and computer printouts. For instance, rather than
searching the printed volumes of *Psychological Abstracts,* researchers will
soon scan terminal screens and, if the list looks good, order a printout.
Already, *Biological Abstracts* is available on B-I-T-S, a floppy disk system. This
new BITTERN software creates files and performs retrospective searches on
the small microcomputers. Many more systems like B-I-T-S are becoming
available.

The appendix, 245–69, lists data base sources most valuable to you.

Citation Searching

The purpose of citation searching is to find the most reliable sources,
which will be those authors and works most often referred to in the literature.
You should scan your bibliography cards to discover three or four journal
articles and books which devote space to the topic. For example, after locating
the "Works Cited" or "List of References" at the end of an article on child
abuse, you would need to study the list for authors whose names appear more
than once:

Fig. 41: A DIALOG Search from the PSYCINFO Data Base

68-03368 Vol. No: 68 Abstract No: 03368
 The relationship between viewing televised violence in ice hockey and sub-sequent levels of personal aggression.
 Celozzi, Mathew J.; Kazelskis, Richard; Gutsch, Kenneth U.
 Journal of Sport Behavior 1981 Dec Vol 4(4) 157-162
 Language: ENGLISH Document Type: JOURNAL ARTICLE
 Descriptors: ADOLESCENTS, TELEVISION VIEWING, AGGRESSIVE BE-HAVIOR, SPORTS, VIOLENCE
 Identifiers: viewing TV violence vs discussion of hockey, subsequent level of personal aggression, male high school students
 Section Headings: 2840 (PSYCHOSOCIAL & PERSONALITY DEVELOP-MENT)

66-05589 Vol No: 66 Abstract No: 05589
 Normative aggression in non-athletic versus ice hockey playing Canadian boys.
 Tyler, Ken; Duthie, J. H.
 U Windsor, Faculty of Human Kinetics, Canada
 International Journal of Sport Psychology 1980 Vol 11(4) 231-239 CODEN: IS-PYAN ISSN: 00470767
 Language: ENGLISH Document Type: JOURNAL ARTICLE
 Descriptors: ADOLESCENTS, SCHOOL AGE CHILDREN, AGE DIFFER-ENCES, COMPETITION, ATHLETIC PARTICIPATION, AGGRESSIVE BE-HAVIOR, SOCIAL VALUES
 Identifiers: age vs competitive level of hockey team, judgment of aggressive vs nonaggressive on-ice behavior, 12-16 yr old league members vs nonathletic males, Canada
 Section Headings: 2840 (PSYCHOSOCIAL & PERSONALITY DEVELOP-MENT)

66-05560 Vol No: 66 Abstract No: 05560
 Aggression by high school basketball players: An observational study of the ef-fects of opponents' aggression and frustration-inducing factors.
 Harrell, W. Andrew
 U Alberta, Edmonton, Canada
 International Journal of Sport Psychology 1980 Vol 11(4) 290-298 CODEN: IS-PYAN ISSN: 00470767

61-08007 Vol. No: 61 Abstract No: 08007
 The stimulating versus cathartic effects of viewing televised violence in ice hockey and the relationship on subsequent levels of aggression and hostility.
 Celozzi, Matthew J.
 U Southern Mississippi
 Dissertation Abstracts International 1978 Apr Vol 38(10-B) 5088

60-05322 Vol No: 60 Abstract No: 05322
 An analysis of the relationship between aggressive sport fan behavior and per-sonality.
 Sysler, Barry L.
 Temple U
 Dissertation Abstracts International 1977 Jul Vol 38(1-A) 159
 Language: ENGLISH Document Type: JOURNAL ARTICLE
 Descriptors: AGGRESSIVE BEHAVIOR (01390), SOCIAL DESIRABILITY (48180), SOCIAL ACCEPTANCE (48040), AGGRESSIVENESS (01400), IN-TERESTS (26080), BASKETBALL (05520), COMPETITION (10750), ADOLES-CENTS (00950), YOUNG ADULTS (57320), ADULTS (01160)
 Identifiers: interest in sport & aggressive personality & desire to be socially ac-ceptable, aggressive behavior at basketball game involving rival team 17-33 yr old sport fans
 Section Headings: 3100 (PERSONALITY)

Fig. 42:
From *Child*
Development
1. Authors who
appear twice on the
list with two
different essays

References

Achenbach, T. M. The child behavior profiles, I: Boys aged 6–11. *Journal of Consulting and Clinical Psychology,* 1978, **46,** 478–488.

Achenbach, T. M., & Edelbrock, C. S. The child behavior profile, II: Boys aged 12–16 and girls aged 6–11 and 12–16. *Journal of Consulting and Clinical Psychology,* 1979, **47,** 223–233

Burgess, B., & Garbarino, J. Doing what comes naturally? An evolutionary perspective on child abuse. In D. Finkelhor, R. Gelles, G. Hataling, & M. Straus (Eds.), *The dark side of families.* Beverly Hills, Calif.: Sage, 1983.

Cicchetti, D., & Aber, J. Abused children—abusive parents: An overstated case? *Harvard Educational Review,* 1980, **50,** 244–255.

Cicchetti, D., & Rizley, R. Developmental perspectives on the etiology, intergenerational transmission, and sequelae of child maltreatment. *New Directions for Child Development,* 1981, No. 11, 31–52.

Cronbach, L. J. Coefficient alpha and the internal structure of tests. *Psychometrika,* 1951, **16,** 297–334.

Daly, M., & Wilson, M. Child maltreatment from a sociobiological perspective. *New Directions for Child Development,* 1981, No. 11, 93–112.

Devereux, E. C., Bronfenbrenner, U., & Rodgers, R. R. Child-rearing in England and the United States. *Journal of Marriage and the Family,* 1969, **31,** 257–270.

Garbarino, J., & Gilliam, G. *Understanding abusive families.* Lexington, Mass.: Lexington, 1980.

Garbarino, J., & Sherman, D. High-risk neighborhoods and high-risk families: The human ecology of child maltreatment. *Child Development,* 1980, **51,** 188–198.

Take note of authors who have more than one article (note especially the name "Cicchetti"). Then shuffle through your cards and mark with stars or special marks any of these sources you have already recorded. Also make new cards for any sources that treat your specific subject. (Note: you could skim the articles now while you have the journal in hand, but the primary goal is to build a bibliography list.) Next you would search out another "List of References" and look for the repetition of key names:

Fig. 43:
From *Child*
Development
1. Name of author
who participated in
writing three
articles on the
subject

References

Alexander, R. D. The evolution of social behavior. *Annual Review of Ecological Systems*, 1974, **5**, 325–383.

Alley, T. Infantile head shape as an elicitor of adult protection. *Merrill Palmer Quarterly*, in press.

Belsky, J. Three theoretical models of child abuse: A critical review. *International Journal of Child Abuse and Neglect*, 1978, **2**, 37–49.

Belsky, J. Child maltreatment: An ecological integration. *American Psychologist*, 1980, **5**, 320–335.

Brooks, J. M. Infant's responses to strangers: Midget, adult, and child. *Child Development*, 1976, **47**, 323–332.

Cicchetti, D., & Rizley, R. Developmental perspectives on the etiology, intergenerational transmission, and sequelae of child maltreatment. *New Directions for Child Development*, 1981, **11**, 31–55.

Cicchetti, D., & Sroufe, A. An organizational view of affect: Illustration from the study of Down's syndrome infants. In M. Lewis & L. A. Rosenblum (Eds.), *The development of affect*. New York: Plenum, 1978.

Cicchetti, D., Taraldson, B., & Egeland, B. Perspectives in the treatment and understanding of child abuse. In A. Goldstein (Ed.), *Prescriptions for child mental health and education*. Elmsford, N..Y.: Pergamon, 1978.

Daly, M., & Wilson, M. I. Child maltreatment from a sociobiological perspective. In R. Rizley & D. Cicchetti (Eds.), *New Directions for Child Development*, 1981, **11**, 93–112.

As circled above, the name "Cicchetti" occurs again, which suggests that (1) he has authority in this field and (2) you should examine his works in more detail. In addition, the article by "Daly and Wilson" appears a second time, which suggests its value.

This citation search should continue through several articles in each of the three or four journals and books chosen for the search. The author cards with stars or circles represent books or articles that have been cited more than once, a fact which suggests significant scholarship. They are "must" reading. In effect, you have accomplished a circular search that allowed the sources themselves to provide the important, relevant books and articles.

Three citation indexes that do some of this work for you are:

Arts and Humanities Citation Index (AHCI) 1977–date.

Science Citation Index (SCI) 1961–date.

Social Sciences Citation Index (SSCI) 1966–date

These citation indexes consist of three separate but related indexes:

(1) *Source Index* lists articles of a given year published in the indexed periodicals (e.g., *SSCI* indexes about 2000 journals).

(2) *Citation Index* lists articles *cited* by authors listed in the *Source Index* (e.g., about 90,000 citations appear in *AHCI*).

(3) *Permuterm Subject Index* suggests the subjects treated in the *Source Index* for those who do not know a specific author.

Supplementing Library Materials and Collecting Data Outside the Library

The library is, without a doubt, an invaluable source of information when writing a research paper, but material exists in other places, too. For instance, a U.S. senator or representative can send you booklets printed by the Government Printing Office. A list of these materials, many of which are free, appears in a monthly catalog issued by the Superintendent of Documents, *Monthly Catalog of United States Government Publications* (Washington, DC: GPO, 1895–date).

Also important are audiovisual materials: films, filmstrips, music, phonograph recordings, slides, audio cassettes, and video cassettes. You may find these in the library or in some other location on or off campus. Your library may have available such guides as *Educators Guide* (film, filmstrips, and tapes), *Media Review Digest* (nonprint materials), *Video Source Book* (video catalog), *The Film File,* or *International Index to Recorded Poetry.*

Other good sources of information are: *radio and television programs,* especially programs of the Public Broadcast System; *lectures,* which you may experience yourself or find reproduced on videotape; *public addresses,* which may touch on your subject or motivate you to write on a topic; *interviews,* which are time-consuming to conduct or to read, but they do elicit the information you need; *letters,* which provide a written record for research; *questionnaires,* which are popular because they produce accurate data that may be tabulated and analyzed quickly (however, varying degrees of bias can creep into the questionnaire unless you remain objective and, if necessary, let somebody else proofread the questions); *observation* and *case studies,* which enable you to examine patterns of behavior and build a profile of a person as based on biographical data, interviews, tests, and observation; *experiments, tests,* and *measures,* which determine why and how things exist, function, or interact with one another.

3

Taking Notes

After preliminary investigation in the library, it's time to take stock of your progress. While gathering materials for your working bibliography cards, you should also have uncovered and skimmed briefly some of the more promising books and articles. From these you will have gained an initial familiarity with your general subject. You must now narrow the focus of your research, as framed by a preliminary thesis sentence and a rough topic outline. You can afford neither the time nor the effort of taking notes on a scattered, hit-or-miss basis. The information in every note should answer a research question or relate to an issue of your topic's preliminary thesis. Careful note-taking will thereby narrow the subject even more.

THE PRELIMINARY OUTLINE

Before progressing very far into note-taking, you should prepare a preliminary outline or, at least, a list of major issues (a final outline comes after note-taking, see 84). Like a grocery list, it identifies necessary items and prevents wasted trips along fruitless aisles.

To develop a preliminary outline, follow two fairly simple steps: (1) jot down ideas or code words in a rough list, and (2) give order to the list by arranging items into major and minor ideas. How you finally organize is a matter of your work habits and the nature of the subject. One researcher, for example, chose the general topic "Child Abuse" and created this preliminary thesis sentence: "The parents, not just the children, should be a major focus of social concern." She roughed out a set of code words:

```
discipline                          agencies and organizations
the battered child                  case studies
social workers                      physical abuse
parents and unfit parents           psychological damage
step-parents                        neglect
sexual abuse                        aggression
short-term effects on child/parents behavioral patterns
```

She could then begin note-taking with only this list or could arrange it according to one of the following plans. (See also "Using Basic Formulas as Paradigms," 91–94, and "Writing a Final Outline," 84–89.)

Using Your Writing Situation

If you have developed a writing situation (see 17), use it to guide note-taking. Tighten it to one aspect of the subject. Note how one writer used her writing situation to frame several important issues:

> I want to address public officials who must find a way
> to control the parents who abuse their children. My role is
> investigation and my purpose is to explore options for
> identifying and then counseling at-risk families. To that
> end I need information on types of abuse, types of parents
> and guardians, behavioral patterns of abused children and
> the abusing parents, and the role of social agencies.

That paragraph effectively outlines the specific information that the writer would seek from source materials or interviews.

Roughing Out a Preliminary Outline

Organize main topics and subordinate related elements to develop a rough outline for a paper, as shown:

```
        The Battered Child
            Discipline
            Physical abuse
            Psychological abuse
        Effects
            Physical
            Mental
        Public Concern
            Governmental agencies
            Private organizations
        Spotting Unfit Parents
            Mothers
            Fathers
            Friends
            Step-parents and relatives
```

The outline, although sketchy, will guide note-taking. Later, it might prove inadequate for writing the first draft, at which time a formal outline would be in order.

Using Questions to Outline Ideas

Another preliminary list for bringing order to note-taking is the question outline:

```
What is child abuse?

How does it differ from "discipline"?

What causes abuse?

How prevalent is it?

What are the short-term consequences?

What are the long-term consequences?

What can the average citizen do about it?
```

This question method develops a clear direction for collection of .data because each note card develops an answer. In fact, one question alone might serve as the focusing agent for an entire paper. Your answer might become your thesis.

Outlining by Methods of Development

A third method uses the modes of paragraph development that best suit the topic:

```
Defining abuse

Contrasting abuse with discipline

Using statistics of incidents (by age, sex, types, etc.)

Writing case studies of abuse

Observing three families to collect data

Searching for causes of abuse with focus on the parents

Determining the consequences of abuse with focus on children
```

Again, the writer has guidelines for collecting data. Other categories might be: examples, process, description, narration, illustration, analysis, division, classification.

Ordering from General Ideas to Particular Items

When you have a clear, well-expressed thesis, you can begin an outline with the thesis and then chart areas that need support, as shown here:

```
Thesis: Child abuse reaches beyond the formative years into
        the adult life of the abused child.
Physical impairment
Psychological disorders
Marital strife
Abuse of his/her own children
```

This outline is deductive in nature because it moves from the general to the specific. It narrows note-taking to areas where evidence is needed.

Ordering from Particular Items to General Issues

If you are still searching for a thesis but haven't discovered one yet, consider the specifics of your problem and then work carefully toward a general attitude. For example, someone researching child abuse might examine several case histories before arriving at any clear generalization:

```
            Case study A
            Case study B
            Case study C
            Comparison of the three cases
            Focus on causal elements
```

This plan invites discovery of the topic as much as it controls note-taking, yet the nature of this inductive procedure assures an orderly search for conclusions. In another case you might read fifteen or twenty poems by Robert Frost, jotting down repetitions of theme, image, character, or language pattern. Inductively, your thinking might lead you to a specific issue worthy of your time and effort.

Revising the Rough Outline During Research

Having a rough outline to refer to as you take notes helps you locate important information. It also eliminates useless information. However, the rough outline is not a binding contract, so let it develop and grow: add new topics and discard others, rearrange the order, evaluate topics, and subordinate minor elements.

Writing a research paper is recursive, which means that you will look back over your paragraphs, adjust your thinking, and more forward again. The outline expands or shrinks throughout the gathering of data and the writing of drafts. With that in mind, use these questions to evaluate your overall plan:

1. What is my role as researcher? Am I reviewing, discovering, interpreting, or theorizing?
2. What is my thesis? Will my notes and records defend and illustrate my proposition? Is it convincing evidence?
3. How specialized is my audience? Do I need to write in a non-technical language or may I assume that the audience is knowledgeable in this field and expects in-depth discussion of substantive issues?

Your answers will determine, in part, the type of notes needed. (For additional tips about outlining, see Chapter 4, 84–89. "Writing a Final Outline.")

EVALUATING YOUR SOURCE MATERIALS

A rough outline can show you where to concentrate your researching efforts, but it can't evaluate the quality of what you find. You must do that yourself. Be curious and track down facts from the library. Be skeptical about accepting every printed word as absolute. Constantly review, verify, and double-check findings and discoveries.

Use Recent Sources

A book may treat a topic extensively, but if its copyright date is 1938, its content is suspect: time and new developments have probably passed it by (unless, of course, the work is a classic in its field). Scientific and technical topics especially require up-to-date research. Learn to depend upon monthly and quarterly journals as well as books (see appropriate indexes for your field on 44–48). Remember too that recent publications review previous works in the field. This year's overview of literature on a topic will cite recognized, reliable sources for you to add to your working bibliography (see "Citation Searching," 50–54).

Use Reliable Source Materials

Beware of biased reporting, both in the writing of others and in your own drafts. In general, scholarly journals offer more reliable evidence than magazines. Unlike magazine free-lancers, journal writers document all sources and publish through university presses and organizations that screen articles before publication. A journal article about child abuse found in *Child Devel-*

opment or in *Journal of Marriage and the Family* should be reliable. A magazine article about child abuse in a Sunday newspaper supplement or in a popular magazine may exaggerate facts to create sensational effects. To examine an author's credentials, consult *Contemporary Authors,* a reference of biographies on contemporary writers.

Many organizations publish slanted, biased articles to promote their viewpoints. There's nothing wrong with the practice, but you should be aware of any biases. For example, the *New Republic* presents a liberal view of society while the *National Review* remains staunchly conservative. A report on health care may seem reasonable on the surface, but if the publication is sponsored by a health care insurance company, you must exercise caution.

Quote the Best Scholars

Influential authorities on a topic are usually mentioned often in various sources, whatever the field. It will pay you to look at their work. Several methods will help you discover the key people in one area: (1) ask your supervisor or instructor; (2) watch for certain names that reappear in scholarly materials (see "Citation Searching," 50–54); or (3) check the credentials of an author in such works as *Who's Who in American Art, Contemporary Authors,* or *Book Review Digest.* Ask these valuable questions: Is the researcher associated with a university? Has he or she written several articles and a book or two? Has the individual been quoted in articles and listed in footnotes and bibliographies? Citing the top men and women in a field will mark you as a perceptive scholar who knows the territory.

Use Relevant Source Materials

Determining the value of a particular book or article can be troublesome. To evaluate magazine and journal articles, read the opening and perhaps the closing for relevance, turning to the body of the article only if it appears promising. Read abstracts, which are brief overviews of articles and books in abstracting services (e.g., *Psychological Abstracts, Abstracts of English Studies*) or in the journal itself at the beginning of the article. Abstracts are available for all university dissertations.

Evaluating a book requires that you check several items:

1. The complete *title* with *subtitle* indicates the book's relevance. For example, *Children and Parents* may look ideal for a child-abuse topic until you read the subtitle: *Children and Parents: Growing Up in New Guinea.*

2. The *table of contents* helps you discover chapters that touch directly or indirectly on the topic. Often, only one chapter is potentially useful.

3. The *preface* or *introduction* serves as a critical overview of the entire book, pinpointing the primary subject of the text and approaches taken by the author toward it.

4. The *appendix* offers additional materials of a supplementary nature not pertinent to the primary text. Valuable charts and graphs are often placed in an appendix.

5. A *glossary* lists and defines complex terminology within the subject area. On this note, you ought to draw appropriate terminology from any such list and learn word meanings for use in your own papers.

6. The *bibliography* and *footnotes* suggest new sources for later investigation. Many new sources can be added to a bibliography list during the note-taking phase of research. The same names appearing time and again in the citations give clues to the best authorities (see "Citation Searching," 50–54).

7. The *index* of a book gives names and terms with page numbers for all items mentioned within the text. For example, the index of a Robert Frost biography will provide page numbers to a discussion of each special poem. One student, for example, planned to research Andrew Wyeth's 1961 painting "Christina's World." She found Wanda Corn's book, *The Art of Andrew Wyeth*, but neither the preface nor table of contents helped, so she turned to the index and found a gold mine: "*Christina's World*, 38, 39, 40, 55, 74, 78, 93, 95, 143, 144, 164." As a side benefit, she also found among the back matter an extensive bibliography to Wyeth's letters and interviews and to books and articles about him.

Examine the Book Reviews

Whenever one book serves as a cornerstone for research, test its validity and critical reputation by reading a review or two. Reviews are hidden here and there in magazines and journals, requiring a search of the following indexes:

Book Review Digest. New York: H. W. Wilson, 1905–date.

> Arranged alphabetically by author, this work provides an evaluation of several thousand books each year. It features summaries and brief quotations from the reviews to uncover the critical reception of the work.

Book Review Index. Detroit: Gale, bimonthly.

> This work indexes reviews in 225 magazines and journals.

Index to Book Reviews in the Humanities. Williamston, Michigan: Phillip Thompson Publ., annually.

> This index to reviews in humanities periodicals has entries listed by author, title, and reviewer.

Index to Book Reviews in the Social Sciences. Williamston, Michigan: Phillip Thompson Publ., annually.

> This index to reviews in social science periodicals has entries listed by author, title, and reviewer.

Current Book Review Citations. New York: H. W. Wilson, annually. This work gives an author-title index to book reviews published in more than 1,000 periodicals.

The Booklist. Chicago: American Library Assn., 1905–date. A monthly magazine that reviews new books for librarians. This work includes brief summaries and recommendations.

A sample page of *Book Review Digest* shows you the type of information available in this type of review survey:

Fig. 44: From *Book Review Digest*

1. Author, title, and facts of publication
2. Dewey call number and subject entries for card catalog 3. Library of Congress call number
4. Description of the work
5. Reviewer's evaluation of the book 6. Facts of publication of the 600 word review: *Library Journal* 98 (1973): 3247.
7. A review that the *Book Review Digest* has not quoted

FONTANA, VINCENT J. Somewhere a child is crying: maltreatment— causes and prevention. 268p $6.95 '73 Macmillan Pub. Co 364.1
Cruelty to children Child welfare LC 78-16566

"The author presents numerous case studies of child battering and deprivation, exploring . . . the factors contributing to abusive parental behavior as well as the reasons why courts and social welfare agencies often fail to protect children. Using the New York City task force on child abuse as an example, Fontana shows how better reporting and disposition of abuse cases, voluntary self-help groups such as Parents Anonymous, and an experimental program of parental retraining have bettered the situation. The conclusion calls for a legal statement of children's rights and the machinery needed to protect them." (Library J) Index

"The author sketches the long history of child maltreatment . . . [and] tells of the increasing rise of conditions which favor [it]. . . . The book then becomes one long account of the sufferings of the children, their causes, and the barriers against their prevention. . . . [It contains] one element notable in these days of public outcry against any use of punishment . . . in dealing with violent offenders and those few of the mentally deranged who are dangerous to themselves or others. Dr. Fontana does not want persons who lose control and harm children to 'get away with it.' . . . For the inexpert who may come in contact with children who are being abused, Dr. Fontana provides a list of tell-tale indications . . . [He] calls for widespread public concern and massive expenditures for the detection of child maltreatment in its earliest stages and for the establishment of a national system of prevention and remedial services. Let us hope that his crusading spirit will prove contagious." E. J. Levinson

Ann Am Acad 415:275 S '74 600w

"The director of pediatrics at New York's Foundling Hospital and chairman of the Mayor's Task Force on Child Abuse and Neglect presents startling descriptions and statistics of a major national problem . . . Fontana's concern for both child and parent, his plea for recognition of the rights of children, and his suggestions for improving both legislation and procedures for detecting, investigating, and preventing maltreatment make this book vital reading for concerned layman and professional alike." J. M. Marey
Library J 98:3247 N 1 '73 110w
Reviewed by George Merrill
Library J 99:586 F 15 /74 130w [YA]

Understanding What You Read

Some student researchers do more copying than thinking. Convinced that they need scores of entries for their "Works Cited" pages, some waste time photocopying entire journal articles and carrying stacks of books home from the library. That sort of diligence is misplaced. The quality of your analysis outweighs the number of source materials; likewise, the content of your finished paper is more important than how many note cards you accumulate. Your thinking comes first. To that end, keep your thesis and outline headings firmly in mind as you open books and leaf through articles. In many instances you may borrow only one idea that you rephrase into your own words. Note B. N. Raina's original statement, especially the highlighted sentence in the middle of this essay:

Fig. 45: From
The Explicator

1. Passage of importance to the researcher. From B. N. Raina, "Dickinson's 'Because I Could Not Stop for Death,'" *The Explicator* 43.3 (1985): 11–12.

Dickinson's BECAUSE I COULD NOT STOP FOR DEATH

It has been the general difficulty with critical exegeses of Emily Dickinson's "Because I could not stop for Death—" that (1) "Death" and "Immortality" in the first stanza seem unaccountably syncopated, and (2) that "I first surmised the Horses' Head/Were toward Eternity—" of the end of the poem remains equally enigmatically without derivation. I offer the following interpretive possibility.

The crux of the poem's meanings, I suggest, is in the first two lines, "Because I could not stop for Death—/He kindly stopped for me—". We have tended mechanically to read this to mean that since the narrative subject of the poem finds herself rather too involved in the humdrum of living, with no thought of death, Death like a civil gentleman-suitor stops by in his chaise and four to take the busy persona out for the final ride, paradoxically, to the accompaniment of "Immortality." I think the lines lead us into a simplistic literalness because of the deceptive surface. Read them as you would a prototypical "romantic" utterance and the problem begins to solve itself.

To wit, translate the persona's not stopping for death into an imaginative perception of the nonreality of death. Death is death only to those who live within the time-bound finite world outside of the imaginative infinity of consciousness. That being so, the "stopped" of the second line takes on a profoundly rich ambiguity. Whereas clearly the metaphor of Death stopping by is to be retained as one level of courtship, more essentially, since the persona's consciousness has negated death, Death in turn stops, that is, *ceases* (so that the full richness of the initial "because" should now be apparent). And, appropriately, from that dialectic of consciousness is *generated* "Immortality."

The rest of the poem carries forward the poetic journey through a necessary but obviously imagined framework of body-consciousness in which the "chill" of the "Setting Sun" is sensually rendered. Yet, when the carriage comes to the grave—"A Swelling of the Ground—" *entrance* is not made: "we *paused* before a House" merely (emphasis added). So that the "Immorality" achieve at the very beginning remains unthreatened even as death is sensibly confronted. And when the retrospective voice comes back after centuries, the poem only returns to its first accomplished vision of the nonreality of death in an unbroken moment of consciousness:

Since then—'tis Centuries—and yet
Feels shorter than the Day
I first surmised the Horses' Heads
Were toward Eternity.

The "first" surmise recalls how "Immortality" was attained at the start of the poem, and in a remarkable conflation of the romantic and the Christian, the dreaded Horses of the Apocalypse are comfortably perceived as yielding only everlasting life in a grand personal apotheosis: "He kindly stopped for *me*" (emphasis added).

Rather than photocopying the entire piece or copying Raina's entire paragraph, the researcher read first, related the reading to her thesis and outline headings, and wrote this:

Fig. 46: Sample note card

> Raina 11-12
>
> B. N. Raina observes that death for this speaker is an "imaginative perception of the nonreality of death" (12) so that death is confronted as a window to everlasting life.
>
> on Dickinson's "Because I Could Not Stop..."

This student's note can slide easily into the finished text. A bibliography card with full information on Raina was also prepared.

Getting the Author's Idea

When faced with an article, read the abstract, if one is available. That is the quickest way to ascertain if the piece will be of use to you. If no abstract is available, read the opening paragraph for clues to the writer's purpose. (See 45 for a sample abstract.)

With a book, skim the author's preface to find a statement of purpose. One folklore student's reading of a preface put new perspectives on a book entitled *The Bell Witch of Tennessee* in which the author, Charles Bailey Bell, says:

> The name "Bell Witch" has always been resented by the family. They are sensitive to such an appellation. . . . The Author shall relate in this book what was handed down to him by his father, Dr. J. T. Bell, he having the recollections of his father, John Bell, Jr.
>
> From: *A Mysterious Spirit: The Bell Witch of Tennessee* (Nashville: Elder, 1972).

The author reveals his built-in bias about the folklore. He is a descendent of one of the principals in the story, which will color his account of what happened. To balance against the Bell book, the student went in search of other sources.

Understanding the Difference Between Primary and Secondary Sources

Primary sources are original words of a writer—novel, speech, eyewitness account, letter, autobiography, interview.

Secondary sources are works about somebody (biography or history) and about their work, including books and articles about a novel, about a speech or document, or about a scientific finding. The subject area of a research paper determines in part the nature of the source materials. Use the following chart as a guide:

	Primary Sources	Secondary Sources
Literary Topics	novels, poems, plays, short stories, letters, diaries, manuscripts, autobiographies	journal articles, reviews, biographies, critical books about writers and their works
Government Political Science History	speeches, writings by presidents and others, the *Congressional Record,* reports of agencies and departments, documents written by historical figures	newspaper reports, news magazines, political journals and newsletters, journal articles, and history books
Social Sciences	case studies, findings from surveys and questionnaires, reports of social workers, psychiatrists, and lab technicians	commentary and evaluation in reports, documents, journal articles, and books
Sciences	tools and methods, experiments, findings from tests and experiments, observations, discoveries, and test patterns	interpretations and discussions of test data as found in journals and books (scientific books, which are quickly dated, are less valuable than up-to-date journals)
Fine Arts	films, paintings, music, sculptures as well as reproductions and synopses of these for research purposes	evaluations in journal articles, critical reviews, biographies, and critical books about the artists and their works

| Business | market research and testing, technical studies and investigations, drawings, designs, models, memoranda and letters, computer data | discussion of the business world in newspapers, business magazines, journals, government documents, and books |
| Education | pilot studies, term projects, sampling results, tests and test data, surveys, interviews, observations, statistics, and computer data | analysis and evaluation of educational experimentation in journals, reports, pamphlets, and books |

TECHNIQUE OF NOTE CARDS

The following tips may prove helpful for attaining accuracy in hand-written notes.

1. **Use ink.** Write notes legibly in ink because penciled notes become blurred after repeated shuffling of the cards.

2. **Use index cards.** In general, use either four-by-six or the smaller three-by-five-inch index cards for recording data. Unlike large sheets of paper, cards are easily rearranged.

3. **One item per card.** One item of information on each card facilitates shuffling and rearranging the data during all stages of organization.

4. **Write on one side of card.** Material on the back of a card may be overlooked. Use the back side, if at all, for personal notes and observations, but mark the front with "OVER."

5. **List the source.** Before writing the note, abbreviate the exact source (for example, "Thornton 431") to serve as a quick reference to the full bibliography card. Note: avoid a key number system or other complex plan because you need author and page number for in-text citation, not a key number. Besides, you might lose your key!

6. **Label each card.** Use the major headings of your preliminary outline for labeling cards. This label, sometimes called a "slug," appears at the top of each card, speeds arrangement of notes in accordance with the outline, and will speed tabulation of data for tables and graphs.

7. **Write a full note.** While you have source materials in your hands, write full, well-developed sentences. Full wording in the note will speed the writing of your first draft (see above, 46, for an example). Avoid the temptation to photocopy everything with the hope that materials will fall miraculously into place later on.

8. **Keep everything.** Try to save every card, sheet, scrap, and note in order to authenticate a date, age, page number, or full name.

METHODS OF NOTE-TAKING
Building a Set of Personal Note Cards

How often have you developed a good thought only to lose it before writing it down? This happens to many researchers; the best way to avoid it is to learn the practice of writing notes to yourself during research reading. After all, when you start writing the rough draft, the contents should be your thoughts and ideas interspersed with and supported by your sources. If you have no personal notes, then your writing will develop slowly.

Let's look at two hypothetical instances. In the first one, a student sits down with his outline and note cards drawn entirely from the sources. He faces a major hurdle: how to write his own paper while avoiding the temptation to string together an endless cycle of quotations and paraphrases. In the second instance, another student uses her personal note cards in combination with the source cards in order to write out her argument as supported by the sources. The difference is monumental.

Two samples of personal notes follow:

Methods of Note-Taking

> *Preventing abuse*   mine
>
> I'm concerned that most of the time the agencies try makeshift remedies after the fact. Maybe the answer lies in preventing abuse. Or am I being too naïve?

> *Parents as victims*   mine
>
> Are the parents victims? The more I read, the more it seems that parents are depressed, not deranged. What causes it? I think maybe a mother who reaches a breaking point just takes it out on the kids. She doesn't hate them; she's just striking out because things are coming down hard on her.

Eventually, these notes became part of a research paper, as reproduced in the following example:

> This case study, moreover, prompts this theory: if people like the Jane Neilsons of our society could be identified and given help in a timely fashion, then perhaps children would not be victimized. Perhaps the answer lies in preventing abuse, not in makeshift remedies after the fact. Can social agencies not predict that Jane Neilson's six children are targets for abuse? After all, child abuse is a symptom of the parent's condition.

Writing Summary Notes

Many times you will want to write a brief sketch of your material without great concern for style or expression. Because the original material is not valuable, not well written, or not pertinent, your purpose is to write quickly and concisely without concern for careful wording or exact paraphrase. The summary note represents borderline information for your study. If more information is needed, you can rewrite it later in a clear, appropriate prose style.

Extract significant facts by focusing on essentials: select the key information, summarize it, and get on with other matters. Remember, however, that even a summary needs documentation of author and page number.

Sample summary note cards follow:

> statistics   from Cohen & Sussman 433
>
> Nobody seems to know for certain, but the Education Commission of the States reports 60,000 cases of abuse every year. Others suggest 75,000 and one argues that figure should be 120,000.

Another summary note card by the same writer contains this information:

> *statistics   from Chase 104*
> *This source says boys outnumber*
> *girls in being abused until*
> *they are teenagers. Parents argue*
> *more with girls who date and*
> *fight less with older boys who*
> *might fight back.*

Eventually, these summary notes were incorporated into a final draft in MLA style:

> Even worse, severe abuse is on the rise. Each year more and
> more children suffer the trauma of physical and emotional abuse.
> Although the exact number remains unknown, the Education
> Commission of the States reports that some 60,000 cases occur
> annually (Cohen and Sussman 433). Boys suffer more abuse than
> girls until the teen years, when girls then suffer more (Chase
> 104).

As demonstrated above, summary notes sketch material to be expressed more fluently for the first draft.

Writing Plot Summaries and Review Notes

Another type of card reviews the contents of an article or book. This note is especially useful for writing an annotated bibliography (see pages 133–34). In truth, it should be called a précis (see below), but standard terms are "review" or "plot summary." You will have occasion to use plot summary notes whenever you write about a novel, short story, drama, or similar literary work. The next note demonstrates the plot summary card:

> plot   Hansberry's *Raisin in the Sun*
> The drama portrays a black family's
> determination to move from the
> ghetto. Mama Younger dominates
> the family members. However, each
> member rebels in his or her own
> way, especially Walter, who squanders
> the family's inheritance and
> brings them to a crisis that threatens
> their survival as a family unit.

As shown, this note briefly clarifies the nature of the work. It seldom extends beyond one paragraph. You can study the abstracts that accompany most professional articles; these are review summaries of entire works (see also "Abstract," 130).

Condensing Sources with Précis Notes

A précis differs from the rough summary by its polished style. It differs from paraphrase by its brevity. The plot summary card, as noted above, is a précis because it condenses into a few words the entire nature of a drama. Usually, information condensed into a précis note has more value than a summary, so it deserves a polished style for transfer later to the first draft. Success with the précis requires the following:

1. Condense the original with precision and directness. Reduce a long paragraph into a sentence, tighten an article into a brief paragraph, and summarize a book into a page.

2. Preserve the tone of the original. If the original is serious, suggest that tone in the précis. In the same way, retain moods of doubt, skepticism, optimism, and so forth.

3. Limit your quotation of the original by writing the précis in your own language. However, retain exceptional phrases from the original, enclosing them in quotation marks.

4. Provide documentation locating the source of your material.

A sample précis note card follows:

> *Loss of jobs + abuse from Steinberg + others*
> *975-85*
> *This article explores the abuse of children*
> *in relation to economic conditions. These*
> *experts are quick to note a correlation*
> *of unemployment in a town or nation*
> *with increased danger to children,*
> *their well being, and even their lives.*
> *This loss of jobs may endanger the*
> *children.*
> *Good conclusion about this on p. 982*

In only a few sentences, the writer has summarized the essential elements of an entire article. Transitions that bridge across the omitted materials are "Thus," "In brief," and "In short." The manner in which she used the précis and the quotation mentioned at the bottom of the card is shown here:

> The year 1982 saw an increase in child abuse all across
> the nation; it was also one of extremely high
> unemployment. Experts note the correlation, saying
> unemployment in a town, state, or whole nation may
> endanger the well-being of the children as well as their
> very lives (Steinberg, Catalano, and Dooley 975-85).
> These three authorities also reach rather distressing
> conclusions:
>
> > Declines in the work force are significantly
> > related to reported child abuse in two
> > metropolitan communities. This finding is
> > consistent with the hypothesis that undesirable
> > economic change causes family stress, resulting
> > subsequently in child abuse. (982)
>
> On an individual basis the family scenario might go like
> this: the father loses his job so the mother enters the

A similar summarization is demonstrated in the following excerpt from the sample research paper:

> Depression also causes a parent to beat his or her
> child, but E. Milling Kinard suggests that treating the
> parent for depression without removing the social problems
> of economic poverty and emotional stress will probably
> have only limited success (403-06).

Note the citation to pages 403–06, which indicates that several pages of the original were condensed into a one-sentence précis. Accordingly, you will have success with précis notes if you tighten into a sentence or two the essence of a much longer statement.

Rewriting Sources with Paraphrased Notes

Paraphrasing is a technique for restating in your own style the thought or meaning expressed by someone else. In other words, you borrow an idea, opinion, interpretation, or statement and rewrite it. By paraphrasing the sometimes elevated style of scholarly writing, you can maintain the stylistic flow of your paper. It prevents obvious jumps back and forth from the language of the sources to your own.

Write paraphrase notes in about the same number of words as the original (hence the distinction between paraphrase and précis, the latter being a very *brief* condensation). You will be wise to paraphrase material during note-taking rather than to fill cards with quoted matter or to photocopy pages of journals. Writing a rough draft goes quickly with paraphrased notes, but not so quickly when shuffling through page after page of photocopied materials. Also, plagiarism is one danger of relying primarily on carelessly documented quoted materials. You are saved from plagiarism when paraphrasing because you credit the borrowed ideas as well as words (see "Avoiding Plagiarism" 77–81). The point of view and the presentation may be yours, but the idea belongs to the original author and deserves proper recognition.

Success with paraphrasing requires the following:

1. Rewrite the original in about the same number of words.
2. Preserve the tone of the original by maintaining moods of satire, anger, humor, doubt, and so on.
3. Retain exceptional words and phrasing from the original and enclose them within quotation marks. Double-check a finished paraphrase with the original to be certain that the paraphrase truly rewrites the original and that it places any retained wording of the original within quotation marks.

4. Provide documentation indicating the source of the material. For example, an original article on childhood aggression states:

> There are many abusive parents for whom groups may be the only answer, not only because of the quality of services offered, or the potential benefits they promise, but chiefly for the fact that a group of this type is the only service that some abusive parents will attend and participate in.
>
> **From "Parents Anonymous and the Private Agency: Administrative Cooperation" by Marlin Blizinsky from *Child Welfare*, 1982, Vol. 61, pp. 305–11. Copyright © 1982 by Child Welfare League of America, Inc. Reprinted by permission.**

The researcher's paraphrased note card, based on this source, is shown next:

> group therapy from Blizinsky 311
>
> This critic reports that group sessions may be the only answer for some folks because group sessions might be the only thing a person will participate in whether he is the abuser or the abused.

Eventually, this note appeared in the final paper, slightly altered, as shown below in MLA style:

>   First, the idea of group therapy and self-help
> sessions for adults seems sound. Marlin Blizinsky reports
> that group sessions may be the only answer for some
> persons because a group session might be the only program
> in which an abusive person will participate (311).

To repeat, paraphrasing keeps the length of the note about the same, but converts the original into your language and style.

Copying Sources with Quotation Notes

Researchers frequently overuse direct quotations in taking notes, and, as a result, in the final paper. In the worst cases, they rush to the photocopier for wholesale copying of page after page. They discover later that the writing still remains to be done. Probably only ten to twenty percent of a final manuscript should appear as directly quoted matter, but textual study of a novel or use of in-depth interviews may increase that quota considerably. In particular, avoid lifting huge pieces of a scholarly article to use in your paper. The overuse of direct quotation indicates either (1) that you did not have a clear focus and jotted down verbatim just about everything related to the subject, or (2) that you had inadequate evidence and used numerous quotations as padding.

Specific cases for using direct quotation of *secondary sources* are these: (1) to display excellence in ideas and expression by the source; (2) to explain complex material; and (3) to set up a statement of your own, especially if it spins off, adds to, or takes exception to the source as quoted.

Direct quotation is necessary with *primary sources* because you should cite poetry, fiction, drama, letters, and interviews. In other cases, you will need to use a phrase from a presidential speech, quote a business executive, or reproduce computer data. Success with quotation note cards requires the following:

1. Place quotation marks around material that is directly copied onto note cards to distinguish the quotes from paraphrases.
2. Copy the exact words of the author, even to the retention of any errors in the original or what might appear to be errors. The word *sic* within brackets signals that an error in the original is being reproduced precisely (see "Sic," 120).
3. For special problems, see 108–21.

The following note card demonstrates a quotation from a secondary source:

TV as breeding violence   from Zigler 40

"One finds violence, hostility and aggression everywhere, including TV, the movies, and in many of our everyday social relations. So long as this preoccupation with and even glorification of aggression is tolerated, so long can we expect the abuse of children both at home and in the school."

For an example of how one researcher worked these two quoted sentences into her paper, see the next sample. Note especially that rather than lumping the sentences together as one long indented quotation, she works them separately into a meaningful paragraph that fits her style and the MLA format:

```
       What's more, the television age may breed violence.

  Zigler laments, "One finds violence, hostility and

  aggression everywhere, including TV, the movies, and in

  many of our everyday social relations" (4).  Violence

  observed becomes, all too often, violence practiced by

  parents on the children as well as by children on their

  brothers and sisters and even against their own parents.

  As Zigler puts it, "So long as this preoccupation with and

  even glorification of aggression is tolerated, so long can

  we expect the abuse of children both at home and in the

  school" (40).
```

In the case of direct quotation from a primary source, be certain to quote exactly. Two samples follow:

> *Images of frustration Eliot's "Prufrock" 5*
> *"For I have known them all already,*
>   *Known them all: —*
> *Have known the evenings, mornings,*
>   *afternoons,*
> *I have measured out my life with*
>   *coffee spoons;*
> *I know the voices dying with a*
>   *dying fall*
> *Beneath the music from a farther room.*
> *So how should I presume?"*

From: T. S. Eliot, "The Love Song of J. Alfred Prufrock."

The student has copied an entire unit of the poem but may use only a line or two. Having an entire verse (or entire paragraph of prose) assures accuracy in handling the quotation within the body of the research paper.

The following note quotes a novel:

From: Renzo Rosso, *The Hard Thorn,* trans. William Weaver (London: Alan Ross, 1966) 43.

Additional examples of handling quoted materials may be found on 79–81 and a discussion of technical matters will be found on 108–21.

Writing Notes into a Computer

The availability of word processing computers offers an alternative for note-taking. However, take advantage of the new technology only if you have the necessary expertise and only if a machine is available to you throughout the project. The computer affects note-taking strategies in several ways:

1. Record the bibliography information for each source you encounter by listing it in a BIBLIO document so that you build the necessary list of references in one alphabetical file. Chapter 6 will show you the correct forms of entries.

2. Write your notes into the word processor using one of two methods.

   a. Write all notes into a single file, labeled with a short title, such as NOTES. Your notes can then be moved around easily within the one document by BLOCK moves which will transfer them quickly into your TEXT document.

   b. Write each note as a separate temporary file so that each can be moved later into the appropriate section of your TEXT file by a COPY or READ command. With either method, you should print out your notes so that you can see them all at once; then edit them on the printed sheets as well as on the computer monitor.

3. During the writing stage copy notes directly into your rough draft by moving blocks or by transferring files. However, keep original notes on file in case they are needed again in the same form. That is, you can build and edit

your TEXT and still keep a copy of each note on the diskette for proofreading against the finished pages of TEXT file.

4. Computer notes often approximate the form of a rough draft, so write your computer notes in a complete, fluid writing style so that, once keyboarded, the material will not need retyping. You need only move the note into your rough draft and then revise it to fit the context.

AVOIDING PLAGIARISM

Plagiarism (the improper use of source materials) is a serious breach of ethics. Most instances of plagiarism are the result of ignorance of rules rather than a deliberate effort on the part of the researcher to deceive instructors and other readers of the research paper.

Purpose of Documentation of Source Materials

The inventor Thomas Edison depended upon documented research by others. He once said that he began his inventions where other men left off; he built upon their beginnings. How fortunate he was that his predecessors recorded their experiments. Scholarship is the sharing of information. The primary reason for any research paper is to announce and publicize new findings. A botanist explains her discovery of a new strain of ferns in Kentucky's Land Between the Lakes. A medical scientist reports the results of his cancer research. A sociologist announces the results of a two-year pilot study of Appalachian Indians. Similarly, you must explain your findings in a psychology experiment, disclose research into shoplifting, or discuss the results of an investigation into schizophrenia of preschool children. A basic ingredient of business and professional life is research, whether by a lawyer, boot maker, or hospital nurse. A management position demands research expertise as well as the ability to examine critically and to write effectively about an issue: a client's liability, a marketing decision, or the design of a work area.

Like Thomas Edison's, your research in any area begins where others leave off. You will report your findings, but whether or not somebody continues the research will depend upon two factors: the quality and significance of the research and the accuracy of the written document. In truth, an undergraduate paper probably will not circulate beyond the immediate classroom; yet the central purpose of all research remains the same—to disclose new findings to the research community. In the process you learn the conventions of scholarship, discover the multiple resources of the library, find methods for recording data, and learn more about a topic than associates and colleagues.

An Explanation of Plagiarism

Fundamentally, plagiarism is the offering of the words or ideas of another person as one's own. While the most blatant violation is the use of another student's work, the more common error is carelessness with reference sources because of mislabeled note cards or a failure to place quotation marks on a note card. Sometimes paraphrase never quite becomes paraphrase—too much of the original is left intact. The obvious form of plagiarism is to copy any direct quotation from a source without providing quotation marks and without crediting the source. The more subtle form, but equally improper, is to paraphrase material that is not properly documented. (For "common knowledge" exceptions, see below, 81.) Remember that an author's ideas, interpretations, and words are his or her property; in fact, they are protected by law and must be acknowledged whenever borrowed. Consequently, the use of source materials requires conformity to a few rules of conduct:

1. Acknowledge borrowed material by introducing the quotation or paraphrase with the name of the authority. This practice serves to indicate where the borrowed materials begin.
2. Enclose all quoted materials within quotation marks.
3. Make certain that paraphrased material is rewritten into your own style and language. The simple rearrangement of sentence patterns is unacceptable. Do not alter the essential idea of the source.
4. Provide specific in-text documentation for each borrowed item. For example, MLA style requires name and page for all in-text references. Requirements differ for other fields, so see the section on your discipline in Chapter 7.
5. Provide a bibliography entry in the "Works Cited" for every source cited in the paper. Omit sources consulted but not used.

The examples provided below in MLA style should reveal the differences between genuine research writing and plagiarism. First is the original reference material; it is followed by four student versions, two of which are plagiarism and two of which are not.

Original Material:

> The extended family is now rare in contemporary society, and with its demise the new parent has lost the wisdom and daily support of older, more experienced family members. Furthermore, many parents are not as well equipped for parenthood as were their parents before them, since over the years most children have been given less responsibility in helping to care for younger siblings.
>
> From Edward F. Zigler, "The Unmet Needs of America's Children," *Children Today* 5.3 (1976): 42.

STUDENT VERSION A (Unacceptable)

```
Today's society and shifting patterns of social order may

dictate, then, a climate for abuse. Many parents are just

not equipped today for parenthood. For instance, the

extended family is rare in contemporary society, and

because of its disappearance new parents have lost the

wisdom and daily support of the wise grandparents. In

truth, a family such as that portrayed by the Waltons on

television seldom exists today with grandparents, parents,

and many children all living together under one roof.

Therefore, today's young parents are not well equipped

because as children they were given less responsiblity in

helping care for younger brothers and sisters.
```

This piece of writing is plagiarism in a most deplorable form. Material stolen without documentation is obvious, and even a casual reader will spot it immediately because of radical differences in the student's style and that of the source. The writer has simply borrowed abundantly from the original source, even to the point of retaining the essential wording. The writer has provided no documentation whatever, nor has the writer named the authority. In truth, the writer implies to the reader that these sentences are an original creation when, actually, only two sentences belong to the writer, and the rest belong to the source.

The next version is better, but it still demonstrates blatant disregard for scholarly conventions.

STUDENT VERSION B (Unacceptable)

```
Too many parents are not equipped today for parenthood.

The extended family with three or more generations under

one roof is now rare. Thus parents have lost the wisdom

of older, experienced persons. In truth, a family such as

that portrayed by the Waltons on television seldom exists

today with grandparents, parents, and many children living

all together under one roof. Therefore, young parents of

today do a poor job because as youngsters they did not

help care for younger brothers and sisters (Zigler 42).
```

Although this version provides a citation to the authority, it contains two serious errors. First, readers cannot know that the citation "(Zigler 42)" refers to most of the paragraph; readers can only assume that the citation refers to the final sentence. Second, the paraphrasing is careless with words that should be enclosed by quotation marks or rephrased into the student's language and style, such as: "not equipped for parenthood, "extended family," and "lost the wisdom of older."

The next version is correct and proper.

STUDENT VERSION C (Acceptable)

```
        Public concerns for the whole fabric of society stand

in conflict with the selfish, private needs of the abusive

parent.  On that point, Edward Zigler argues that many

parents are just not equipped today for parenthood (42).

He states that the "extended family is now rare in

contemporary society, and with its demise the new parent

has lost the wisdom and daily support of older, more

experienced family members" (42).  In truth, a family such

as that portrayed by the Waltons on television seldom

exists today with grandparents, parents, and many children

all living together under one roof.  If children do not

learn by caring for their younger siblings, then, as

Zigler warns, they cannot be prepared for handling their

own children (42).
```

This version represents a satisfactory handling of the source material. The authority is acknowledged at the outset, the key phrases are directly quoted so as to give full credit where credit is due. The student has been completely honest to the source.

Let's suppose, however, that the writer does not wish to quote directly. The following example shows a paraphrased version:

STUDENT VERSION D (Acceptable)

```
Today's society and shifting patterns of social order may

dictate, then, a climate for abuse.  Edward Zigler argues

that many parents are just not equipped today for

parenthood (42).  He insists that the "extended family"

with several generations under one roof no longer exists
```

```
and parents, who have little expereince and no wise adults

around, are therefore ill equipped to handle their duties

toward family members (Zigler 42). In truth, a family

such as that portrayed by the Waltons on television seldom

exists today with grandparents, parents, and many children

all living together under one roof.
```

This shortened version also represents a satisfactory handling of the source material. In this case, no direct quotation is employed, and the authority is acknowledged and credited, yet the entire paragraph is written in the student's own language.

Common Knowledge Exceptions

Finally, consider the typical complaint: "When I started this research, I didn't know *anything* about child abuse. Does that mean I must document every sentence in the paper?" No, not at all. Personal notes and synthesis of library sources are one's own, along with the thesis, topic sentences, analyses, and surely most of the opening and concluding discussion. In addition, factual information of a general nature, called "common knowledge," recurs in source after source. For example, most sources on Franklin Pierce will report common knowledge: his birth and death, 1804–69, his role at age 48 as 14th President of the United States from 1853–57, and even his role as supporter of the Compromise of 1850 and his later criticism of Abraham Lincoln. However, if one historian comments that Pierce's handling of the slavery issue ruined his effectiveness as President, a citation to the source would be in order.

Remember this general rule: information that occurs in five or more sources may be considered general knowledge. The fact that General Custer lost the battle at Little Big Horn is common knowledge and need not be documented even though you record it while reading an encyclopedia. Required instances for citing a source are:

1. An original idea derived from a source, whether quoted or paraphrased.
2. Factual information borrowed directly from a source that is not common knowledge.
3. Wording that is exceptional in expression or style, even if it repeats common knowledge information.
4. Any exact wording copied from a source.
5. Your summary of original ideas by a source.

4

Writing the Paper

Your task now centers on coordinating all materials and developing a rough draft. You will work best if you have a final thesis sentence, a title, and usually a final outline. Your preliminary thesis helped control note-taking, and now a final thesis will direct your writing. A title identifies your key terms (see 84), and a final outline (see 84–89) helps order your note cards and brings unity and coherence to the final draft.

WRITING A FINAL THESIS SENTENCE

Before writing the entire draft you should reevaluate all materials and frame a final thesis sentence which will (1) control and focus the entire paper, (2) give order to details of the essay by providing unity and a sense of direction, and (3) specify to the reader the point of the research.

You are not bound to an early working thesis (see 17–18) because research may have led you to new, different issues. For example, one writer began "child abuse" research with this preliminary thesis: "A need for a cure to child abuse faces society each day." Investigation, however, directed her away from her first obvious reaction and toward a narrowed focus: "Parents who abuse their children should be treated as victims, not criminals." The writer moved, in effect, to a specific position from which to argue that social organizations should serve abusing parents in addition to helping the abused children.

The final thesis should conform to several conventions:

1. It expresses your position in a full, declarative sentence, which is not a question, not a statement of purpose, and not merely a topic.
2. It limits the subject to a narrow focus that grows out of research.
3. It establishes an investigative, inventive edge to your research and thereby gives a reason for all your work.
4. It points forward to the conclusion.
5. It conforms to your note card evidence and your title.

Every research writer should ask this question: "What is the point of my research?" The answer might very well be the thesis. Other possible questions are:

Can I tell the reader anything new or different?
Do I have a solution to the problem?
Do I have a new slant and new approach to the issue?
Should I take the minority view of this matter?
What exactly is my theory about this subject?

Although a good thesis statement cannot guarantee a good paper, it offers a tool for unifying and controlling any drifting, shifting thoughts about the subject. The following examples have served effectively as thesis sentences for student papers:

Title: The Theme of Black Matriarchy in *A Raisin in the Sun*

Thesis: Hansberry uses the sociological concept of black matriarchy to create dramatic conflict among the members of the Younger family.

Title: Geological Predictions: Sinkholes

Thesis: It is possible within certain guidelines to predict the location of potential sinkholes.

Title: The Language of Television Advertising

Thesis: The rhetorical schemes of repetition enable advertisers to pitch their products effectively within a thirty-second time slot.

Title: Computer Control in Business Applications

Thesis: A company should program the computer to safeguard both valuable documents and its own software.

These samples have three things in common: (1) a declarative sentence that (2) focuses the argument toward an investigative issue that (3) will be resolved in the paper's general discussion and conclusion.

WRITING A TITLE

Your title should clearly describe the contents of the research paper. Imagine that somebody must catalog, file, or index the paper by its title; then provide key words of identification, as with the following:

Poor: Gothic Madness
Better: Gothic Madness in Three Southern Writers
    Key words: gothic and southern writers

Poor: Saving the Software
Better: Computer Control: Software Safeguards and Computer Theft
    Key words: computer theft and software safeguards

Poor: The Joys of Music
Better: The Joys of Music: Special Effects With Pizzicato
    Key words: music and pizzicato

Fancy literary titles may fail to label issues under discussion. The title "Let There Be Hope" offers no clue for a reader; use it with a personal essay or fiction, not with a research paper. A better title would be "Let There Be Hope: A View of Child Abuse." A precise title would be: "Child Abuse: A View of the Victims." For placement of the title, see "Title Page or Opening Page," 128–29.

WRITING A FINAL OUTLINE

An outline classifies the segments of the investigation into clear, logical categories. Understand that not all papers require the formal outline, nor do some researchers need one. After all, the outline and first draft are preliminary steps to discovering what needs expression. Modify your outline throughout the writing of the rough draft as you discover new ideas and reorganize your evidence.

Use Standard Outline Symbols

List your major categories and subtopics in this form:

I. _____ **First major heading**
  A. _____ **Subheadings of first degree**
    1. _____ **Subheadings of second degree**
    2.
      a. _____ **Subheadings of third degree**
      b.
        (1) _____ **Subheadings of fourth degree**
        (2)
          (a) _____ **Subheadings of fifth degree**
          (b)

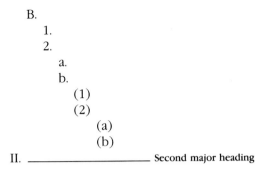

   B.
      1.
      2.
         a.
         b.
           (1)
           (2)
              (a)
              (b)

II. _____ Second major heading

Indenting signifies progress from major concepts to minor ones. The degree to which you continue the subheads will depend, in part, upon the complexity of the subject; generally, subheads seldom carry beyond the first series of small letters.

An alternative form, especially for papers in business and the sciences, is the *decimal outline,* which divides material by numerical divisions, as follows:

1. _____
   1.1. _____
      1.1.1. _____
      1.1.2. _____
      1.1.3. _____
   1.2. _____
      1.2.1. _____
      1.2.2. _____
2. _____

Use Balanced and Parallel Form

Headings of like rank on the same margin should have equal importance. Use grammatical balance to coordinate ideas that relate logically, as with a series of representative examples, the opposition of two ideas, a set of cause/ effect relationships, or a sequence of steps. As equal ideas develop, give them parallel form in the outline. Note the mistake in the following:

```
I. Spring sports

  A. Golf

  B. To swing a baseball bat

  C. Swinging a tennis racket
```

This writer has not balanced items logically or grammatically. Make each item a noun or a phrase, either infinitive or participle, but do not mix the forms. Subordinate balanced ideas, but *not* as shown in the following:

```
I.  Spring sports

    A. Baseball

        1.  Swinging the bat

    B. Tennis

        1.  Swinging the racket

    C. Golf

        1.  Swinging the club
```

This writer probably researched one sports technique—the swing, suggesting the arrangement on the left below where all parts now balance logically in sequence. However, the outline on the right below classifies by elements of the swing to discuss one sport in depth or to compare all three sports under each subheading:

```
The Sports Swing                    The Elements of a Sports Swing

A.  The baseball swing              A.  Setup

    1. Setup                            1. Balance

    2. Mechanics of the swing           2. Addressing the ball

    3. Follow through                   3. Grip and hand position

B.  The tennis swing                B.  Mechanics of the swing

    1. Setup                            1. Backswing

    2. Mechanics of the swing           2. Hand-eye contact

    3. Follow through                   3. Acceleration

C.  The golf swing                  C.  Follow through

    1. Setup                            1. Steady head

    2. Mechanics of the swing           2. Body rotation

    3. Follow through                   3. Extension
```

Use Content-Oriented Headings

Avoid the terms "introduction," "body," and "conclusion" in the outline. Instead of writing "I. Introduction," write instead:

```
I.  The Role of Repetition in Television Advertising
```

Instead of writing "IV. Conclusion," write instead:

```
IV.  Advertising Copywriters Defend Their Craft
```

In this way the outline headings specify content and allow for subheadings. An alternative includes both the descriptive heading and the content heading, as with: "Introduction: The Role of Repetition in Television Advertising."

List the Thesis Sentence Separately Above the Outline

Because a thesis is the main idea of the entire paper, do not label it as Item I in the outline. Otherwise, you may search fruitlessly for parallel ideas to put in II, III, and IV. Instead, write the thesis separately, placing it above the actual outline. Then, as the rough draft develops, the thesis appears naturally as the motivating part of the paper, usually in the general opening. (See also page 99 on using the thesis in the opening.)

Use Dynamic Order with the Outline

The outline should trace the issues, defend and support a thesis, and provide dynamic progression of issues and concepts that point forward to the conclusion. Outline headings generally move from explanation of the theory, to evidence, and then to answers. In other cases, headings move from explanation of the issues to analysis of parts, and then to synthesis. Some headings follow chronological order for events in time or items in sequence. The report of an empirical study has headings that move from the introduction of the problem to tools and methods and then to results and discussion. In every case, the issues and the handling of evidence will generate the dynamics of the closing. The outline on pages 162–64, for example, establishes the issues of child abuse, traces the causes and effects, progresses to its focus on parents as victims, and moves to a conclusion about necessary treatment.

CHOOSING A FINAL OUTLINE FORM

Outlines appear in topic, sentence, or paragraph form. Avoid mixing the forms within a given outline, and use either standard outline symbols or the decimal plan (see above, 84–85). In every case treat the outline as a tool. It should contribute to the writing process, not inhibit it.

Topic Outline

With the topic outline, every heading is a noun phrase ("Prevention of abuse") or its equivalent, a gerund phrase ("Preventing abuse"), or an infinitive phrase ("To prevent abuse"). A brief sample follows:

```
II.  The Issues of Child Abuse

     A.  The Problems

         1.  Recognition that there is a problem

         2.  Myth that America is child-oriented

         3.  Problems of discovering abuse

         4.  Help after the fact

     B.  Statistics of Abuse

         1.  Abuse on the increase

         2.  Specific examples

         3.  Absence of professional help

         4.  Prevention of rather than coping with
```

This form, the most popular, establishes succinctly and precisely the main areas of investigation. Its weakness is brevity because the incomplete headings can hide any organizational problems.

Sentence Outline

This outline includes full sentences that you would transcribe into the rough draft. Some outline entries can serve as topic sentences for paragraphs, thereby speeding the writing process. In addition, the subject/verb pattern establishes the logical direction of your thinking (for example, the phrase "myths about abuse" becomes "We must avoid myths and distortions"). Thereby, the sentence outline brings into the open any possible organizational problems rather than hiding them, as a topic outline might do. The time devoted to a complete sentence outline, like complete, polished notes (see 96–97) will serve you well by speeding the entire writing process. A brief sample follows:

```
II.  The issues of child abuse are multiple and complex.

     A.  The problems center on recognition and discovery
         of abuse.

         1.  First, we need to recognize that there is a
             problem.

         2.  Next, we must avoid mythic distortions.

         3.  We should discover potential abusers.

         4.  Help after the fact of abuse is limited help
             at best.
```

```
B.  Statistics reveal the extent of the problem.

    1.  Abuse increases yearly.

    2.  All types of abuse take place daily.

    3.  Professional help is too often absent before abuse.

    4.  We cope with abuse more than we prevent it.
```

Paragraph Outline

Write the paragraph outline with every section as a paragraph or as full paragraphs under noun headings. The dangers of the paragraph outline are twofold: you may try to write the paper when developing only an outline or you may carry weak, undeveloped outline paragraphs directly into the rough draft. A brief sample follows:

```
II.  The Issues

    A.  Experts say public recognition of the degree of

        child abuse is a serious problem. Too many myths

        and distortions of the truth exist in the public

        mind. Generally, we think everybody should love

        their children. Therefore, the discovery of abuse

        after a child is battered arrives too late. We

        need a way to discover potential abusers.

    B.  Statistics startle us by revealing the annual

        increase in reported cases of all types--beatings,

        burnings, neglect, etc. There is an absence of

        professional help before abuse. Thus, we cope

        with it rather than prevent it.
```

REVIEWING YOUR NOTES AND PREPARING TO WRITE

Begin the actual writing of your paper several days before it is due to provide sufficient time for drafting, revising, and rewriting. Prior to the final deadline, you should (1) examine the thesis sentence and outline to see that they provide a well-rounded, logically organized plan, (2) examine various approaches to the topic, (3) review all note cards, and (4) write a rough draft to get a feel for your materials with the understanding, of course, that you must reorganize and rewrite with exacting care.

Reviewing the Thesis Sentence and Outline

Constantly ask, "Do I know my main idea?" If in doubt, rethink and rework the thesis sentence. Also ask, "Do I have sufficient supporting ideas?" If not, build a better outline and add supporting note cards. In particular, examine all ideas and their logical progression through the outline because each paragraph should develop and expand a principal concept.

For example, one writer on "child abuse" decided that unemployment in a community causes an increase in the abuse of children. That clear thesis joined with evidence outlined in notes defended the researcher's generalization that job loss produces mental stress, which causes, in some cases, parental abuse of children. The clarity of the writer's thesis sentence and outline helped maintain the unity of the writing.

Reviewing Your Approach to the Topic

Ask yourself, "Do I know my purpose?" To answer this question, consider both the intellectual framework (the facts of the study) and the emotional framework (your feeling about the topic). The writing needs to be exact, but it should also be human.

Take another look at your writing situation to consider purpose, audience, and your persona as writer. For example, one writer's intellectual choice about child abuse predictably condemned the practice, but her emotional framework became more sensitive and responsive to the abused victims. Should she select an objective approach and, with a degree of detachment, present an analysis of the issues for an inquisitive audience? Or could she assume an involved, subjective position, negative in tone at times, positive at others, so that her presentation would persuade readers and call them into action?

Objective writers offer evidence and analysis with detached distance from the subject. Subjective writers argue with flashes of human passion toward predetermined conclusions, answers, or principles. Of course, complete objectivity is unlikely for any research paper, which displays in fact and form an intellectual argument. At the same time, you should avoid the extremes of subjective writing—demanding, insisting, or quibbling. Try to maintain a quiet prose style, offer rational reasons, and cite precedents. Moderation of your voice, even during argument, suggests control of the situation—both emotionally and intellectually. For example, one writer chose the world energy crisis as her topic. Obviously, she faced an intellectual choice: to defend or condemn the energy policies of the Department of the Interior. As she narrowed the topic to an issue, clean water, and generated ideas about it, she could not remain wholly objective. She wished to destroy misconceptions and quietly rally the audience to her position. Yet, while ridiculing the government agencies with flashes of irony, she had to avoid displays of bias and prejudice. The writing remained based in scholarly evidence, not entertaining fancy. Thus she balanced human concern with research writing.

Using Basic Formulas as Paradigms for Papers in Special Fields

A paper needs to find its own way as an independent writing process; however, your reading of various scholarly articles should have convinced you that writers conform to similar patterns in the development of their papers. These basic formulas are paradigms or general models for papers of a given type. Specifically, a paradigm is an ideal pattern for the paper. It differs from the outline by serving as a basic pattern of reasoning, whereas a traditional outline, with its specific detail on various levels of subdivision, is useful for only one paper.

The most rigid paradigm of all is the one for reports of original research. It demands development, in order, of an introduction, methodology, results, and discussion. Other types of papers fall into patterns less rigid but nevertheless highly formulated.

PARADIGM FOR ADVANCING YOUR IDEAS AND THEORIES

When advancing theory, use this guide, but adjust it as necessary by eliminating some items and adding new elements of your own.

Introduction: Establish the problem or question
Discuss its significance
Introduce experts who have addressed the problem
Provide a thesis sentence that addresses the problem from a perspective not yet advanced by others

Body: Trace issues involved in the problem
Develop a past-to-present examination
Compare and analyze the details and subissues
Cite experts who have addressed the same problem

Conclusion: Advance and defend your theory as it grows out of evidence in the body
Offer directives or a plan of action
Suggest additional work and investigation that is needed

PARADIGM FOR ANALYSIS OF ARTISTIC WORKS

If you plan a literary analysis of poetry, fiction, or drama, keep in mind this overall formula and adjust it to your subject and purposes:

Introduction: Identification of the work
Brief summary in one sentence
Background information that relates directly to the thesis

Biographical facts about the author that relate to
the specific issues
Quotations and paraphrases of authorities that
establish the scholarly traditions
Thesis sentence that establishes your particular
views of the literary work

Body: An analysis divided according to such elements as
imagery, theme, character development, structure,
symbolism, narration, language, and so forth. Your
thesis sentence serves as unifying element for
exploration of these elements.

Conclusion: A fundamental focus on the author of the work, not
just the elements of analysis as explained in the
body. In particular, the conclusion explores the
contributions of the writer in concord with your
thesis sentence.

Use this same pattern, with appropriate modifications, for a study of music, art,
and the other fine arts.

PARADIGM FOR POSITION PAPERS

Position papers for philosophy, religion, political science, and other
fields conform in general to this basic formula:

Introduction: A statement that establishes the problem or contro-
versial issue that your paper will examine
A summary of the issues.
Definition of key terminology
Quotation and paraphrase of sources to build the
controversial nature of the subject
Background to establish a past/present relationship
A thesis to establish your position

Body: Arguments in defense of one side
Analysis of the issues, both pro and con
Evidence from your reading, including quotations
as appropriate

Conclusion: Reestablishment of your thesis to make clear your
position, which should be one that grows logi-
cally from your analysis and discussion of the issues.

PARADIGM FOR ANALYSIS OF HISTORIC EVENTS

Writing the historical or political science paper that analyzes events and
their causes and consequences would need to conform in general to the
following plan:

Introduction: Identification of the event
The background leading up to the event
Quotations and paraphrases from experts
A thesis sentence

Body: Thorough analysis of the background events leading up to the event
A tracing from one historic episode to another
A chronological sequence that explains how one
event relates directly to the next
Citation of authorities who have also investigated
this piece of history

Conclusion: The consequences of this event on the course of
history.
Reaffirmation of your thesis and, if possible, an
explanation on how the course of history was
altered by this one event.

PARADIGM FOR A COMPARATIVE STUDY

Writing a comparative study will require you to examine two schools of
thought, two issues, or the positions taken by two persons. In general the
paper both compares and contrasts the issues and subissues, as suggested by
the following general plan. Note that you have three choices for the body. The
first two serve for comparison of two people, two schools of thought, or two
positions. The third establishes divisions of the subject by comparative
issues.

Introduction:
Establish A
Establish B
Briefly compare the two
Introduce the central issues
Cite source materials on the subjects
Present your thesis

Body (choose one):

Examine A	Issue 1: Discuss A & B	Similarities of A & B
Examine B	Issue 2: Discuss A & B	Differences of A & B
Compare and	Issue 3: Discuss A & B	Discussion of central
contrast A & B		issues

Conclusion:
Discussion of significant issues
Conclusion that ranks one over the other or
Conclusion that rates the respective genius of each side

Remember that the formulas provided here are general guidelines, not iron-clad rules. Use them in that spirit and adjust each as necessary to meet your special needs. No single magic paradigm exists; every paper must find its own path of development and every writer must put personal flourishes on the design.

DRAFTING THE PAPER

At some point you must systematically write a draft of the whole paper. Working through the outline for order and using the note cards for evidence and support, you will create the paper in rough fashion. Transcribe personal notes directly into the draft. Rephrase source material into your writing style, giving credit for any paraphrased ideas and citing only one source at a time in order to control the coherence of ideas and to maintain proper documentation. Weave quotations into the text smoothly. You can offer a blanket citation to several sources, but it needs special in-text citation (see 108–21) or use of a content endnote (see 138–41). You may and should cite more than one source in a paragraph, as with the following:

> Each year more and more children suffer the trauma of physical and emotional abuse. Although the exact number remains unknown, the Education Commission of the States reports that some 60,000 cases occur annually (Cohen and Sussman 433). Boys outnumber girls as victims of abuse until the teen years (Chase 104). One authority even notes that the death rate from cruelty actually exceeds that from infectious disease (Fontana 196).

This example illustrates two points: this writer cites each source separately, one at a time, and provides three different in-text citations.

Readers want your thoughts and ideas with a variety of sources adding contrast, evidence, or defense. You should explain, analyze, and support a thesis, not merely string together research information. Remember this general rule: a paragraph should seldom contain source material only; it needs at least a topic sentence to establish a point for the research evidence.

Adjusting to the Long, Recursive Nature of Research Writing

Writing your paper will occupy many days, during which you may think the paper will never become whole. Supporting evidence may seem weak or may be missing entirely. As a result, you will find yourself retracing previous steps, even to the point of returning to the library for bits of information.

If you get stuck and find yourself staring at the wall, relax and enjoy the break, instead of getting frustrated. Lean back in your chair and change depression into time for reflecting. Nature has a way of reminding each of us that we need to pause now and then, catch our breath, and rethink our problems. Even if you only have a page or two in manuscript form, you would do well occasionally to read back over your progress so far. That period of rereading might restart your motivation and send you into a period of writing once again.

Feel free to write out of sequence, writing a piece of material when you are ready, not when you arrive there by following the outline. For example, when Jo Walker wrote her child abuse paper she penned a section of her closing early in her writing. She knew the material—the four positive steps (see 174–76)—would fit the outline at a set point, so when she was ready she wrote it and set it aside.

Leave yourself time for drafting the paper, revising it with care, and preparing the final manuscript. In particular, worry about the context of your paper more than the intrinsic beauty of the finished document. Perfect typing and an attractive folder do not disguise a poorly conceived design and weak, ineffective development of ideas. Instructors, given a choice, will appreciate a thoroughly developed paper in hand-written form more than a beautifully typed manuscript which has little substance.

Remembering Your Audience as You Write

A research paper assignment inevitably has impact on you, the researcher and writer. In fact, many instructors consider the assignment as a learning process, one that affects you as principal player in the drama. Nevertheless, your work can affect the world around you and influence readers, especially when you address a particular audience. Consequently, recall your early efforts to develop a writing situation (see 17) which included a sense of audience. Jo Walker, for example, wanted to address the social organizations that have power to effect changes in child abuse policies. As a result, she formulated early in her draft the set of four directives for positive action (see 174–76).

You can do the same. Your business paper analyzing the bear market of the stock exchange can address a young investment club. Your interpretation of Dali's paintings might address fellow art students who will be quizzed on Dali, or it might address local museum directors who need an evaluation of Dali's stature in the art world.

Adapting Your Language to Your Purpose and Audience

Many words and phrases will be peculiar to your topic. Therefore, while reading and taking notes, jot down words and phrases relevant to the study. Get comfortable with them so that you can use them effectively. For example, a child abuse topic requires the language of sociology and psychology, thereby demanding an acquaintance with:

social worker	maltreatment	battered child
aggressive behavior	poverty levels	recurrence
behavioral patterns	incestuous relations	formative years
hostility	stress	guardians

In like manner, a poetry paper might require *symbolism, imagery, rhythm, persona,* or *rhyme.* Every discipline and every topic has its own vernacular. In fact, many writers compose a terminology list to strengthen noun and verb usage.

However, nothing betrays weakness about subject matter more quickly than a writer's awkward, distorted usage of technical terminology. For example, the following sentence uses big words, but it distorts and scrambles the language:

```
The impediment of maltreatment documents the national

compulsion toward crippling economically deprived children.
```

The words may be large, but what does the passage mean? This writer is attempting to impress the reader, not communicate.

Writing in Third Person and First Person Voice

Write your paper with a third person voice that avoids "I believe" or "It is my opinion." See the sample paper, 161–82, for correct voice. However, use first person *I* when speaking of personal efforts, as with: "I attempted to identify. . . ." or "In this experiment I placed one of the mice. . . ." Attribute human functions to yourself, but not to non-human sources (Inaccurate: "The total study considered several findings").

Writing with Unity and Coherence

Your paper needs unity and coherence so that all pieces fit the whole. It has *unity* if it explores one topic in depth, with each paragraph carefully expanding upon a single aspect of the narrowed subject. The outline controls unity (see above, "Choosing a Final Outline Form," 87–89). A paper has *coherence* if your ideas and evidence function as an interrelated whole. Coherence requires that quotations and paraphrases be logical extensions of your writing, not intrusions or mere padding. Coherence also demands clear transitions that highlight the logical progression of ideas by repetition of key words, use of pronouns and synonyms, and effective placement of transitional words and phrases (e.g., *also, furthermore, therefore, in addition,* and *thus*). Pay special attention to progression of ideas and to smooth incorporation of quoted materials, as shown below:

> Family troubles will most likely affect the
> delicate members of our society, the children. The
> recognition of causes for their mistreatment and a
> possible cure face this society each day if we are to
> defeat what one authority calls "the greatest
> crippler and killer of our children--child abuse and
> neglect" (Fontana xvi). In fact, another writer
> argues that the "single greatest impediment to our
> improving the lives of America's children is the myth
> that we are a child-oriented society" (Zigler 39).
> This sociologist suggests that too many Americans
> will not respond to documented findings about child
> abuse (Zigler 39). However, a growing concern among
> many segments of the population has spurred passage
> of laws to protect the rights of children. These
> new laws are difficult to enforce.

Writing in the Proper Tense

When dealing with an event or concept of the past, express it in past tense, as in the following example:

> In the face of ever increasing incidents of abuse,
> can our social organizations not do better? For
> instance, let's look at one case study, summarized
> here from Leontine Young (76-77). Jane Neilson was
> the oldest of ten children of an alcoholic father and
> a promiscuous mother. Jane became a prostitute and
> her mother shared the income. Along with three of
> her sisters, Jane was arrested and spent time at the
> state correctional school. . . .

Clearly, the history of Jane Neilson requires the past tense. However, use the present tense to indicate what is true at the present time and will remain true in the future:

> In truth, Jane Neilson is a victim of her own background.
> How she might serve as role model to her children is
> difficult to imagine.

Use present tense for comments by you and other sources because they remain in print and continue to be true in the present. Good usage demands "Richard Ellmann argues" or "Eudora Welty writes" rather than past tense verb forms: "argued" or "wrote." Note the use of present tense by both the research writer and the source in this segment:

> Today's society and shifting patterns of social class may
>
> dictate, then, a climate for abuse. Edward Zigler argues
>
> that many parents are just not equipped today for parenthood
>
> (42). He says, for instance, that the "extended family is
>
> now rare in contemporary society, and with its demise the
>
> new parent has lost the wisdom and daily support of older,
>
> more experienced family members" (42).

Follow this general rule: write the paper in the historical present tense except when reporting historic happenings:

> John F. Kennedy, who was assassinated in 1963, serves
>
> as a trumpet of challenge to all Americans when he
>
> says in his famous inaugural address: "And so, my
>
> fellow Americans: ask not what your country can do
>
> for you--ask what you can do for your country."

WRITING AN INTRODUCTION

Your opening must establish several things within the first three to six paragraphs:

Subject.   You must identify or define your specific topic, especially the manner in which you have limited and narrowed it to one issue.

Significance.   Convince the reader that he or she *needs* to read what you have to say on this topic. For example, stress the validity of an issue, such as the social influence of specialized magazines or the role of symbolism in the short stories of one writer. Quoting an authority or two, or citing other evidence in the opening, establishes a critical focus for the paper's reader.

Background.   Develop a brief discussion of relevant literature on the topic, but avoid a long review in the opening. Discuss only a few key authors who touch on your specific issue. If writing about a major figure, give only relevant biographical facts, not an encyclopedia-type survey (see below, "Providing Background Information").

Appeal. Attract the attention of your audience with an effective opening. In general, your reader has an intellectual interest in the topic, but he or she often needs motivation beyond a dull, dry opening (see below "Relating to the Well Known" and "Challenging an Assumption").

Thesis. Early in the study, within the first few paragraphs, state your position in order to establish the direction of the study and to point toward your eventual conclusions.

How you work these essential elements into the framework of your opening will depend upon you and your style. They need not appear in this order. Nor should you cram all these items into the opening paragraph. For instance, with the sample research paper on child abuse, 161–82, the thesis is not stated until the sixth paragraph, after the writer has established child abuse as an issue and moved to her focus on parents as victims.

The following techniques are effective individually as opening paragraphs. When you combine several of these, you can build a full introduction of several paragraphs.

Opening with Your Thesis Statement

Generally, the thesis statement will appear in the final paragraph of the general opening, although it sometimes begins a research paper. The following paragraph could appear as either the first or final paragraph of a long introduction:

> Parents who abuse their children are victims and should be treated as such, not as criminals. Granted, they are not battered like the youngsters, but society must understand that child abuse can be a symptom of the parent's economic condition and social background. Reaching out to the parent before a child appears in an emergency room may prove difficult, yet theoretically solving the causes, not just treating the effects, may be the only way to stop this escalating maltreatment of America's greatest resource, the children.

Relating to the Well Known

The following opening suggests the *significance* of the subject as it appeals to the interest and knowledge of the reader:

> Television transmits images into our living rooms,
> radios invade our automobiles, and local newspapers flash
> their headlines to us daily. However, one medium that has
> gained great popularity and influence within the past decade
> is the specialized magazine.

Providing Background Information

This opening offers essential background matter, not information that is irrelevant to the thesis. For example, explaining that Eudora Welty was born in Jackson, Mississippi, in 1909 would contribute little to the following opening:

> In 1941 Eudora Welty published her first book of short
> stories, A Curtain of Green. That group of stories was
> followed by The Wide Net (1943) and The Bride of the
> Innisfallen (1955). Each collection brought her critical
> acclaim, but taken together the three volumes established
> her as one of America's premier short story writers.

Reviewing the Literature

The opening shown here cites only books and articles relevant to the specific issue. It distinguishes the new study from previous works by explaining the logical connections between previous research and the present work:

> Billy Budd possesses many characteristics of the Bible.
> Melville's story depicts the "loss of Paradise" (Arvin 294);
> it serves as a gospel story (Weaver 37-38); and it hints at
> a moral and solemn purpose (Watson 319). Throughout his
> tale, Melville intentionally uses biblical references as a
> means of portraying and distinguishing various characters,
> ideas, and symbols, and of presenting different moral
> principles by which people may govern their lives. In
> brief, it explores the biblical passions of one man's
> confrontation with good and evil (Howard 327-328; Mumford
> 248).

Reviewing and Quoting the Literature

This method combines the background review with source quotations.

> Family troubles will most likely affect the delicate
> members of our society, the children. The recognition of
> causes for their mistreatment and a need for a cure face
> this society each day if we are to defeat what one critic
> calls "the greatest crippler and killer of our children--
> child abuse and neglect" (Fontana xvi). Another writer
> argues that "the greatest impediment to our improving the
> lives of America's children is the myth that we are a child-
> oriented society" (Zigler 39). This sociologist suggests
> that too many Americans will not respond to documented
> findings about child abuse(39). Yet the death rate from
> cruelty exceeds that from infectious disease (Fontana 196).
> The situation is so bad that Kratcoski (437) warns parents
> to prepare for their children to turn on them and to become
> parent abusers.

Taking Exception to Critical Views

The next identifies the subject, establishes a basic view taken by the literature, and then differs with or takes exception to the critical position of other writers:

> Lorraine Hansberry's popular and successful <u>A Raisin in
> the Sun,</u> which first appeared on Broadway in 1959, is a
> problem play of a black family's determination to escape a
> Chicago ghetto to a better life in the suburbs. There is
> agreement that this escape theme explains the drama's
> conflict and its role in the black movement (e.g., Oliver,
> Archer, and esp. Knight, who describes the Youngers as "an
> entire family that has become aware of, and is determined to
> combat, racial discrimination in a supposedly democratic
> land" [34]). Yet another issue lies at the heart of the
> drama. Hansberry develops a modern view of black
> matriarchy in order to examine both the cohesive and
> conflict-producing effects it has on the individual members
> of the Younger family.

Challenging an Assumption

This opening establishes a well-known idea or general theory in order to question, analyze, challenge, or refute it:

```
Christianity dominates the religious life of most
Americans to the point that many Christians mistakenly
assume that it dominates the world population as well.
However, despite the denominational missionaries who have
reached out to every corner of the globe, only one out of
every four people on the globe is a Christian, and far fewer
than that practice their faith.
```

Providing a Brief Summary

When the subject is a novel, long poem, book, or other work that can be summarized, refresh the memory of the reader:

```
Ernest Hemingway's novel The Old Man and the Sea
narrates the ordeal of an old Cuban fisherman, Santiago, who
manages to endure a test of strength when he is first locked
in a tug of war with a giant marlin that he hooks and second
when he fights sharks who attack his prize catch.  The
heroic and stoic nature of this old hero reflects the
traditional Hemingway code.
```

Supplying Data, Statistics, and Special Evidence

This opening uses special evidence both to attract the reader and to establish the subject:

```
Severe abuse of children is on the rise.  Each
year more and more children suffer the trauma of physical
and emotional abuse.  Although the exact number remains
unknown, the Education Commission of the States reports that
some 60,000 cases occur annually (Cohen and Sussman 433).
Boys outnumber the girls in suffering from abuse until the
teen years (Chase 104).  The death rate from cruelty exceeds
that from infectious disease (Fontana 196).  In truth, few
young persons reach maturity without a severe spanking from
an angry parent.
```

Defining Key Terms

Some openings explain difficult terminology, as shown with the following example:

```
      Black matriarchy, a sociological concept with origins
in slavery, is a family situation, according to E. Earl
Baughman (80-81), in which no husband is present or, if he
is present, in which the wife and/or mother exercises the
main influence over family affairs.  Hansberry develops a
modern view of black matriarchy in order to examine the
conflict-producing effects it has on the individual members
of the Younger family.
```

Avoiding Certain Mistakes in the Opening

Avoid a purpose statement, such as "The purpose of this study is . . ." unless your writing reports empirical research, in which case you *should* explain the purpose of your study.

Avoid repetition of the title, which should appear on the first page of the text anyway.

Avoid complex or difficult questions that may puzzle the reader. However, general rhetorical questions are acceptable.

Avoid simple dictionary definitions, such as "Webster defines monogamy as marriage with only one person at a time." See above for an acceptable definition opening.

Avoid humor, unless the subject deals with humor or satire.

Avoid artwork and cute lettering unless the paper's nature requires it (for example, "The Circle as Advertising Symbol").

WRITING THE BODY OF THE PAPER

The main body of the paper features a logical development of your outline subdivisions. If the outline has dynamic order, the body will develop a sequential argument in defense of the thesis sentence (see "Dynamic Order," 87). Orderly presentation of ideas, well-reasoned statements, and proper documentation will provide continuity and thematic development from one paragraph to another. The sample research paper (161–82) may prove helpful in demonstrating how one writer sequentially explored her complex topic.

Strategies of Writing

Strategies of writing the body of a paper vary from writer to writer. In general, quality research writing develops in three steps:

1. Use both a writing paradigm (see 91–94) and an outline (see 84–89) to maintain order because they locate main issues and define subtopics. In addition, consider the following possibilities:

Use *criteria* of judgment for examination of performances and works of arts. For example, analyze the films of George Lucas by critical response to story, theme, editing, photography, sound track, special effects, and so forth. Use *structure* to control papers on architecture, poetry, fiction, and biological forms. For example, divide a study of fiction into six distinct parts to match the story's natural structure. Use *chronology* for tracing subjects in history, political science, and others. For example, a study of Mason and Dixon's Line would examine several periods: the early 1700s, then 1763–67 when Charles Mason and Jeremiah Dixon made their survey in Pennsylvania and Maryland, and other later periods. Use *location* and *setting* for arranging papers in which geography and locale are key ingredients. For example, the settling of Wyoming could feature both locations and chronology, or the settings for several Faulkner novels might control a literary study, while the location of land features (lakes, springs, sinkholes) can key a geology paper's organization. Sometimes *importance* will establish a dynamic order. For example, examining President Harry Truman's decision to use the atomic bomb to bring World War II to an end would invite your consideration of several minor criteria and then a study of Truman's major reason(s) for his decision. Dividing the body by important *issues* is standard fare in many research papers. Jo Walker, for example, uses the first half of the body of her paper to develop major issues of child abuse (see her outline, 162). Building the body by *causal* links has merit in many papers. Jo Walker, for example, explores the causes and cycles of child abuse in part two of her paper (see her outline, 163).

2. Follow stylistic conventions, especially with regard to technical matters and documentation standards as explained at the end of this chapter and in Chapters 5 and 6. Your stylistic conformity gives a professional touch to your paper. Accuracy with documentation signals to the reader that you have both researched the subject and given proper credit to other scholars, rather than plagiarizing the sources by borrowing without acknowledgement.

3. Revise the first draft carefully. Rereading and revising the first draft is essential for clarity and accuracy. During both writing and editing, consult 132–55 for handling technicalities of preparing the manuscript, such as abbreviations, margins, Arabic numerals, or numbering.

Finally, keep in mind that the paper's body needs no subtitles, centered headings, or Roman numerals to mark divisions of the text (see "Headings," 143).

WRITING THE CONCLUSION OF YOUR PAPER

Your conclusion should be neither summary nor restatement of your thesis. Instead, it must go beyond the thesis to reach a judgment, to endorse one side of an issue, to discuss findings, or to offer directives. To put it succinctly, it should say something worthwhile. After all, readers who stay with a long research paper deserve a concluding statement. The following techniques suggest closing paragraphs. You can employ only one, yet the use of several techniques will build a longer, more involved conclusion.

Restate the Thesis and Reach Beyond It

As a general rule, restate your thesis, but do not assume that your reader will generate final conclusions about the issues. Instead, establish the essentials of your study: a literary study should turn from analysis of the work to a discussion of the author's accomplishments, a business paper should establish guidelines and directives, and a geology study should explain the significance of its findings. Note the following example:

> Health authorities should look to parents or guardians
> as victims and try, difficult though it may be, to identify
> adults who suffer from loneliness, isolation, and
> alienation. Their violent beating of a child, though it
> cannot be condoned, may be a cry for help. Good family life
> breeds love and affection for one's fellow human beings.
> Helen Perlman calls it the "art of caring." Unfortunately,
> children who lack loving care fall victims to hostile,
> aggressive physical abuse. They may, because they cannot
> give love, grow up to be abusers themselves.

Close with an Effective Quotation

Sometimes a source may provide a striking commentary that deserves special placement:

> Billy Budd, forced to leave the Rights of Man, goes
> aboard the Bellipotent where law, not morality, is supreme.
> His death is an image of the crucifixion, but the image is

not one of hope. William Braswell best summarizes the

mystery of the novel by suggesting that the crucifixion, for

Melville, "had long been an image of human life, more

suggestive of man's suffering than of man's hope" (146).

Return the Focus of a Literary Study to the Author

In the body of your paper analyze the characters, images, and plot of a literary work, but in your conclusion explain the author's accomplishments:

By her characterization of Walter, Lorraine Hansberry

has raised the black male above the typical stereotype.

Walter is not a social problem, nor a mere victim of

matriarchy. Rather, Hansberry creates a character who

breaks out of the traditional sociological image that

dehumanizes the black male. By creating a character who

struggles with his fate and rises above it, Hansberry has

elevated the black male. As James Baldwin puts it, "Time

has made some changes in the Negro face" (24).

Compare Past to Present

You can use the conclusion rather than the opening to compare past research to the present study or to compare the historic past with the contemporary scene:

In the traditional patriarchal family, the child was

legal property of the parents. But the idea that children

are the property of the parents and, therefore, may receive

whatever punishment seems necessary, no longer holds true.

Social organizations and governmental agencies now help

young victims in their search for preventive measures.

Unlike the past, children today have rights too!

Offer a Directive or Solution

After analyzing a problem and synthesizing issues, offer your theory or solution, as demonstrated below:

> The four points above defend a central theory: the troubled parents who were victims in their own childhood and those who are victimized by circumstances today need to be identified by social agencies and helped to recognize their real potential as human beings and parents. The responsibility rests with health professionals who can prevent abuse before it occurs. Major cities across the nation and many rural communities are establishing child abuse centers and parental self-help groups. A few of the most successful community involvement programs are the Child Abuse Prevention Center in Toledo, the Johnson County Coalition for Prevention of Child Abuse in Kansas City, and the Council for Prevention of Child Abuse and Neglect in Seattle. More cities should establish such programs.

Discussion of Test Results

Discuss your findings and identify implications of a study, as shown:

> The results of this experiment were similar to expectations, but perhaps the statistical significance, because of the small subject size, was biased toward the delayed conditions of the curve. The subjects were, perhaps, not representative of the total population because of their prior exposure to test procedures. Another factor that may have affected the curves was the presentation of the data. The images on the screen were available for five seconds, and that amount of time may have enabled the subjects to store each image effectively. If the time period for each image were reduced to one or two seconds, there could be lower recall scores, thereby reducing the differences between the control group and the experimental group.

Avoiding Certain Mistakes in the Conclusion

Avoid afterthoughts or additional ideas; now is the time to end the paper, not begin a new thought. However, empirical studies often discuss options and possible alterations that might affect test results (see above, "Discussion," 107).

Avoid the use of closing transitional words, such as "thus," "in conclusion," or "finally" at the beginning of the last paragraph where readers can see plainly the end of the paper. However, such tags are sometimes advisable when a conclusion begins several paragraphs before the final one.

Avoid stopping at an awkward spot or trailing off into meaningless or irrelevant information.

Avoid questions that raise new issues, but rhetorical questions that restate the issues are acceptable.

Avoid fancy artwork.

BLENDING REFERENCE MATERIALS INTO YOUR WRITING

Citation of sources should conform to standards announced by your instructor. This book uses the standards established by the Modern Language Association, known as MLA style. Some instructors may require a different form of documentation, such as APA style or the traditional footnote style; if so, consult Chapter 7.

The MLA style requires brief in-text citations to sources and *no* documentation footnotes. Only content footnotes are permitted (see 138–41 for discussion and examples of content footnotes). Full documentation of sources appears on a "Works Cited" page at the end of your paper, so be certain that you have a bibliography card that contains full information on each in-text source.

As a general policy, provide just enough information within the text to locate a source, which will have full documentation listed on the "Works Cited" page. Sometimes you will need no parenthetical reference, as with: "Baird has devoted his entire text to the subject of Melville's mythology" (if Baird has only one book in the "Works Cited"). However, if you cite a specific part of a book, add page numbers. Conform to the following stipulations.

Provide Both Name of Authority and Page Number

1. **Signal the beginning and end of quotations and paraphrases.** Introduce each paraphrase or quotation, whenever convenient, with the name of the authority and end it with a page reference:

> ```
> James Baird argues convincingly that Melville shaped
> a new symbolistic literature (19).
> ```

This standard citation informs the reader of the beginning and the end of borrowed materials. An alternative places the page citation immediately after the authority's name: "James Baird (19) argues. . . ."

2. If necessary, use both the authority's name and the page number inside the parenthetical citation. Include the authority's name within the parenthetical citation when you cannot successfully introduce the material with the name of the authority:

> ```
> This point of Melville's contribution to the American
> symbolist movement has been argued successfully (Baird 19).
> ```

3. Cite every borrowed sentence. Every sentence with borrowed materials must contain a signal to the reader: an authority's name, quotation marks, page number, or pronoun reference. Avoid quoting or paraphrasing a full paragraph with only one citation to the source at the very end. The following sample is acceptable because after her topic sentence the writer credits an authority for the second and third sentences, she has obviously written the fourth, she credits another authority for the fifth, and the sixth again belongs to her:

> ```
> Second, parenthood courses for adolescents are
> positive actions. Zigler advocates an expanded effort to
> educate young people for parenthood. He would extend sex
> education to include information on child care, at least for
> older children of child bearing age (42). Such a program
> makes sense because it seeks prevention and not remedies
> after the act of child abuse. Another sociologist concurs,
> saying, "A central notion in the treatment model is the
> building of a social responsibility, the realization that
> each of us is an important element of society" (Giarreto 5).
> Youngsters who are future parents should be helped toward
> responsible social behavior.
> ```

4. Introduce sources that have no author listed. When no author is listed for a source, introduce the borrowed materials with a general reference to the magazine, report, agency, or authority and then within the in-text citation use an abbreviated title of the work:

```
One regional magazine correctly locates the Jesuit settlement

of St. Gall, Texas, as the modern city of Fort Stockton

("Crossroads" 49).
```

or

```
The regional magazine Southern Living correctly locates

the Jesuit settlement of St. Gall as the modern city of

Fort Stockton, Texas ("Crossroads" 49).
```

The Works Cited entry would read: "A Crossroads of West Texas History." *Southern Living* Dec. 1984: 49.

5. **Cite corporate authors.** Name the company, corporation, or committee when it publishes a work:

```
The National Committee on Careers for Older Americans

urges greater awareness of the vital resources that too

often lie dormant and unused (19).
```

The Works Cited entry would read: National Committee on Careers for Older Americans. *Older Americans: An Untapped Resource.* Washington: Acad. for Educ. Dev., 1979.

6. **Combine paraphrase and quotation.** Combine your words with the source's to form a unified whole, yet let the reader know who says what. Note how the next passage moves the reader smoothly through the diverse materials while it cites accurately each source:

```
A recognition of causes for their mistreatment and a need

for a cure face this society each day if we are to defeat

what one authority calls "the greatest crippler and killer

of our children--child abuse and neglect" (Fontana xvi). In

fact, another writer argues that "the single greatest

impediment to our improving the lives of America's children

is the myth that we are a child-oriented society" (Zigler

29). This sociologist suggests that too many Americans will

not respond to documented findings about child abuse (39).
```

7. **Include page number(s) with all quotations.** Keep page citations outside quotation marks but inside the final period (except in cases of long, indented quotations as shown below, 115). Note the following examples:

```
     "The marriage contract," according to Dr. Clifford

Sager (48), "becomes a therapeutic and educational concept

that tries to spell out the vague and intuitive."


     Dr. Clifford Sager says, "The marriage contract becomes

a therapeutic and educational concept that tries to spell

out the vague and intuitive" (48).


     For one critic the contract of marriage is an attempt

"to spell out the vague and intuitive" (Sager 48).
```

Punctuate Quotations Accurately

Quotation marks should enclose all direct quotations. Place commas and periods *inside* the closing quotation marks in every instance, with the one exception of intervening documentation shown below. Place colons and semicolons *outside* the quotation marks. Place the question mark and the exclamation mark inside the quotation marks if the mark is part of the quoted matter; otherwise, place it outside the quotation marks. Place single quotation marks around short quotations set within longer quotations.

1. **Place commas and periods inside quotation marks.** For example, if the original material states:

> The Russians had obviously anticipated neither the quick discovery of the bases nor the quick imposition of the quarantine. Their diplomats across the world were displaying all the symptoms of improvisation, as if they had been told nothing of the placement of the missiles and had received no instructions what to say about them.
>
> From: Arthur M. Schlesinger, Jr., *A Thousand Days,* (New York: Houghton, 1965) 820.

Write one of the following (MLA style):

```
"The Russians," writes Schlesinger, "had obviously

anticipated neither the quick discovery of the [missile]

bases nor the quick imposition of the quarantine" (820).

Schlesinger notes, "Their diplomats across the world were

displaying all the symptoms of improvisation . . ." (820).

Schlesinger observes that the Russian failure to anticipate

an American discovery of Cuban missiles caused "their diplomats

across the world" to improvise answers as "if they had been

told nothing of the placement of the missiles . . ." (820).
```

This last example correctly changes the capital "T" of "their" to lowercase to match the grammar of the restructured sentence and does not use ellipsis points before "if" because it flows smoothly into the textual matter.

2. **Place semicolons and colons outside quotation marks.** For example, if the original states:

> The extended family is now rare in contemporary society, and with its demise the new parent has lost the wisdom and daily support of older, more experienced family members. (Zigler 42)

Note the following possibilities:

```
Zigler admits that "the extended family is now rare in
contemporary society"; however, he stresses the greatest loss
as the "wisdom and daily support of older, more experienced
family members" (42).

Zigler laments the demise of the "extended family": that is, the
loss of the "wisdom and daily support of older, more experienced
family members" (42).
```

3. **Retain question marks and exclamation marks.** Arrange your page citations so that they do not interfere with question marks and exclamation marks:

```
The philosopher Thompson (16) asks, "How should we order our
lives?"

How should we order our lives, asks Thompson (16), when we face
"hostility from every quarter"?

Thompson (16) passionately shouted to union members, "We must
bring order into our lives even though we face 'hostility from
every quarter!'"
```

4. **Place single quotation marks inside regular quotation marks.** Note the following:

```
George Gilder (32) believes that "monogamy is central to any
democratic social contract, designed to prevent a breakdown of
society into 'war of every man against every other man.'"
```

Remember that the period always goes inside quotation marks with the one exception shown here:

```
George Gilder believes that "monogamy is central to any
democratic social contract, designed to prevent a breakdown of
society into 'war of every man against every other man'" (32).
```

Provide Extra Information Within Citations If Necessary

1. **Add a volume number with the page numbers for a multivolume work.** Provide a volume number, colon, space, and page number(s) for any work that has more than one volume:

```
Joseph Campbell suggests that man is a slave yet also the
master of all the gods (1: 472).
```

2. **Place shortened titles within the citation.** Include a shortened title within the parentheses whenever an author has two or more works listed in your "Works Cited."

```
Because he stresses the nobility of man, Joseph Campbell
suggests that the mythic hero is symbolic of the "divine
creative and redemptive image which is hidden within us
all . . ." (Hero 39). He elevates the human mind to an
"ultimate mythogenetic zone--the creator and destroyer, the
slave and yet the master, of all the gods" (Masks 1: 472).
```

Note: Complete titles of the two works by Campbell are: *The Hero With a Thousand Faces* and *The Masks of God,* a 4-volume work.

3. **Cite more than one author of a work.** For two authors, employ both names: "(Torgerson and Andrews 16–17)." For three or more authors use the abbreviation "et al.," which means "and others" as in: "(Smith et al. 344–55)."

4. **Cite several works in one parenthetical citation.** You may include two or more works within one citation. Provide normal entries with semicolons separating them, as shown:

```
This point about Melville's thesis is disputed
by two critics (Baird 34; Arvin 21).
```

```
One authority places importance on Melville's fantastical
episodes (Seelye 15; cf. Arvin 21 and Baird 34).
```

Note: The abbreviation "cf." means "compare with."

5. **Supply more than the page number.** If necessary, specify additional information:

```
Horton (22, n. 3) suggests that Melville forced the
symbolism, but Welston (199-248, esp. 234) reaches
an opposite conclusion.
```

Classical prose works such as *Moby Dick* or *Paradise Lost* may appear in two or more editions. Courtesy dictates that you provide extra information to chapter, section, or part so that readers can locate a quotation in any edition of the work.

```
Melville uncovers the superstitious nature of Ismael by
stressing Ismael's fascination with Yojo, the little
totem god of Queequeg (71; ch. 16).
```

6. **Use a double reference when one source quotes another.** Sometimes one author will quote another person, and the latter is the one you want to use. Such citations to quoted words of a person other than the author requires clear introduction of the speaker and a detailed citation to the source:

```
As an echo to Melville, Albert Schweitzer states that "the
world is inexplicably mysterious and full of suffering" (qtd.
in Baird 19).
```

Your "Works Cited" would then list Baird's book; do not list Schweitzer because you consulted the Baird book, not a book or article by Schweitzer.

Handling Frequent Page References to the Same Work

Frequent references to the same novel, drama, or long poem need not repeat the author's name in every instance; a specific page reference is adequate, or you can provide act, scene, and line if appropriate. Note the following example:

```
When the character Beneatha denies the existence of God in
Hansberry's A Raisin in the Sun, Mama slaps her in the face
and forces her to repeat after her, "In my mother's house
there is still God" (37). Then Mama adds, "There are some
```

```
ideas we ain't going to have in this house. Not long as I
am at the head of the family" (37). Thus Mama meets Beneatha's
challenge head on. The other mother in the Younger household
is Ruth, who does not lose her temper, but through kindness
wins over her husband (79-80).
```

Omitting Parenthetical Citation for Nonprint Sources

For sources with no page numbers (e.g., television speeches, interviews, and lectures), introduce the quotation or paraphrase with the name of the speaker and omit a citation at the end. Your "Works Cited" entry will make clear the nature of the nonprint source.

```
Governor Thorton defends the merits of prayer in public
schools, saying recently, "Every child has the right to
pray." However, he faces opposition from several quarters.
```

An alternative is to place the reference at the end of the quotation:

```
One public figure defends the merits of prayer in public
schools, saying recently, "Every child has the right to
pray" (Thorton). However, he faces opposition from several
quarters.
```

Handling Long Quotations of Prose and Poetry

1. **Set off long quotations.** Use a block indented 10 spaces and without quotation marks for a quotation of more than four lines. Double space between your text and the quoted materials. Don't indent the first line of the paragraph more than the rest. Place the parenthetical citation *after* the final mark of punctuation, as shown next:

```
The prophecy, spoken by the angel Gabriel, states:
        Seventy weeks are determined upon thy people and
        upon thy holy city, to finish the transgression,
        and to make an end of sins, and to make
        reconciliation for iniquity, and to bring an
```

> everlasting righteousness, and to seal up the
>
> vision and prophecy, and to anoint the most
>
> Holy. (Dan. 9.24)
>
> Scholars generally agree on interpretation of this prophecy.

Note: If you quote more than one paragraph, indent each paragraph three (3) extra spaces (see "Paragraph Omitted," 119).

2. **Incorporate short passages of poetry into your text.** Short passages of quoted poetry (one or two lines) should be incorporated into your text as in the following:

> Eliot's "The Waste Land" (1922) remains a springtime search
>
> for nourishing water: "Sweet Thames, run softly, for I speak
>
> not loud or long" (3.12) says the speaker in "The Fire
>
> Sermon," while in Part 5 the speaker of "What the Thunder
>
> Said" yearns for "a damp gust / Bringing rain" (5.73-74).

As the example demonstrates, set off the material with quotation marks and indicate separate lines by using a virgule (/) with a space before and after the slash mark. Place line documentation within parentheses immediately following the final quotation mark and inside the period. Use Arabic numerals for books, parts, volumes, and chapters of works; acts, scenes, and lines of plays; cantos, stanzas, and lines of poetry (see "Arabic Numerals," 134–35).

3. **Indent poetry of three or more lines.** Several lines of poetry should appear as follows:

> The king cautions Prince Henry:
>
>   Thy place in council thou has rudely lost,
>
>   Which by thy younger brother is supplied,
>
>   And art almost an alien to the hearts
>
>   Of all the court and princes of my blood.
>
>   (3.2.32-35)

Reference to act, scene, and lines is sufficient only after you have established Shakespeare's *Henry IV, Part 1* as the central topic of your study; otherwise, write "(1H4 3.2.32-35)." (See also "Arabic Numerals," 134–35, and "Shakespearean Plays," 152–53.)

4. **Signal turnovers of long lines of poetry.** If one line of poetry is too long for your right margin, indent the continuation five spaces more than the

longest indentation and type "[t/o]" at the end of the line to indicate that this line is a turnover:

```
      In the first section of Ash-Wednesday Eliot lets
despair spill out:
            Because I do not hope to know again
            The infirm glory of the positive hour
            Because I do not think
            Because I know I shall not know
            The one veritable transitory power
            Because I cannot drink
            There, where trees flower, and springs flow, for
                  there is nothing again            [t/o]
```

Alter Initial Capitals in Some Quoted Matter

In general, you should reproduce quoted materials exactly, yet one exception is permitted for logical reasons: if the quotation forms a grammatical part of the sentence in which it occurs, you need not capitalize the first word of the quotation, even though it is capitalized in the original, as in:

```
Another writer argues that "the single greatest impediment
to our improving the lives of America's children is the myth
that we are a child-oriented society" (Zigler 39).
```

Restrictive connectors, such as "that" or "because," limit the information and make it essential to the sentence; therefore, a comma is inappropriate before the quotation, and without a comma the capital letter is unnecessary. However, if the quotation follows a formal introduction set off by a comma or colon, you must capitalize the first word as in the original:

```
      Another writer argues, "The single greatest. . . ."
                        or
Zigler states: "The single greatest. . . ."
                        but
Zigler says that "the single greatest. . . ."
```

Use Ellipsis Points to Omit Portions of Quoted Matter

Omit quoted material with ellipsis dots when you want to quote only part of a sentence. However, incorporating fragments of the quotation into your prose can be more effective than sprinkling your paper with too many ellipsis points:

> The long-distance marriage, according to William
> Nichols, "works best when there are no minor-aged children to
> be considered," the two people are "equipped by temperament
> and personality to spend a considerable amount of time
> alone," and both are able to "function in a mature, highly
> independent fashion" (54).

This writer's grammatical styling handles the omissions smoothly. The phrases fit into the sentence and ellipsis points would only disturb the reader. In other cases, however, you may need to indicate an omission by the use of three spaced dots for an omission and a fourth dot as the period to end the sentence. Ellipsis points must *not* be used to change the spirit or essential meaning of the original. Quote your sources in correct grammatical structure and use brackets (see esp. 120) to add a verb or other essential word(s).

Conform to usage shown below:

1. Ellipsis points for material omitted from the middle of a sentence:

> Phil Withim objects to the idea that "such episodes are
> intended to demonstrate that Vere . . . has the intelligence
> and insight to perceive the deeper issue" (118).

2. Ellipsis points for material omitted from the end of a source:

> R. W. B. Lewis declares that "if Hester has sinned, she
> has done so as an affirmation of life, and her sin is
> the source of life . . ." (62).

or

> R. W. B. Lewis (62) declares that "if Hester has sinned,
> she has done so as an affirmation of life, and her sin
> is the source of life. . . ."

Note: as shown in this sample, use a period with no space and then three spaced ellipsis points.

3. **Ellipsis points for material omitted from the beginning of a source:**

> He states: "... the new parent has lost the wisdom and
> daily support of older, more experienced family members"
> (Zigler 34).

Caution: It would read better as: He states that "the new parent has lost. . . ."

4. **Ellipsis points for complete sentence(s) omitted from the middle of a source:**

> Zigler reminds us that "child abuse is found more
> frequently in a single (female) parent home in which the
> mother is working. . . . The unavailablity of quality day
> care can only make this situation more stressful" (42).

5. **Ellipsis points for line(s) of poetry omitted:**

> Do ye hear the children weeping, O my brothers,
> Ere the sorrow comes with years?
> They are leaning their young heads against their mothers,
> And _that_ cannot stop their tears.
> . . . .
> They are weeping in the playtime of the others,
> In the country of the free. (Browning 382)

6. **Ellipsis points for paragraphs omitted:**

> Zigler makes this observation:
>
> > With many others, I am nevertheless optimistic
> > that our nation will eventually display its
> > inherent greatness and successfully correct the
> > many ills that I have touched upon here.
> > . . . .
> > Of course, much remains that could and should
> > be done, including increased efforts in the area of
> > family planning, the widespread implementation of
> > Education for Parenthood programs, an increase in
> > the availability of homemaker and child care

> services, and a reexamination of our commitment to
> doing what is in the best interest of every child
> in America. (42)

Note: If you are quoting two or more paragraphs, indent the first line of each paragraph an extra three (3) spaces in addition to the standard indention of ten spaces.

Use Brackets to Insert Your Words Inside Quoted Matter

Use brackets for interpolation, which means to insert new matter into a text or quotation. The use of brackets signals the insertion. Note the following:

1. Use brackets to clarify:

This same critic indicates that "we must avoid the temptation to read it [The Scarlet Letter] heretically" (118).

2. Use brackets to establish correct grammar:

"John F. Kennedy . . . [was] an immortal figure of courage and dignity in the hearts of most Americans," notes one historian (Jones 82).

3. Use brackets to note the addition of underlining:

He says, for instance, that the "extended family is now rare in contemporary society, and with its demise the new parent has lost the wisdom [my emphasis] and daily support of older, more experienced family members" (Zigler 42).

4. Use brackets with *sic* to indicate errors in the original:

Lovell says, "John F. Kennedy, assassinated in November of 1964 [sic], became overnight an immortal figure of courage and dignity in the hearts of most Americans" (62).

Note: The assassination occurred in 1963. However, do not burden your text with the use of "sic" for historical matter in which misspellings are obvious, as with:

"Faire seemely pleasauance each to other makes."

5. Use brackets to enclose additional material within parentheses:

The escape theme explains the drama's racial conflict

(see esp. Knight, who describes the Younger family as one

that opposes "racial discrimination in a supposedly

democratic land" **[34])**.

or

(e.g., the results for the experimental group **[n = 5]** are

also listed in Figure 3, page 16.)

6. Use brackets to present fractions:

$$a = [(1 + b)/x]^{1/2}$$

To present fractions in a line of text, use a slanted line (/) and parentheses first ( ), then brackets [( )], and finally the braces {[( )]}. Most typewriters do not have brackets or braces; therefore, leave extra space for the brackets and braces and write them in with ink.

REVISING, EDITING, AND PROOFREADING

After completing the rough draft, begin revising and rewriting. Be critical and exacting—this is no time for any complacent pride of accomplishment. *Revising* means to alter, amend, and improve the entire whole. *Editing* means preparing the draft for final typing by checking your style, word choice, and grammar. *Proofreading* means examining the final typed manuscript to spot any last-minute errors. All three stages are important.

Revising Your First Draft

Arrange for time to examine the draft as a whole. Does it flow smoothly according to your outline plan? If not, is your new order effective? If it isn't, begin global revision, which means that you focus on the whole and rearrange large blocks of the paper.

Examine your *introduction* for the presence of several items: a thesis, a clear direction or plan of development, and a sense of your involvement. See 98–103 for additional tips and guidelines.

Examine your *body* for: a clear sequence of major statements, appropriate and effective evidence to support your key ideas, and transitions that move the reader effectively from one block of material to another. See 103–104 for additional guidelines.

Examine your *ending* for: a conclusion that is drawn from the evidence, one that evolves logically from the introduction and the body, and one that clearly conveys your position and interpretation. See 105–108 for additional information about writing the conclusion.

When satisfied that the paper flows effectively point by point and fulfills the needs of your intended audience, you can begin editing.

Editing Before You Type the Final Manuscript

The cut-and-paste revision period is complemented by careful editing of paragraphs, sentences, and individual words. Travel through the paper one time to examine each paragraph as a whole for logical development of one central idea. A few will need extra development or more evidence from primary and secondary sources. One or two paragraphs may rely too heavily on sources and not enough on your own input. Some woefully short paragraphs can be combined with others. Long, difficult paragraphs may need to be divided because you crammed too much into them.

Next, read through the paper again to study your sentences and word choices. Cut phrases and sentences that do not advance your main ideas or that merely repeat what your sources have already stated. Look for ways to change "to be" verbs (is, are, was) to stronger active verbs. Maintain the present tense in most verbs. Convert passive structures to active if possible. In particular, confirm that your paraphrases and quotations flow smoothly within your text (see "Blending Reference Materials into Your Writing," 108–21). Check individual words for their effectiveness and appropriateness. The language of a research paper should be slightly formal, so be on guard against trendy expressions and slang.

Note the editing by one student in the following example:

Family troubles will most likely affect the ~~The most~~ delicate members of our society, ~~appear the most~~ the children.

The
~~awfully affected by family troubles.~~ Our recognition of causa̶l̶ es

for their treatment
~~elements~~ and a ⌃cure ~~always~~ face this society each and every day
⌞ need for a

one
of the year if we are to defeat what ~~a real good~~ authority calls

> "the greatest crippler and killer of our children--child abuse
>
> and neglect" (Fontana, ~~7~~). ~~Another~~ writer ~~suggested~~ that

(handwritten edits: xvi; In fact,; argues)

As shown above, the writer conscientiously edited the paragraph. You too should delete unnecessary material, add supporting statements and evidence, relate facts to one another, rearrange for active voice, and rewrite for clarity. Review earlier sections of this text, if necessary, on unity and coherence (96–97) and writing the body (103–104).

Editing to Avoid Discriminatory Language

You must exercise caution against words that may stereotype any person, regardless of gender, race, nationality, creed, age, or handicap. Reevaluate words for accuracy; there is no need to avoid gender when writing about the difficulty of working during the ninth month of pregnancy. Be specific. Unless your writing is precise, readers might make assumptions about race, age, and handicaps. To many people, a reference to a doctor or governor may bring to mind a white male, while a similar reference to a teacher or homemaker may bring to mind a woman. In truth, no characteristic should be assumed for all members of a group.

The first step to avoiding language which discriminates is to review the accuracy of your statements.

Example: Old people walk with difficulty.
1. How old is old?
2. Do *all* old people walk with difficulty?
3. Are the elderly the only persons who walk with difficulty?

Second, use plural subjects so that nonspecific, plural pronouns are grammatically correct. For example, do you intend to specify that Judy Jones maintains *her* lab equipment in sterile condition or to indicate that technicians, in general, maintain *their* own equipment? Do be careful, though, because the plural is easily overused and often inappropriate.

A third strategy is to reword the sentence so that a pronoun is unnecessary:

> The doctor prepared the necessary surgical equipment without
>
> interference.

or

> Each technician must maintain laboratory equipment in
>
> sterile condition.

Fourth, use pronouns denoting gender only when necessary or when gender has been previously established. The use of a specifier (the, this, that) is often helpful. In directions and informal settings, the pronoun "you" is appropriate. Note these examples:

```
Mary, as a new laboratory technician, must learn to maintain
her equipment in sterile condition.

The lab technician maintains that equipment in sterile
condition.

Each of you should maintain your equipment in sterile
condition.
```

A fifth strategy is necessary for courtesy titles. In general, avoid formal titles (Dr., Gen., Mrs., Ms., Lt., Professor, and so forth). Avoid their equivalents in other languages (Mme., Dame, Monsieur). First mention of a person requires the full name (for example, Ernest Hemingway or Margaret Mead) and thereafter requires only usage of the surname (Hemingway or Mead). Use Emily Brontë and thereafter use Brontë, *not* Miss Brontë.

Editing with an eye for the inadvertent bias should serve to tighten up the expression of your ideas. However, beware of the pitfalls. If your attempt to be unbiased draws more attention than your arguments, it will ultimately detract from the paper.

Proofreading the Final Typed Manuscript Before Submitting It

After the typed copy is finished, proofread carefully because mechanical and stylistic errors suggest carelessness that can seriously weaken your credibility. Typing a paper, or having it typed by somebody else, does not relieve you of the responsibility of proofreading; if anything, it requires you to be doubly careful. Typographical errors often count against the paper just as heavily as other shortcomings. If necessary, make corrections neatly in ink; marring a page with a few handwritten corrections is better than leaving damaging errors in your text.

Specifically, check for errors in sentence structure, spelling, and punctuation. Avoid dividing a word at the end of a line. Read each quotation for accuracy in wording and documentation. Double-check citations to be certain that each one is listed on your "Works Cited" page at the end of the paper. Before and during final typing of the manuscript, consult "Handling General Technicalities," 132–55, which provides tips on handling technicalities of the margins, content notes, and many other matters.

WRITING WITH WORD PROCESSORS

Many students now use word processing computers for writing their research papers. This new technology has several advantages. It saves time in that you keyboard the text just once, and the printer produces various drafts for you. It enables you to store and retrieve notes and sources and makes it easy to move blocks of material when you revise the paper. In some instances it will even review your writing style and spelling.

Storing and Retrieving Notes, Documents, and Bibliography Sources

Writing your notes into a computer is discussed above in Chapter 3, 76–77. It explains the importance of establishing a BIBLIO document for storing full information on your sources, which will form your "Works Cited" page. It also explains two methods for writing and storing your notes, one that keeps all notes in a single file and one that creates each note as a separate temporary file.

Entering Your Text into a Computer

Once you learn a few new commands, the word processing system on any computer functions much like a typewriter. If you did not use the word processor to store your notes, you should now gather all materials and begin typing, much as you would at a regular typewriter.

If you used the word processor to write your notes into a single file, such as NOTES, begin writing your draft at the beginning of this NOTES file (which will push your notes downward as you type). When you need a certain note, scroll downward to find it, mark it as a block, scroll upward to your text, and move it into place. Then blend it into your textual discussion with necessary rewording. An important alternative for a long set of notes, 12 or more, would be to label each note with a brief heading so that when you need one, you can employ the FIND feature, block the note, and move it into your text. Keep a separate, written list of these special headings.

If you developed each note as a separate file using a different code word for each, you can pause during your writing and ask the computer to READ or COPY a file into your text. For example, let's suppose you have labeled and filed your notes by key words of your outline, such as MYTHABUSe, DISCOVERy, INCREASE of abuse (Note: names of files are generally limited to eight characters). You would now retrieve those files and blend them into your rough draft. This system is more rapid than the first because you will not scroll through note after note looking for the right one. However, you must keep a written record of file names and the contents of each file.

During your entry of text be sure to SAVE the material every page or so. This command inscribes your writing onto the diskette or tape. If the computer suddenly shuts down for any reason, your copy will not be lost.

When finished with your initial typing, have the computer produce a copy of your paper in double or triple spacing. If you use a 40 character screen, print a DRAFT copy that duplicates screen spacing to ease your revision efforts.

Revising Your First Draft

The word processor enables you to make major and minor changes in the text and then quickly print various drafts of the paper. Consider the following:

Using Global Revision of the Whole Work.   Once you keyboard the entire paper, you can redesign and realign sentences, paragraphs, and entire pages without bothering to cut pages and paste them back together. You can add, delete, or rewrite material anywhere within the body.

Move and rearrange material with the MOVE or MOVE BLOCK commands. After each move remember to rewrite and blend the words into your text. Then reformat your paragraph. Use the FIND command to locate some words and phrases in order to eliminate constant scrolling up and down the screen. Use the FIND/REPLACE to change wording or spelling throughout the document.

Editing Your Text.   In some situations you may have a software program that examines the style of your draft. Such a program tells you: total number of words, number of sentences, average sentence length in words, number of paragraphs, and the average length of paragraphs in words. It provides a list of your most active words and counts the number of monosyllabic and polysyllabic words. Its analysis then suggests, for example, "Your short paragraphs suggest a journalistic style that may not be appropriate for scholarly writing" or "Your writing demonstrates strong use of short words on a colloquial level." You would then revise and edit the text to improve certain stylistic weaknesses. Some software programs examine your grammar, looking for a parentheses that you have opened but not closed, unpaired quotation marks, passive verbs, and other specific items that the computer will flag for your correction. A spelling checker moves through your text to flag misspelled words and words not in the diskette dictionary, such as proper names. You must then move through the text and correct misspellings. Whether such sophisticated software is available or not, you should work through the text on the screen of your monitor and make all necessary editorial changes.

Proofreading the Final Printout

After you have edited the text to your satisfaction, print a hard copy as formatted by your final specifications, such as double spacing, one inch margins, page numbers, a running head, and so forth. See 000–00 for details of page format. Proofread this version for correctness of the format and spelling, punctuation, alphabetizing of the Works Cited page, and so forth.

If at all possible, print your final version on a typewriter quality printer, sometimes called a daisywheel printer. Such a printer with sheet-fed paper or razor-cut continuous forms paper will produce a manuscript of the best typewriter quality. Perforated paper in continuous forms will leave the ragged edges along the top, sides, and bottom of sheets. A dot-matrix printer will not give the black sharpness of detail that many instructors require. You can overcome that obstacle by using the double-strike feature available on most dot matrix printers. This feature commands the printer to strike each letter twice, with the second strike slightly off center, giving letters a darker quality.

5

Handling the Format and Mechanics of Your Paper

PREPARING THE FINAL MANUSCRIPT

In its basic organization the format of a research paper consists of the following parts:

1. Blank sheet (optional)
2. Title page
3. Outline (if required)
4. Abstract (if required)
5. The text of the paper
6. Content notes (if used)
7. Appendix (if needed)
8. List of works cited
9. Blank sheet (optional)

If you don't include a separate title page, use the first page of the text to list your name and affiliation (see 156).

Title Page or Opening Page

On the opening page of text identify yourself as the author, give the date, and supply course information; however, if you provide an outline or other prefatory matter, you will need a title page. It contains three main divisions: the title of the paper, the author, and the course identification. Conform to the following example and general guidelines (see also the sample opening page on 156 and the sample title page on 161):

```
              An Interpretation of Melville's

              Use of Biblical Characters

                    in Billy Budd



                         by

                   Doris Singleton


            Freshman English II, Section 108b

                   Mr. Crampton

                   April 23, 1985
```

The following guidelines govern title pages:

1. If the title requires two or more lines, double-space the lines and balance the lines on the page.

2. Write the title in capitals and lowercase letters without underlining and without enclosing it in quotation marks. However, do underline published works that appear as part of your title. Do not use a period after a centered heading.

3. Place your full name below the title, usually in the center of the page.

4. Provide the course information or name of the institution, along with the date, centered below your name.

5. Employ separate lines for each item.

6. Provide balanced, two-inch margins for all sides of the title page.

7. You may omit the title page if you have no outline, abstract, or other prefatory matter, in which case you place identification in the upper left corner of your opening page, as in the following:

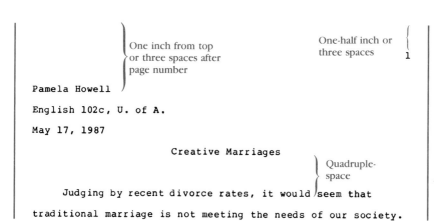

```
Pamela Howell

English 102c, U. of A.

May 17, 1987

                    Creative Marriages


        Judging by recent divorce rates, it would seem that

traditional marriage is not meeting the needs of our society.
```

Outline

Include the outline only if your instructor requires it as part of the finished manuscript. Place it after the title page on separate pages and number these pages with small Roman numerals (for example, "iii," "iv," "v") at the top right-hand corner of the page. For full information on outlining, see 55–59 and 87–89. For a sample outline in manuscript form see 162–64.

Abstract

Include an abstract only if your instructor requires one. An abstract summarizes the essential ideas of the paper in about 100 words. Provide a *brief* digest of the paper's argument. Exact terminology specifies the narrow focus of your research paper. Include within a sentence or two your conclusions(s) and/or finding(s). Place the abstract on the opening page (page 1) below the title and before the first lines of the text. Indent it five spaces and set it off from the text by quadruple-spacing. You may also place it on a separate page between the title page and first page of text. Remember that the abstract is usually read first and may be the *only* part read; therefore, make it accurate, specific, objective, and self-contained (i.e., it makes sense alone without references to the main text). Note this example:

```
              Child Abuse:  A View of the Victims


     This study examines the problems of child abuse,

especially the fact that families receive attention after

abuse occurs, not before.  With abuse statistics on the

rise, efforts devoted to prevention rather than coping

should focus on parents in order to discover those adults

most likely to commit abuse because of heredity, their own

childhood, the economy, and other causes of depression.

Viewing the parent as a victim, not just a criminal, will

enable social agencies to institute preventive programs that

may control abuse and hold together family units.


     Family troubles will most likely affect the delicate members

of our society, the children.  The recognition of causal elements
```

The Text of the Paper

The three dominant parts of the text, introduction, body, and conclusion, are discussed under "Writing the Paper," 98–108. In general, you should *not* use subtitles or numbered divisions in a thesis paper, even if it becomes 20 pages long. Therefore, use continuous paragraphing without subdivisions or headings. Some scientific and business reports demand underlined side headings.

The opening page of your text should begin with the title of the paper centered one inch below the top edge of the sheet. Quadruple-space between the title and your first line of text. A page number appears on the opening page, one-half inch from the top of the sheet and even with the right margin (see page 165 for a sample). If you have no title page, this opening page should contain your name and classroom information in the upper left corner (see above, 129).

The closing page of your text should end with a period and blank space on the remainder of the page. Do not write "The End" or provide artwork as a closing signal. Do not start "Notes" or "Works Cited" on this final page of text.

Content Endnotes Page

Label this page with the word "Notes" centered and one inch from the top edge of the sheet. Continue your page numbering sequence in the upper right corner. Double-space between this heading and the first note. The notes should be numbered in sequence with raised superscript numerals to match those placed within your text at appropriate locations. Double-space all entries and double-space between the entries. See below, "Content Endnotes," 138–41, and the sample "Notes" page, 179.

Appendix

Place additional material, if necessary, in an appendix immediately preceding the "Works Cited." It is the logical location for numerous tables and illustrations, computer data, questionnaire results, complicated statistics, mathematical proofs, or detailed descriptions of special equipment. Double-space appendixes and begin each appendix on a new sheet, identifying each one as Appendix A, Appendix B, and so forth (however, the word "Appendix" is sufficient if you have only one).

Works Cited Page

Label this page with the words "Works Cited" centered and one inch from the top edge of the sheet. Continue your page numbering sequence in the upper right corner. Double-space between your centered heading and the first entry. Double-space all entries and double-space between the entries. For samples and additional information see Chapter 6, "Works Cited," 183–209, and also the sample "Works Cited" pages on 160 and 180.

HANDLING GENERAL TECHNICALITIES OF PREPARING THE MANUSCRIPT

The alphabetical glossary which follows answers miscellaneous questions about matters of form, such as margins, pagination, dates, and numbers. For matters not addressed below, consult the index, which will direct you to appropriate pages elsewhere in this text.

Abbreviations.   Employ abbreviations often and consistently in notes and citations, but avoid them in the text. In your documentation entries always abbreviate dates (Jan. or Dec.), institutions (acad. and assn.), names of publishers (McGraw or UP for University Press), and states (OH or CA). See "Postal Abbreviations" for correct abbreviations of states; see "Names of Persons," 148, for comments on the abbreviation of honorary titles; see also "Place, Publisher, and Date," 188.

AD *anno Domini* 'in the year of the Lord'; precedes numerals with no space between letters, as in "AD 350"

anon. anonymous

art., arts. article(s)

assn. association

assoc. associate, associated

BC 'Before Christ'; follows numerals with no space between letters, as in "500 BC"

bk., bks. book(s)

ca., c. *circa* 'about,' used to indicate an approximate date, as in "ca. 1812"

cf. *confer* 'compare' (one source with another); not, however, to be used in place of "see" or "see also"

ch., chs., chap., chaps. chapter(s)

col., cols. column(s)

comp. compiled by or compiler

diss. dissertation

doc. document

ed., eds. editor(s), edition, or edited by

e.g. *exempli gratia* 'for example,' preceded and followed by a comma

enl. enlarged, as in "enl. ed."

esp. especially, as in "312–15, esp. 313"

et al. *et alii* 'and others'; "John Smith et al." means John Smith and other authors

et pas. *et passim* 'and here and there' (see "passim")

et seq. *et sequens* 'and the following'; "9 et seq." means page nine and the following page; compare "f." and "ff."

f., ff. page or pages following a given page; "8f." means page eight and the following page; but exact references are sometimes preferable, for example, "45–51, 55, 58" instead of "45ff." Acceptable also is "45+."

fl. *floruit* 'flourished,' which means a person reached greatness on these dates, as in "*fl.* 1420–50"; used when birth and death dates are unknown.

ibid. *ibidem* 'in the same place,' i.e., in the immediately preceding title, normally capitalized and underlined as in "<u>Ibid.</u>, p. 34"

i.e. *id est* 'that is,' preceded and followed by a comma

illus. illustrated by, illustrations, or illustrator

infra 'below,' refers to a succeeding portion of the text; compare "supra." Generally, it is best to write "see below."

intro., introd. introduction (by)

loc. cit. *loco citato* 'in the place (passage) cited'

ms, mss manuscript(s); but followed by a period ("MS.") when referring to a specific manuscript

n., nn. note(s), as "23, n. 2" or "51 n."

n.d. no date (in a book's title or copyright pages)

no., nos. number(s)

n.p. no place (of publication)

ns new series

op. cit. *opere citato* 'in the work cited'

p., pp. page(s); do not use "ps." for "pages"

passim 'here and there throughout the work,' e.g., "67, 72, et passim," but also acceptable is "67+."

proc. proceedings

pseud. pseudonym

pt., pts. part(s)

rev. revised, revised by, revision, review, or reviewed by

rpt. reprint, reprinted

sec., secs. section(s)

ser. series

sess. session

sic 'thus,' placed in brackets to indicate that an error was made in the quoted passage and the writer is quoting accurately; see example on page 120

st., sts. stanza(s)

sup., supra 'above,' refers to a preceding portion of the text; it is just as easy to write "above" or "see above"

suppl. supplement(s)

s.v. *sub voce (verbo)* 'under the word or heading'

trans., tr. translator, translated, translated by, or translation

viz. namely

vol., vols. volume(s), as in "vol. 3"

vs., v. versus 'against' as used in citing legal cases

Acknowledgments. Generally, acknowledgments and prefaces are unnecessary. Use a superscript reference numeral to your first sentence and then place any obligatory acknowledgments or explanations into a content endnote (see also 138):

> [1] I wish here to express my thanks to Mrs. Horace A. Humphrey for permission to examine the manuscripts of her late husband.

Ampersand. Avoid using the ampersand symbol "&" unless custom demands it, e.g., "A & P." Use *and* for in-text citation (Smith and Jones, 1984), *but* use "&" in APA style references (Spenser, L. M., & Wilson, Z. W.).

Annotated Bibliography. An annotation describes the essential details of each book and article of your "Works Cited." Place it just below the facts of publication. Follow these suggestions:

1. Explain the main purpose of the work.
2. Briefly describe the contents.
3. Indicate the possible audience for the work.
4. Note any special features.
5. Warn of any defect, weakness, or suspected bias.

Provide enough information in about three sentences for a reader to have a fairly clear image of the work's purpose, contents, and special value. A sample APA entry follows:

```
Kissinger Henry.  (1979).  The White House Years.  Boston:

Little, Brown.  Kissinger discusses his first four

years (1969-1973) as Assistant to the President for

National Security Affairs during the Nixon presidency.

He gives personal, sometimes biased reflections on a

variety of events.  His art of diplomacy is uncovered.
```

Apostrophe.   To form the possessive of singular nouns add an apostrophe and *s* (e.g., "the typist's ledger"), but use only the apostrophe with plural nouns ending in *s* (e.g., "several typists' ledgers"). Singular proper nouns of people and places form the possessive with the apostrophe and *s* (e.g., "Rice's story," "Rawlings's novel," "Arkansas's mountains," *but* "the Rawlingses' good fortune"). Use apostrophes to form plurals of letters (a's and b's) but not numbers or abbreviations (ACTs in the 18s and 19s, the 1980s, sevens, three MDs).

Arabic Numerals.   MLA style demands Arabic numerals whenever possible: for volumes, books, parts, and chapters of works; acts, scenes, and lines of plays; cantos, stanzas, and lines of poetry.

Use Arabic figures to express all numbers 10 and above (such as 154, 1,269, the 10th test, the remaining 12%). Write as Arabic numerals any numbers below 10 that cannot be spelled out in one or two words (such as 3½ or 6.234). Numbers below 10 grouped with higher numbers should appear as Arabic numerals (such as "3 out of 42 subjects" or "lines 6 and 13" *but* "15 tests in three categories").

Large numbers may combine numerals and words (such as 3.5 million). For inclusive numbers that indicate a range, give the second number in full for numbers through 99: 3–5, 15–21, 70–96. With three digits or more give only the last two in the second number unless more digits are needed for clarity: 98–101, 110–12, 989–1001, 1030–33, 2766–854.

Commas in numbers are usually placed between the third and fourth digits from the right, the sixth, and so on, as with "1,200" or "1,200,000." Exceptions are page and line numbers, addresses, four digit year numbers, and zip codes: page 1620, at 12116 Nova Road, in 1985, or New York, NY 10012.

Spell out the initial number that begins a sentence, e.g., "Thirty people participated in the first test."

Use the number "1" in every case for numbers, not the lowercase "l" or uppercase "L," especially if you type into a word processor or computer.

Usage of numbers in your text:

AD 200 *but* 200 BC
in 1974–75 *or* from 1974 to 1975, *but not* from 1974–75
lines 32–34 *but not* ll. 32–34
32–34 or pages 32–34 *but not* pp. 32–34
45, *but not* the forty-fifth page
6.213
0.5 *but not* .5
March 5, 1985 or 5 March 1985, *but not* both styles
1960s or the sixties
one-fifth *but* 153½
six percent *but* 6 percent and 15 percent were low scores
six o'clock or 6:00 P.M.
twentieth century *but* twentieth-century literature *and* 20th century in "Works Cited" entries
three-dimensional
zero-based budget
one response *but* 1 of 15 responses
one fifth of the session
twelve 6-year-olds or 12 six-year-olds, *not* 12 6-year-olds

Usage of numerals with in-text citations and "Works Cited" entries:

(*Ham.* 5.3.16–18)
(*Faust* 2.140)
(2 Sam. 2.1–8)
(Fredericks 23–24) (MLA style)
(Fredericks, 1985, pp. 23–24) (APA and CBE style)
2 vols.
Rpt. as vols. 13 and 14
MS CCCC 210
95th Cong., 1st sess. S. 2411
16mm., 29 min., color
Monograph 1962–M2
College English 15 (Winter 1974): 3–6 (MLA style)
Memory and Cognition, 3, 562–590 (APA style)
J. Mol. Biol. 149:15–39; 1981 (CBE style)
Journal of Philosophy 26 (1981): 172–89 (footnote style)

Asterisks. Do not use asterisks for content notes or illustrations or tables (see 138).

Bible. Use parenthetical documentation for biblical references in the text—that is, place the entry within parentheses immediately after the quotation, for example, "(2 Kings 18.13)." Do not underline titles of books of the

Bible. Abbreviations of most books of the Bible follow, but do not abbreviate one-syllable titles, such as "Mark" or "Acts."

1 and 2 Chron.	1 and 2 Chronicles
Col.	Colossians
1 and 2 Cor.	1 and 2 Corinthians
Dan.	Daniel
Deut.	Deuteronomy
Eccles.	Ecclesiastes
Eph.	Ephesians
Exod.	Exodus
Ezek.	Ezekiel
Gal.	Galatians
Gen.	Genesis
Hab.	Habakkuk
Hag.	Haggai
Heb.	Hebrews
Hos.	Hosea
Isa.	Isaiah
Jer.	Jeremiah
Josh.	Joshua
Judg.	Judges
Lam.	Lamentations
Lev.	Leviticus
Mal.	Malachi
Matt.	Matthew
Mic.	Micah
Nah.	Nahum
Neh.	Nehemiah
Num.	Numbers
Obad.	Obadiah
1 and 2 Pet.	1 and 2 Peter
Phil.	Philippians
Prov.	Proverbs
Ps. (Pss.)	Psalm(s)
Rev.	Revelation
Rom.	Romans
1 and 2 Sam.	1 and 2 Samuel
Song of Sol.	Song of Solomon
1 and 2 Thess.	1 and 2 Thessalonians
1 and 2 Tim.	1 and 2 Timothy
Zech.	Zechariah
Zeph.	Zephaniah

Capitalization. Titles of books, journals, magazines, and newspapers: capitalize the first word and all principal words, but not articles, prepositions, conjunctions, and the *to* in infinitives, when these words occur in the middle of the title (for example, *The Last of the Mohicans*). Titles of articles and parts of books: capitalize as for books (for example, "Appendix 2," "Writing the Final Draft"). If the first line of the poem serves as the title, reproduce it exactly as it appears in print ("anyone lived in a pretty how town"). Some fields capitalize only the first word and proper names of reference titles (including the first word of subtitles), as in this APA entry:

```
Baron, James N., & William Bielby. (1980). Bring the firms

    back in: Stratification, segmentation and the organization

    of work. American Sociological Review, 45, 737-765.
```

Study the appropriate style for your field as found in Chapter 7.

If a *complete* sentence of text follows a colon, the first word after the colon need not be capitalized:

```
    This decision has far-reaching consequences: each

division of the corporation will be required to cut

twenty percent of its budget within this fiscal year.
```

Capitalize the second part of a hyphenated compound word only when it is used in a heading with other capitalized words:

```
Low-Frequency Sound Equipment
```

but

```
Low-frequency sound distortion is caused by several factors.
```

Capitalize trade names:

```
Pepsi, Plexiglass, Dupont, or Dingo
```

Capitalize proper names used as adjectives *but not* the words used with them (for example, "Einstein's theory" or "Salk's vaccine").

Capitalize a specific department or specific course:

```
Department of Psychology but the psychology department

Psychology 314 but an advanced course in psychology
```

Capitalize nouns followed by numerals or letters when they denote a specific place in a numbered series:

```
during Test 6, we observed Group C

as shown in Table 5 and also Figure 2
```

But do not capitalize nouns that name common parts of books or tables followed by numerals:

| chapter 12   page ix   column 14 |

Content Endnotes.   Content notes, as distinguished from documentation notes, have limited use in undergraduate research. As a general rule, put important matters into the text and omit entirely the unimportant and marginally related items. However, when circumstances call for content notes, they should conform to these rules:

1. Content notes are *not* documentation notes. Make references to your sources by in-text citations, although instructors in some fields, especially history, philosophy, and the fine arts, may ask for documentation footnotes (see below, "Footnotes for Documentation," 142).

2. Place endnotes on a separate page(s) following the last page of text, unlike footnotes, which go at the bottom of pages. See page 131 for specifications on typing notes.

3. Place superscript numerals within the text by turning the roller of the typewriter so that the Arabic numeral strikes about half a space above the line, like this.[3] Each numeral immediately follows the material to which it refers, usually at the end of a sentence, with no space between the superscript numeral and a word or mark of punctuation.

| Third, a program to advise young girls and boys about |
| incest could warn many children about aggressive adults and |
| perhaps help them preserve the family unit.[1] Amazingly, |
| many children feel responsible and accept guilt for forced |
| incestuous behavior. |

Note: This superscript numeral refers to note 1 in part 5 below.

4. Complete documentation to endnote sources must appear in your "Works Cited" just as with your in-text citations. That is, you may mention a source in a content endnote that is not mentioned in the main text; nevertheless, this source requires citation in the note and full documentation in "Works Cited."

5. The sample notes below demonstrate information supplied by content notes:

Related matters not germane to the text

| [1] The problems of incest and sexual abuse are explored in |
| Adams-Tucker, Giarretto (4-5), Walters, and also De Young (583). |
| These authorities cite the need for preventive measures, if |
| possible, before damage occurs to the children; nevertheless, |

sexual abuse, like a disease, is here today in horrifying case after case, and we do not have a cure. Patricia Herman offers 11 clear guidelines for teaching children about abuse (170-72).

Blanket citation

2 On this point see Giarrett (3-4), de Young (579), Kinard (405-07), and Young (119).

3 Cf. Campbell (Masks 1: 170-225; Hero 342-45), Frazer (312), and Baird (300-344).

Literature on a related topic

4 For additional study of the effects of alcoholics on children, see especially the Journal of Studies on Alcohol for the article by Wolin et al. and the bibliography on the topic by Orme and Rimmer (285-87). In addition, group therapy for children of alcoholics is examined in Hawley and Brown.

Major source requiring frequent in-text citations

5 All citations to Shakespeare are to the Parrott edition.

6 Dryden's poems are cited from the California edition of his Works and documented in the text with first references to each poem listing volume, page, and lines and with subsequent references citing only lines.

Compare textual commentary with another source

7 Cf. James Baird who argues that the whiteness of Melville's whale is "the sign of the all-encompassing God" (257). Baird states: "It stands for what Melville calls at the conclusion of the thirty-fifth chapter of Moby-Dick 'the inscrutable tides of God'; and it is of these tides as well that the great White Whale himself is the quintessential emblem, the iconographic representation" (257).

[8] On this point see also the essay by Patricia Chaffee in which she examines the "house" as a primary image in the fiction of Eudora Welty.

Explain tools, methods, or testing procedures

[9] Water samples were drawn from the identical spot each day at 8 a.m., noon, 4 p.m., and 8 p.m. with testing done immediately on site.

Note: A report of an empirical study would require this type of information in the text under "Methods."

[10] The control group continued normal dietary routines, but the experimental group was asked to consume nuts, sharp cheeses, and chocolates to test acne development of its members against that of the control group.

[11] The initial sample was complete data on all twins born in Nebraska between 1920 and 1940. These dates were selected to provide test subjects 60 years of age or older.

Provide statistics (see also "Illustrations and Tables," p. 143)

[12] Database results show 27,000 pupil-athletes in 174 high schools with grades 0.075 above another group of 27,000 non-athletes at the same high schools. Details on the nature of various reward structures are unavailable.

Acknowledge assistance or support

[13] Funds to finance this research were graciously provided by the Thompson-Monroe Foundation.

[14] This writer wishes to acknowledge the research assistance of Pat Luther, graduate assistant, Physics Department.

Note: Acknowledge neither your instructor nor typist for research papers, though such acknowledgments are standard with graduate theses and dissertations.

Explain variables or conflicts in the evidence

> [15] Potlatch et al. includes the following variables: the positive acquaintance, the equal status norm, the various social norms, the negative stereotypes, and sexual discrimination (415-20). However, racial barriers cannot be overlooked as one important variable.
>
> [16] The pilot study at Dunlap School, where sexual imbalance was noticed (62 percent males), differed sharply from test results compared with those of other schools. The male bias at Dunlap thereby eliminated those scores from the totals.

Copyright Law. Your "fair use" of the materials of others is permitted without the need for specific permission as long as your usage is noncommercial for purposes of criticism, scholarship, or research, which means you can quote from sources and reproduce artistic works within reasonable limits. The law is vague on specific amounts that can be borrowed, suggesting only the "substantiality of the portion used in relation to the copyrighted work as a whole." You should be safe in reproducing the work of another as long as the portion is not substantial. To protect your own work, if necessary, you need only type in the upper right-hand corner of your manuscript, "Copyright © 19__ by _____." Fill the blanks with the proper year and your name. Then to register a work, order a form from the U.S. Copyright Office, Library of Congress, Washington, D.C. 20559.

Definitions. For definitions within your text, use single quotation marks without intervening punctuation, for example:

> The use of et alii `and others' has diminished in scholarly writing.

Endnotes for Documentation of Sources. An instructor or supervisor may prefer traditional superscript numerals within the text and documentation notes at the end of the paper. If so, see Chapter 7, 210–44, especially 240.

Enumeration of Items. Incorporate short items into the text with parenthetical numbers:

> College instructors are usually divided into four ranks: (1) instructors, (2) assistant professors, (3) associate professors, and (4) full professors.

Present longer items in tabular form:

1. Full professors generally have 15 or more years experience, the Ph.D. or other terminal degree, and have achieved
   distinction in teaching and scholarly publications.
2. Associate professors. . . .

Etc.   *Et cetera* 'and so forth'; avoid using this term by adding extra items
to the list or by saying "and so forth."

Footnotes for Documentation.   If your instructor requires you to
use footnotes, see Chapter 7, 237, for discussion and examples.

Foreign Cities.   In general, spell the names of foreign cities as they are
written in original sources. However, for purposes of clarity, you may substitute an English name or provide both with one in parentheses:

Köln (Cologne)   Braunschweig (Brunswick)

München (Munich)   Praha (Prague)

Foreign Languages.   Underline foreign words used in an English
text:

Like his friend Olaf, he is aut Caesar, aut nihil, either
overpowering perfection or ruin and destruction.

Do not underline quotations of a foreign language:

Obviously, he uses it to exploit, in the words of Jean
Laumon, "une admirable mine de themes poetiques."

Do not underline foreign titles of magazine or journal articles:

Brandt, Von Thomas O. "Brecht und die Bibel."
     PMLA 79 (1964): 171-72.

Do not underline foreign words of places, institutions, proper names, or titles
that precede proper names:

> Of course, Racine became extremely fond of Mlle Champmesle,
> who interpreted his works at the Hotel de Bourgogne.

Titles of French, Italian, and Spanish works: capitalize the first word and the proper nouns, but not adjectives derived from proper nouns: *La noche de Tlatelolco: Testimonios de historia oral* or *Realismo y realidad en la narrativa Argentina.*

Titles of German works: capitalize the first word, all nouns, and all adjectives derived from names of persons: *Über die Religion: Reden an die Gebildeten unter ihren Verächtern.*

Headings. Begin every major heading on a new page of your paper (title page, opening page, notes, appendix, works cited). Center the heading in capital and lowercase letters one inch from the top of the sheet. MLA style uses a quadruple space between the title and the first line of text; other headings for MLA style, such as "Works Cited," are set off by double-spacing. APA style double-spaces between headings and text. CBE style triple-spaces between headings and text. Number *all* text pages, including those with major headings.

Illustrations and Tables. A table is a systematic presentation of materials, usually in columns. An illustration is any nontext item that is not a table: blueprint, chart, diagram, drawing, graph, photo, photostat, map, and so on. Note the following samples:

Fig. 44:
Illustration

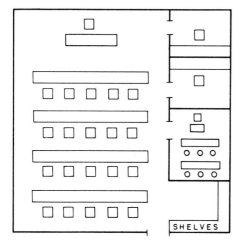

SHELVES

Fig. 44: Audio Laboratory with Private
Listening Rooms and a Small Group Room

Fig. 45: Table

Table 1

Response by Class on Nuclear Energy Policy

	Freshmen	Sophomores	Juniors	Seniors
1. More nuclear power	150	301	75	120
2. Less nuclear power	195	137	111	203
3. Present policy is acceptable	87	104	229	37

When you present an illustration or table in your paper, conform to the following guidelines:

1. Present only one kind of information in each illustration, and make it as simple and as brief as possible. Frills and fancy artwork may distract rather than attract the reader.

2. Place small illustrations and tables within your text, but large illustrations, sets of illustrations, or complex tables should go on separate pages in an appendix (see "Appendix," 131).

3. Place the figure or table as near to your textual discussion as possible, although the illustration should not precede your first mention of it.

4. Make certain that the text adequately explains the significance of the illustration. Follow two rules: (1) label the illustration so that your reader can understand it without reference to your discussion; and (2) write the description of the illustration so that your reader may understand your observations without reference to the illustration. But avoid giving too many numbers and figures in your text.

5. In the text refer to illustrations by number (for example, "Figure 5" or "Table 4, col. 16"), not by vague reference ("the table above," "the following illustration," or "the chart below").

6. Number illustrations consecutively throughout the paper with Arabic numbers, preceded by "Fig." or "Figure" (for example, "Figure 4"), placed one double-space above the caption flush left on the page *below* the illustration.

7. Number tables consecutively throughout the paper with Arabic numerals, preceded by "Table" (for example, "Table 2"), placed one double-space above the caption and flush left on the page *above* the table.

8. Always insert a caption that explains the illustration, placed *above* the table but *below* the illustration, flush left, in full capital letters or in capitals and lowercase, but do not mix forms in the same paper. An alternative is to place the caption on the same line with the number (see Fig. 46 below).

9. Insert a caption or number for each column of a table, centered above the column or, if necessary, inserted diagonally or vertically above it.

10. When inserting an explanatory or reference note, place it below both a table and an illustration; then use a lowercase letter as the identifying super-script, not an Arabic numeral (see Figs. 48 and 49).

11. Sources are abbreviated as in-text citations and full documentation must appear in the "Works Cited."

The charts and illustrations on the following pages are examples of design strategies.

Fig. 46:
Illustration

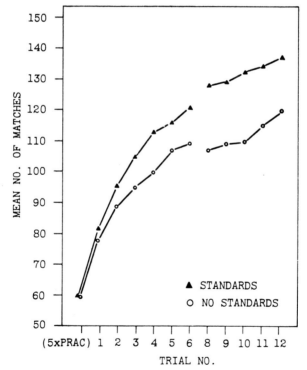

Fig. 46: Mean Number of Matches by Subject with and without
Standard (By Trial). Source: Locke and Bryan (289).

Fig. 47:
Illustration

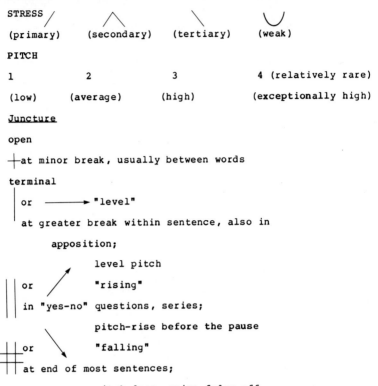

SUPRASEGMENTAL

STRESS /   ∧   \   ∪

(primary)   (secondary)   (tertiary)   (weak)

PITCH

1   2   3   4 (relatively rare)

(low)   (average)   (high)   (exceptionally high)

Juncture

open

─┼─at minor break, usually between words

terminal

│ or ──────► "level"

at greater break within sentence, also in

    apposition;

            level pitch

‖ or ╱   "rising"

in "yes-no" questions, series;

        pitch-rise before the pause

─╫─ or ╲   "falling"

at end of most sentences;

      pitch-drop, voice fades off

Fig. 47: Phonemes of English. Generally, this figure
follows the Trager-Smith system, used widely in Amer-
can linguistics. Source: Anna H. Live (1066).

Fig. 48: Table

Table 2[a]

Mean Scores of Six Values Held by College Students According to Sex

All Students		Men		Women	
Pol.	40.61	Pol.	43.22	Aesth.	43.86
Rel.	40.51	Theor.	43.09	Rel.	43.13
Aesth.	40.29	Econ.	42.05	Soc.	41.62
Econ.	39.45	Soc.	37.05	Econ.	36.85
Soc.	39.34	Aesth.	36.72	Theor.	36.50

[a] Carmen J. Finley, et al. (165).

Fig. 49: Table

Table 3

Inhibitory effects of sugars on the growth of *Clostridium*

histoylticum (11 strains) on nutrient agar[a]

Sugar added 2%	Aerobic incubation (hr)		Anaerobic incubation (hr)	
	24	48	24	48
None	11[b]	11	11	11
Glucose	0	0	11	11
Maltose	0	0	11	11
Lactose	1	1	11	11
Sucrose	3	6	11	11
Arabinose	0	0	0	0
Inositol	0	0	11	11
Xylose	0	0	0	0
Sorbitol	2	7	11	11
Mamnitol	9	10	11	11
Rhamnose	0	0	11	11

[a] Nishida and Imaizumi (481).

[b] No. of strains which gave rise to colonies in the presence
of the sugar.

Indention.   Indent paragraphs of your text five spaces. Indent long quotations 10 spaces. The opening sentence of a full paragraph receives no extra indentation; however, if you indent quotations of two or more paragraphs, indent each paragraph an extra three spaces. Indent "Works Cited" entries five spaces on the second and succeeding lines. Indent the first line of content footnotes five spaces. Other styles (APA or CBE) have different requirements (see Chapter 7, 210–44).

Italics.   Show italics in a typed manuscript by underlining; see "Underlining Titles," 154.

Length of the Research Paper.   It is difficult to set an arbitrary length for a research paper because the ideal length depends on the nature of the topic, the reference material available, the time allotted to the project, and the initiative of the researcher. Your instructor or supervisor may set definite restrictions concerning the length of your paper. Otherwise, plan generally a paper of 2,000 to 3,000 words, about ten typewritten pages, excluding the title page, outline, endnotes, and works cited pages.

Margins.   A basic one-inch margin on all sides is recommended. Place your page number one-half inch down from the top edge of the paper and one inch from the right edge. You should then triple-space (MLA style) between the page number and your text so that you place the first line of text one inch from the top of the page. If you use your name as a running head (MLA style), place both name and page number on the same line, flush with the right margin (for examples, see 165–82).

Monetary Units.   Spell out percentages and monetary amounts only if you can do so in no more than two words. Conform to the following:

$10 or ten dollars
$14.25 *but not* fourteen dollars and twenty-five cents
$4 billion or four billion dollars
$10.3 billion or $10,300,000,000
$63 or sixty-three dollars
the fee is one hundred dollars ($100) *or* the fee is one hundred
    (100) dollars
two thousand dollars or $2,000
thirty-four cents

Names of Persons.   As a general rule, first mention of a person requires the full name (e.g., Ernest Hemingway or Margaret Mead) and there-after requires only usage of the surname (Hemingway or Mead). Omit formal titles (Mr., Mrs., Dr., Hon.) in textual and note references to distinguished persons, living or dead. Convention suggests that certain prominent figures (Lord Byron, Dr. Johnson, Dame Edith Sitwell) require the title while others, for no apparent reason, do not (for example, use Tennyson, Browne, and Hillary rather than Lord Tennyson, Sir Thomas Browne, or Sir Edmund Hil-lary). Where custom dictates, you may employ simplified names of famous persons (for example, use Dante rather than the surname Alighieri and use Michelangelo rather than Michelangelo Buonarroti). You may also use pseud-onyms where custom dictates (for example, George Eliot, Maxim Gorky, Mark Twain). Refer to fictional characters by names used in the fictional work (e.g., Huck, Lord Jim, Santiago, Capt. Ahab).

Numbering (Pagination).   Number pages in the upper right-hand corner of the page, one-half inch down from the top edge of the paper and one inch from the right edge. Triple-space between the page number and a heading or the first line of text so that your top margin is one inch from the top of the sheet. Pages preceding your opening page of text require lowercase Roman numerals (ii, iii, iv). Don't put a page number on a separate title page, but include one on the opening page of text. From page two on, your last name precedes the number. If anonymity is required, use a shortened version of your title rather than your name (see sample on 216).

Paper.   Type on one side of white bond paper, sixteen- or twenty-pound weight, 8 1/2 by 11 inches. Avoid erasable paper. If you write the final draft in longhand, use ruled theme paper. If you write the paper by word processor or computer, use the best quality paper available.

Percentages. Use numerals with appropriate symbols (3%, $5.60), otherwise use numerals only when they cannot be spelled out in one or two words:

percent *not* per cent
one hundred percent *but* 150 percent
a two point average *but* a 2.5 average
one metric ton *but* 0.907 metric ton or 3.150 metric tons
forty-five percent *but* 45 1/2 percent *or* 45 1/2%

In business, scientific, and technical writing that requires frequent use of percentages, write all percentages as numerals with appropriate symbols:

100%   45 1/2%   12%   6 @ 15.00   £92 $99.45

Postal Abbreviations. Use this chart for reference:

AL	Alabama	MT	Montana
AK	Alaska	NB	Nebraska
AZ	Arizona	NV	Nevada
AR	Arkansas	NH	New Hampshire
CA	California	NJ	New Jersey
CO	Colorado	NM	New Mexico
CT	Connecticut	NY	New York
DE	Delaware	NC	North Carolina
DC	District of Columbia	ND	North Dakota
FL	Florida	OH	Ohio
GA	Georgia	OK	Oklahoma
GU	Guam	OR	Oregon
HI	Hawaii	PA	Pennsylvania
ID	Idaho	PR	Puerto Rico
IL	Illinois	RI	Rhode Island
IN	Indiana	SC	South Carolina
KS	Kansas	TN	Tennessee
KY	Kentucky	TX	Texas
LA	Louisiana	UT	Utah
ME	Maine	VT	Vermont
MD	Maryland	VI	Virgin Islands
MA	Massachusetts	VA	Virginia
MI	Michigan	WA	Washington
MN	Minnesota	WV	West Virginia
MS	Mississippi	WI	Wisconsin
MO	Missouri	WY	Wyoming

Punctuation.   Consistency is the key to punctuation. Careful proof-reading of your paper for punctuation errors will generally improve the clarity and accuracy of your writing.

1. *Commas* are used in a series of three or more before "and" or "or." The comma follows a parenthesis if your text requires the comma:

```
How should we order out lives, asks Thompson (22-23), when

we face "hostility from every quarter"?
```

The comma goes inside single quotation marks as well as double quotation marks:

```
Such irony is discovered in Smith's article, "The Sources

of Franklin's `The Ephemera,'" but not in most textual

discussions.
```

2. *Colons* introduce examples or further elaboration on what has been said in the first clause. *Semicolons* join independent clauses. (For proper use of colons and semicolons within quotations see 112, and for usage within documentation see 113). Skip only one space after the colon or semicolon. Do not capitalize the first word after a colon or semicolon, but see 186 for an exception to this rule. Do not use a colon where a semicolon is appropriate for joining independent clauses.

```
Weathers reminds us of crucial differences in rhetorical

profiles that no writer should forget: a colloquial language

differs radically from a formal language and a plain texture

of writing differs greatly from a rich texture.
```

but

```
Weathers reminds us of crucial differences in rhetorical

profiles that no writer should forget; the writer who does

forget may substitute colloquial language where formal is

appropriate or may use a plain texture when language

intensity is needed.
```

3. *Dashes* are formed with your typewriter by typing two hyphens with no blank space before or after––as shown here.

4. *Exclamation marks* are seldom used in research writing. A forceful declarative sentence is preferable.

5. *Hyphens* that separate words at the end of a typed line are unacceptable in research papers. Both MLA style and APA style discourage division of words at the end of a line, asking instead that you leave the lines short, if necessary, rather than divide a word. If you *do* hyphenate, you should always double-check word division by consulting a dictionary. Also double-check automatic hyphenation by a word processor. Do not hyphenate proper names. Avoid separating two letters at the end or beginning of a line (for example, use "depend-able," not "de-pendable").

When using hyphens, follow a few general rules. First, do not hyphenate unless the hyphen serves a purpose. The example, "a water treatment program" makes sense without hyphens. Second, compound adjectives that *precede* a noun usually need a hyphen but those which follow do not. For example, "same-age children" but "children of the same age." Third, when a common base serves two or more compound modifiers, omit the base on all except the last modifier, but retain the hyphens on every modifier: right- and left-hand margins or 5-, 10-, and 15-minute segments. Fourth, write most words with prefixes as one word (for example, "overaggressive," "midterm," "antisocial"), but there are exceptions: self-occupied, self-paced, self-protection, post-1980 *but* postwar, anti-Reagan *but* antisocial. Fifth, use a hyphen between pairs of coequal nouns: scholar-athlete or trainer-coach.

6. *Periods* end complete sentences of the text, endnotes, footnotes, and all bibliography entries. Periods between numbers indicate related parts (e.g., 2.4 for act 2, scene 4). The period normally follows the parenthesis. (The period is placed within the parenthesis only when the parenthetical statement is a complete sentence, as in this instance.) See also 118, for explanation of the period in conjunction with ellipsis points.

7. *Brackets* are used to enclose phonetic transcription, mathematical formulas, and interpolations into a quotation. They should be inserted by hand if these figures are not on your keyboard (see "Brackets," 120–21, for examples).

8. *Quotation marks* should enclose all quotations used as part of your text. Quotations in your text require proper handling for stylistic effects and documentation purposes. In general, work the quotation into your text smoothly (see examples and discussion on pages 112-13).

In addition, use quotation marks for *words discussed,* such as slang, words cited as words, or words purposely misused or misspelled; however, linguistic studies require underlining for all linguistic forms (letters, words, and phrases) that are subjects of discussion and require single quotation marks for definitions that appear without intervening punctuation (for example, *nosu* 'nose'). In all other studies use quotation marks for English translations of foreign words.

9. *Parentheses* are used to enclose these items:

In-text citations

> Larson (23-25) and Mitchell (344-45) report. . . .

Independent matter

> The more recent findings (see Figure 6) show. . . .

Headings for a series

> The tests were (a) . . ., (b) . . ., and (c). . . .

First use of an abbreviation

> The test proved reaction time (RT) to be. . . .

Roman Numerals.   Use capital Roman numerals for titles of persons (Elizabeth II) and major sections of an outline (see 84–89). Use small Roman numerals for preliminary pages of text, as for a preface or introduction (iii, iv, v). Otherwise, use Arabic numerals (e.g., Vol. 5, Act 2, Ch. 16, Plate 32, 2 Sam. 2.1–8, or *Iliad* 2.121–30), *except* when writing for some instructors in history, philosophy, religion, music, art, and theater, in which case you may need to use Roman numerals (e.g., III, Act II, I Sam. ii.1–8, *Hamlet* I.ii.5–6). Here is a list of Roman numerals:

	Hundreds	*Tens*	*Units*
1	c	x	i
2	cc	xx	ii
3	ccc	xxx	iii
4	cd	xl	iv
5	d	l	v
6	dc	lx	vi
7	dcc	lxx	vii
8	dccc	lxxx	viii
9	cm	xc	ix

Thus: xxi equals 21, cx equals 110, and clv equals 155.

Running Heads.   MLA style requires that your name precede page numbers on all pages after the first (see the sample paper, 161–82). APA style requires a short title at the top of each page preceding the page number (see "Short Titles in the Text," 153).

Shakespearean Plays.   For use in parenthetical documentation, the editorial board of the *Shakespeare Quarterly* approves the following abbreviations of titles of Shakespearean plays: *Ado; Ant.; AWW; AYL; Cor.; Cym.; Err.; Ham.; 1H4; 2H4; H5; 1H6; 2H6; 3H6; H8; JC; Jn; LLL; Lr.; Mac.; MM; MND; MV; Oth.; Per.; R2; R3; Rom.; Shr.; TGV; Tim.; Tit.; Tmp.; TN; TNK; Tro.; Wiv.; WT;* and his poems: *LC; Luc.; PhT; PP; Son.; Ven.*

Short Titles in the Text. Shorten titles of books and articles mentioned often in the text after a first, full reference. For example, *Backgrounds to English as Language* should be shortened, after initial usage, to *Backgrounds* both in the text, notes, and in-text citations (see also 113) but not in the bibliography entry. When typing a manuscript according to APA style, shorten your own title to the first two or three words and place it at the top, right corner of each page for identification purposes (for example, "Discovering Recall Differences of the Aged" would be shortened to "Discovering" or "Discovering Recall Differences"). See pages 215–19 for examples of the short title as a page heading.

Slang. Avoid the use of slang terminology. When using it in a language study, enclose in double quotation marks any words to which you direct attention. Linguistic studies, however, require underlining (see item 8, page 151).

Spacing. As a general rule double-space everything—the body of the paper, all indented quotations, and all reference entries. MLA style quadruple-spaces between the title and first line of text but double-spaces in all other instances. Footnotes, if used, should be single-spaced, but endnotes should be double-spaced (see 238). APA style double-spaces after all headings and separates text from indented quotes or figures by double-spacing; however, APA advocates quadruple-spacing above and below statistical and mathematical expressions.

Spelling. Spell accurately. When in doubt, always consult a dictionary. If the dictionary says a word may be spelled in two separate ways, be consistent in the form employed, as with *theater* and *theatre,* unless the variant form occurs in quoted materials. Use American (as opposed to English) spelling throughout. In addition, proofread carefully for errors of hyphenation.

Statistical and Mathematical Copy. Use the simplest form of equation that can be made by ordinary mathematical calculation. If an equation cannot be reproduced entirely by keyboard, type what you can and fill in the rest with ink. As a general rule, keep equations on one line rather than two:

Acceptable: $\dfrac{a + b}{x + y}$

Better: $(a + b)/(x + y)$

Superscript Numerals in the Text. Place the raised note numerals, like this,[14] into the text by turning the roller of the typewriter so that the Arabic numeral strikes about half a space above the line. (See also "Footnote System," 237–40.)

Table of Contents. Seldom is a table of contents necessary, but in isolated cases, as with a complicated grant proposal, it may be advisable. Usually, listing section or chapter headings is adequate.

Typing. Submit the paper in typed form, although some instructors will accept handwritten manuscripts, if neat, legible, and written in blue or black ink on ruled paper. If you produce the paper by a word processor, keep in mind that you are responsible for correct pagination and accuracy of the manuscript. See also "Revising, Editing, and Proofreading," 121–24.

Underlining Titles. Underlining takes the place of italics in a typed manuscript. Use a continuous line for titles with more than one word. Always underline titles of the following types of works:

aircraft	Enola Gay	play	Cat on a Hot Tin Roof
ballet	The Nutcracker	poem	Idylls of the King
book	Earthly Powers		(only if book length)
bulletin	Production Memo 3	radio show	Grand Ole Opry
drama	Desire Under the Elms	recording	The Poems of Wallace Stevens
film	Treasure of the Sierra Madre	sculpture	David
journal	Journal of Sociology	ship	Titanic
magazine	Newsweek	short novel	Billy Budd
newspaper	The Nashville Banner	symphony	Beethoven's Eroica *but* Beethoven's Symphony no. 3 in A (to identify form, number, and key)
novel	The Scarlet Letter		
opera	Rigoletto		
painting	Mona Lisa	television	Tonight Show (title of program, but not of a single episode)
pamphlet	Ten Goals for Successful Sales		
periodical	Scientific American		
		yearbook	The Pegasus

By contrast, place *quotation marks* around: articles, essays, chapters, sections, short poems, stories, songs, lectures, sermons, reports, and individual episodes of television programs.

If separately published, underline titles of essays, lectures, poems, proceedings, reports, sermons, and stories. However, these items are usually published as an anthology of sermons or a collection of stories, in which cases you would underline the title of the anthology or collection.

Do not underline sacred writings (Genesis or Old Testament); series (The New American Nation Series); editions (Variorum Edition of W. B. Yeats); societies (Victorian Society); courses (Greek Mythology); divisions of a work (preface, appendix, canto 3, scene 2); or descriptive phrases (Nixon's farewell address or Reagan's White House years).

Underlining for Emphasis. On occasion, you may use underlining to emphasize certain words or phrases in a typed paper, but positioning the key word accomplishes the same purpose:

Expressed Emphasis: `Perhaps an answer lies in` <u>`preventing`</u> `abuse,`
`not in makeshift remedies after the fact.`

Better: `Prevention of abuse is a better answer than`
`makeshift remedies after the fact.`

Some special words and symbols require underlining: (1) Species, genera, and varieties (<u>Penstemon caespitosus</u> subsp. <u>thompsoniae</u>): (2) Letter, word, or phrase cited as a linguistic sample (the letter <u>e</u> in the word <u>let</u>); (3) Letters used as statistical symbols and algebraic variables (trial <u>n</u> of the <u>t</u> test or <u>C</u>(3, 14) = 9.432).

Word Division. Avoid dividing any word at the end of a line. Leave the line short rather than divide a word (see Hyphens, 151).

SAMPLE PAPER: A SHORT ESSAY WITH DOCUMENTATION

The following paper demonstrates the correct form for short papers that use only one or two sources. Keep in mind that short papers, like the long formal research paper, require correct in-text citations and a list of references.

1/2 inch {

1

} 1 inch

A separate title page is unnecessary with short papers (see 129)

Jon Ashley Ezell

Professor Welker

English 1010

22 September 1985

An Interpretation of "A & P"

Quadruple space {

    John Updike's "A & P" is a short story about a young grocery clerk named Sammy who feels trapped by the artificial values of the small town where he lives. Sammy describes the store and its customers as evidence to this artificiality: "records at discount of the Carribbean Six or Tony Martin Sings or such gunk you

Ellipsis points signal omission from a quotation (see 118)

wonder they waste the wax on . . . and plastic toys done up in cellophane that fall apart when a kid looks at them anyway" (Updike 1088).[1] Sammy observes the

Inform readers with footnotes when you plan to omit author from citations
Introduce and identify any authorities that you quote or paraphrase and supply an in-text citation to page number(s)

customers daily and proclaims them to be "houseslaves in pin curlers" (1087), suggesting thereby that all are stereotypes who no longer care about their appearances. This attitude, according to Gilbert Porter, reveals "that implicit set of values which will ultimately set him against community mores" (1155). In effect, the A & P store serves as "the common denominator of the

---

[1]Future citations to the story will be to page numbers only.

Ezell 2

middle-class suburbia, an appropriate symbol for the mass
ethic of a consumer-conditioned society" (Porter 1155).
Yet Porter fails to place proper emphasize on Sammy's
perceptive eye. Sammy looks at these people and sees,
through them, his own future if he lets himself be
subjected to society's rules of conformity. In throwing
off bonds of conformity he takes all responsibility for
his actions onto himself, and in so doing he sells his
innocence for freedom, a fair trade-off in the rites of
passage from child to adult.

> Identify your special view of the story, which is your thesis statement

    In his peculiar fashion Sammy, who does not like
artificiality, questions the decency of everyone else
in the supermarket, referring to them as dehumanized
"sheep." He comments, "I bet you could set off dynamite
in an A & P and the people would by and large keep
reaching and checking oatmeal off their lists . . ."
(1087). Therefore, when three girls come into the A & P
wearing only bathing suits and looking natural, Sammy
perceives them to be the only decent things in the
entire store. He becomes particularly offended when
the store manager, Lengel, criticizes the girls for
indecency. Sammy believes the girls are only out of
place in the A & P because of its "fluorescent lights,"

> All references to the story serve to develop this writer's thesis

"stacked packages," and "checkerboard green-and-cream-
rubber-tile floor," all artificial things.

　　Lengel is the voice of the community. He manages
the store in a conservative routine. For him, the
girls pose a disturbance to his store, so he expresses
his displeasure of their attire by reminding them that
the A & P is not the beach (1088). "Decently dressed"
to a man like Lengel means that girls must dress in
apparel that will not draw attention. Calling attention
to oneself should be reserved for the beach, not the middle
of town in front of "two banks and the Congregational
church and the newspaper store and three real estate
offices and about twenty-seven old freeloaders tearing
up Central Street because the sewer broke again"
(1087). The manager prefers customers that are like
sheep, which are routine animals that never sway from
the herd and in times of crisis crowd together as a
futile means of survival. In contrast, the entrance of
the three girls is a refreshing breath that blows away
Sammy's mood of oppression. He refers to them as "my
girls" (1089) and labels one of them as "Queenie" to
represent that she is the Queen Bee whom others follow.
She is special as a member of a higher social class

Note how this
writer blends
quotation and
paraphrase into
his textual
discussion

Ezell 4

because there are few leaders and many followers in our society.

The eventual confrontation of Sammy with Lengel serves as the climax of the story. Sammy grows angry because Lengel, noticing that one girl was wearing only a two-piece suit, says, "We want you decently dressed when you come in here" (1088). This social condemnation angers Sammy so much that he quits, an act that Porter labels as Sammy's "rejection of the A & P and the misplaced values for which it stands" (1157).

John Updike thereby suggests that the easy way, a conventional conformity to routine, is not always the best way. Updike suggests that young individualists, like Queenie and Sammy, will travel rough roads ahead in their lives, yet he also suggests that a clear conscience which results from a refusal to conform will prove profitable in the long run of life. The world can be hard on all individuals, so Sammy is right in taking responsibility for himself and his actions.

The writer returns his focus to the author after analysis of the story

The writer extends the thesis into a conclusion

Ezell 5

Works Cited

A separate
"Works Cited"
page lists the
two works used
in the study

Porter, M. Gilbert. "John Updike's 'A & P': The

      Establishment and an Emersonian Cashier." <u>English</u>

      <u>Journal</u> 61 (1972): 1155-58.

Updike, John. "A & P." <u>Pigeon Feathers and Other</u>

      <u>Stories</u>. New York: Knopf, 1962. Rpt. in

      <u>Fiction 100</u>. Ed. James H. Pickering. 4th ed.

      New York: Macmillan, 1982. 1086-1089.

SAMPLE PAPER:
A FORMAL RESEARCH PAPER
WITH OUTLINE AND CONTENT NOTES

The following paper illustrates the style and form of the fully developed research paper. It includes a title page, outline pages, a variety of in-text citations, superscript numerals to content endnotes, and a fully developed "Works Cited" page. Notations in the margins signal special circumstances in matters of form and style.

Child Abuse

The Parents as Victims

by

Jo Walker

Professor James Marsh

Composition 1010

16 May 1986

Sample Research Paper

The following marginal comments clarify the form of the research paper and explain specific problems you may encounter.

The title page is a three-part balance of title, author, and course information (see 128).

ii

Outline

Repeat your thesis at the beginning of the outline, though it may take a different form in the paper itself (see 87).

Employ standard outline symbols (see 84).

Thesis: Parents who abuse their children should be
        treated as victims, not criminals.

I. The Issues of Child Abuse

    A. The Problems

        1. Recognition of a problem

        2. Myth of America as child-oriented

        3. Problems of discovery of potential child
           abuse

        4. Help after the fact

    B. Statistics and Examples of Abuse

        1. Abuse on the increase

        2. Specific examples

        3. Absence of professional help before the
           abuse

        4. Prevention of rather than coping with

        5. Case study of Jane Neilson

    C. A Possible Answer

        1. Help for the Jane Neilsons before, not after

        2. Prevention of abuse before the fact

        3. Thesis: Parents as victims

        4. Reaching parents before abuse

iii

II. The Causes and Cycles of Abuse

    A. Potentials for Abuse

        1. Parents who abuse as having been abused themselves

        2. Predisposition to be abusive

        3. Social levels as climates for abuse

        4. Absence of the extended family

        5. Television violence

        6. Depression as a causal element

    B. Cycles of Child Abuse

        1. High unemployment in 1982

        2. Increase in child abuse in 1982

        3. Declines in work force and increases in child abuse

        4. Sample of scenario of unemployed father

        5. The cycle as escalating even more in years to come

        6. The cycle as breeding itself: the abused become abusive

This writer uses the topic outline (see 87).

iv

III. Focus on the Parents as Victims

    A. A Look at the Evidence

        1. Help for the parents, not just the children

        2. Facts to be faced

    B. Therapy and Study Groups

        1. Parents Anonymous

        2. Courses on parenthood

        3. Warnings against incest

        4. Aid for alcoholics

IV. The Necessary Treatment

    A. Community involvement programs

    B. The parent as victim as well as the child

    C. The character of the community

The headings for both the introduction (I) and conclusion (IV) are content oriented like other outline entries (see 86).

Walker 1

Child Abuse: The Parents as Victims

Family troubles will most likely affect the delicate members of our society, the children. The recognition of causes for their mistreatment and a need for a cure face this society each day if we are to defeat what one authority calls "the greatest crippler and killer of our children-- child abuse and neglect" (Fontana xvi). In fact, another writer argues that "the single greatest impediment to our improving the lives of America's children is the myth that we are a child-oriented society" (Zigler 39). This sociologist suggests that too many Americans will not respond to documented findings about child abuse (30). However, a growing concern among many segments of the population has spurred passage of laws to protect the rights of children. These new laws are difficult to enforce because, according to several sources, the families and the abused children themselves often lie to protect both the abusing parent and the family unit (e.g., Giarretto 2; de Young 581; Kinard 406-08; Young 81).

In addition, social agencies find it difficult to prevent abuse when they can't discover it until a battered child is brought into an emergency room. Law

Margin annotations:

1/2 inch

1 inch

Quadruple space

1 inch

Both running head and page number are given (but see 128).

Repeat the title on the first page of text.

Use parenthetical citations to your sources.

This writer identifies the issue, but a thesis comes later (see paragraph 5).

Note: most research papers have openings that extend over several paragraphs.

For tips on building opening paragraphs, see 98.

Walker 2

This writer begins
narrowing her
thesis about
parents as victims.

enforcement must then enter the picture and, as often as
not, a judge splits up the family structure and the
child no longer has a father or a mother and, in the
worst of cases, has neither parent. At this point the
parent is treated as a criminal. It becomes a cycle,
says Giarretto, and it goes somewhat like this: the
father is usually convicted on a felony charge and
spends months, perhaps years, in jail; the mother is
left in shock and terror and feels herself a failure;
and the child, now under protective custody, feels
banished and punished even though he or she is the
victim (2-3).

Even worse, severe abuse is on the rise. Each year
more and more children suffer the trauma of physical and
emotional abuse. Although the exact number remains

Use of statistics
from several
sources reinforces
the
generalizations.

unknown, the Education Commission of the States reports
that some 60,000 cases occur annually (Cohen & Sussman
433). Boys outnumber girls as victims of abuse until
the teen years (Chase 104). The death rate from
cruelty exceeds that from infectious disease (Fontana

This paragraph
blends paraphrase
with a long
quotation (see
110).

196). In truth, few young persons reach maturity
without a severe spanking from an angry parent. One
critic of the system puts it this way:

Walker 3

More often than not an object such as
a hairbrush, switch, belt, or ironing cord is
used to inflict pain on the child. In some
instances children suffer a whip, fan belt,
clothesline, steam, fire, cigarette burn, or a
blowtorch. Some spend long hours tied to a
bed, in basements or attics, or locked out of
the house. Some are not fed. Relatively few
die, however, yet most who do are young, very
young. Few parents who abuse their children
are reported to the authorities, and most of
those who are reported deny the abuse. Few
are prosecuted and few are treated by
professionals. (Walters 3)

It is important that we note the last phrase above, that
few are treated by professionals either after or before
the abuse. After abuse takes place, most agencies cope
with it rather than work to prevent this painful menace.

In the face of ever increasing incidents of abuse,
can our social organizations not do better? For
instance, let's look at one case study, summarized here
from Leontine Young (76-77). Jane Neilson was the
oldest of ten children of an alcoholic father and

Long quotes
are introduced
by a colon,
indented, without
quotation marks,
double spaced,
with source
cited at the end
(see 115).

The shift into past tense is correct, but regular text should use historical present tense (see 97).

promiscuous mother. Jane became a prostitute and her mother shared the income. Along with three of her sisters, Jane was arrested and spent time at the state correctional school. Later, Jane had six children of her own, two of whom were illegitimate (my underlining). She married a man with a criminal record who abused her and her children. Jane and her husband frequently separated; after he was arrested again, she began to drink heavily. Three of her children were placed under

Blend quotations into your text smoothly (see 108).

the care of agencies. Young (76) points out that Jane Neilson's entire life has been "dreary misery, a saga of exploitation, deprivation, indifference, and hate," and then concludes: "What she could have given any child is hard to see." In truth, Jane Neilson is a victim of her own background; little wonder that her children would suffer.

This case study, moreover, prompts this theory: If people like the Jane Neilsons of our society could be identified and given help in a timely fashion, then perhaps children would not be victimized. Prevention of abuse is unquestionably a better answer than makeshift remedies after the fact. Can social agencies not predict that Jane Neilson's six children are targets

Walker 5

for abuse? After all, child abuse is a symptom of the parent's condition. The preventive measure would be to treat abusing parents as victims, not criminals. They are usually victims of their own childhood. Reaching out to these parents before a child appears in the emergency room may prove difficult, yet theoretically solving the causes of abuse, not just treating the effects, may be the only way to stop this escalating maltreatment of America's greatest resource, the children.

The thesis comes late in the opening; it could also appear early (see 99).

It is generally agreed (Fontana 44; Giarretto 4-5; Kinard 410; Zigler 41-42) that parents who abuse children were abused themselves as children. Many abusive parents had poor role models as parents and did not experience the love between parent and child that most of us know. Julianne Wayne and Nancy Avery stipulate that some parents do not see themselves as people with real potential, and they believe themselves to be black sheep of the family (10). Another expert states that "a number of psychiatrists believe that there is an organic or constitutional factor involved" with parents who abuse a child, and adds that some people have "a predisposition toward this kind of [violent] personality" (Young 78). Thus heredity and childhood

Note the blend of paraphrase and quotation so that text flows smoothly with proper introductions and in-text citations (see 108).

Use brackets to add words to a quotation (see 120).

environment or both may determine such personality
development, which often causes "the gap in
communications so often experienced with abusive
parents, as if they acted on different premises
than other people" (Young 78).

Public concerns for the whole fabric of society
stand in conflict with the selfish, private needs of
the abusive parent. On that point Edward Zigler argues
that many parents are just not equipped today for
parenthood (42). He states that the "extended family is now
rare in contemporary society, and with its demise the
new parent has lost the wisdom and daily support of
older, more experienced family members" (42). In truth,
a family such as that portrayed by the Waltons on
television seldom exists today with grandparents, parents,
and many children all living together under one roof. If
children do not learn by caring for their younger siblings,
then, as Zigler warns, they cannot be prepared for handling
their own children.

What's more, television may breed violence.
Zigler laments, "One finds violence, hostility and
aggression everywhere, including TV, the movies, and in
many of our everyday social relations" (40). Violence
observed becomes, all too often, violence practiced by

Walker 7

parents on the children as well as by children on their
brothers and sisters and even against their own parents.
As Zigler puts it, "So long as this preoccupation with
and even glorification of aggression is tolerated, so
long can we expect the abuse of children both at home
and in the school" (40).

Depression also causes a parent to beat a child,
but E. Milling Kinard suggests that treating the
parent for depression without removing the social
problems of economic poverty and emotional stress will
probably have only limited success (403-06). The
causal chain leading to abuse may be complex to the
point that social workers need to dip into the life
history of the parent/abuser, asking always: How is
this adult a victim who needs help as much as his or
her battered child?

Cycles of child abuse appear regularly on a
community-wide level, even on a national scope. The year
1982 saw an increase in child abuse all across the
nation; it was also a year of extremely high
unemployment. Experts note the correlation, saying
unemployment in a town, state, or whole nation may
endanger the well-being of the children as well as their
very lives (Steinberg, Catalano, and Dooley 975-85).

Even paraphrased materials should be introduced and documented in the text (see 108).

These three authorities reach rather distressing conclusions:

> Declines in the work force are significantly
> related to reported child abuse in two
> metropolitan communities. This finding is
> consistent with the hypothesis that
> undesirable economic change causes family
> stress, resulting subsequently in child
> abuse." (Steinberg, Catalano, and Dooley 982)

On an individual basis the family scenario might
go like this: the father loses his job, so the mother
enters the job market, leaving the children to a man
without the experience or the patience for managing and
properly disciplining the children. Thereafter, the
entire family is victimized. In the worst of cases the
children are harmed physically, even sexually molested,
the father is placed in jail, the children are split up
for placement in foster homes, and the mother struggles
to hold together what is left--all events triggered, in
large part, by unemployment. Unfortunately, these
cycles of child abuse may be expected to escalate for
years to come as economic disaster strikes more and
more adults to the point that children are raised in
violent and hostile environments.

On that point, Peter Kratcoski suggests that

If quoting the beginning of a paragraph, do not indent the first line more than the other lines, but see 119–20 if you quote two or more paragraphs.

Three authors can be listed in a citation, but use "et al." with more than three (see 113).

This writer effectively summarizes the basic problem, then moves to additional issues.

For tips on building the body of your paper, see 103–104 and the section on paradigms, 91–94.

Walker 9

childhood experiences help form basic personalities
that "shape the individual's relationship with his or
her own children" (436). Kratcoski makes this significant
point: "Children reared with love and respect mature
adequately and become loving, responsible, and productive
parents and spouses, while children who are disliked and
abused by their parents may turn out to be abusers" (436-
37). Thus children who experience violence as children
tend to incorporate such behavior for handling stress
later as adults.

In theory, troubled parents can be treated as
victims of their heritage and social conditioning. In
practice, we can do more for them prior to abuse.
Health professionals and social support organizations
need to rededicate themselves to a focus on causes, not
just on remedies after the fact. They may help the
child after a battering episode of abuse, but they are
probably too late to help the parent. As a
consequence, child abuse grows more and more every day.
The main reason for the increasing number of cases
might be our "unwillingness to accept the truth, look
ugliness in the eye, to draw upon our reserves of
courage, and fight back" (Fontana xii). All the people
who fail to get involved or who don't report a case of

The writer reasserts her thesis and moves toward her conclusion.

abuse say to themselves--if I don't look, if I don't get
involved, if I don't think about it, abuse will go away.
But the truth of the matter is, it does not go away, the
problem of abuse just gets greater and greater.

The writer offers
the first of four
directives.

   Therefore the time has arrived to apply theory in
several positive steps. First, the idea of group
therapy and self-help sessions for adults seems sound.
Marlin Blizinsky reports that group sessions may be
the only answer for some persons because a group
session might be the only program in which an abusive
person will participate (311). Blizinsky cites
Parents Anonymous, a self-help group, which has begun
to gain national attention and Seattle's Children's
Home Society (307). The Armstrong/Fraley study proved
that one Family Support Center affected families in a
positive manner long after treatment ceased. Also,
Zigler cites a successful program of emergency services

Some lines may
appear extremely
short, but do *not*
hyphenate words
at the ends of
lines.

The second
directive is now
presented.

to families in Nashville where the number of children
institutionalized because of abuse dropped
substantially: "The Nashville program is an excellent
one and there is no reason that it cannot be implemented
in every community in America" (41).

   Second, parenthood courses for adolescents are

positive actions. Zigler advocates an expanded effort
to educate young people for parenthood. He would extend
sex education to include information on child care, at
least for older children of child bearing age (42).
Such a program makes sense because it seeks prevention
and not remedies after the act of child abuse. Another
sociologist observes, "A central notion in the treatment
model is the building of social responsibility, the
realization that each of us is an important element of
society" (Giarretto 5). Youngsters who are future
parents should be helped toward responsible social behavior.

    Third, a program to advise young girls and boys
about incest could warn many children about aggressive
adults and perhaps help them preserve the family
unit.[1] Amazingly, many children feel responsible and
accept guilt for forced incestuous behavior. The case
study of Leigh, as described below, seems typical:

> Leigh, now 25, had been sexually abused
> by her father for five years. He continually
> told her that if she would only stop acting
> like such a "slut" he would quit having sex
> with her. Early attempts to tell her mother
> what was happening only reinforced her
> father's claim: her mother told her that only

Step three is advanced next.

Superscript numerals signal content endnotes (see 138). Do not use superscript numerals and endnotes for documentation of sources unless you need to cluster several sources.

This description may seem bizarre, but the message is effective under conditions of the paper.

a "whore" would accuse her father of such
things. "So here I was, 11 years old,
standing in front of a mirror thinking, You
filthy slut! You deserve everything you
get!' Then I'd go into a trance almost, and
cut my arms and legs with a razor blade."
(de Young 581)

Counseling for a person like Leigh at 25 may help her
to adjust today and even to be a good parent tomorrow,
but how much better it would be if women like Leigh
were counseled as children before self-injurious
behavior marred their bodies, their lives, and
eventually their own children.

The fourth
directive is now
given.

Fourth, in a related area, identifying and
offering aid to alcoholic parents and their children
may serve to reduce child abuse because studies
demonstrate that a high percentage of abused children
have alcoholic parents or guardians.[2]

The conclusion
now officially
begins. Note
how the writer
develops a full
judgment on the
issue and does
not merely
summarize the
paper.

The four points above defend a central theory: the
troubled parents who were victims in their childhood
and those who are victimized by circumstances today
need to be identified by social agencies and helped to
recognize their real potentials as human beings and

Walker 13

parents. The responsibility rests with health
professionals who can prevent some abuse before it
occurs. Major cities across the nation and many rural
communities are establishing parental self-help groups
as well as child abuse centers. A few of the most
successful community involvement programs are the Child
Abuse Prevention in Toledo, the Johnson County
Coalition for Prevention of Child Abuse in Kansas City,
and the Council for Prevention of Child Abuse and
Neglect in Seattle. More cities should establish such
programs. The organization Mothers Against Drunk
Drivers (MADD) has inspired tough new measures
nationwide, and the crusade to find missing children
has national exposure. Next we need a total national
commitment to serve potential abusers before the fact
as well as to help children after abuse has occurred.

Health authorities should look to parents or
guardians as victims and try, difficult though it may
be, to identify adults who suffer from loneliness,
isolation, and alienation. Their violent beating of a
child, though it cannot be condoned, may be a cry for
help. Good family life feeds love and affection for
one's fellow human beings. Helen Perlman calls it the
"art of caring." Unfortunately, children who lack

For tips on writing paragraphs of the conclusion, see 105–108.

Reference to an entire article needs no in-text citation of page number.

loving care fall victims to hostile, aggressive physical
abuse. They may, because they cannot give love, grow up
to be abusers themselves.

Repeatedly, social agencies destroy family life by
institutionalizing family members after abuse occurs
even though warning notices have been issued by neighbors,
relatives, and even the social workers themselves.
Authorities participate in criminal abuse by failure with
preventive measures. If authorities, in truth, cannot
act until they suspect that a crime has been committed,
then perhaps we need new legislation that will allow
professionals to effectively enter the lives of children,
teenagers, and aggressive adults. In that way we might
succeed in reversing the present growing trend in child
abuse.

Walker 15

Notes

[1] The problems of incest and sexual abuse are explored in Adams-Tucker, Giarretto (4-5), Walters, and also de Young (583). These authorities cite the need for preventive measures, if possible, before damage occurs to the children; nevertheless, sexual abuse, like a disease, is here today in horrifying case after case, and we do not have a cure. Patricia Herman offers 11 clear guidelines for teaching children about abuse (170-72).

[2] For additional study of the effects of alcoholics on children see especially the Journal of Studies on Alcohol for the article by Wolin et al., and the bibliography on the topic in Orme and Rimmer (285-87). In addition, group therapy for children of alcoholics is examined in Hawley and Brown.

Content notes appear on a separate page.

This note offers additional literature on a point.

This note offers sources on a related topic.

For tips on writing content notes, see 138.

Walker 16

Start the "Works Cited" on a new page.

Works Cited

Adams-Tucker, Christine. "Defense Mechanisms Used By
    Sexually Abused Children." <u>Children Today</u> 14.1
    (1985): 8-12, 34.

For tips on writing the bibliography entries, see 185–209.

Armstrong, D. A., and Y. L. Fraley. "What Happens to
    Families After They Leave the Program?" <u>Children</u>
    <u>Today</u> 14.3 (1985): 17-20.

Blizinsky, Marlin. "Parents Anonymous and the Private
    Agency: Administrative Cooperation." <u>Child Welfare</u>
    61 (1982): 305-11.

Chase, Naomi F. <u>A Child Is Being Beaten</u>. New York:
    Holt, 1975.

Cohen, Stephan J., and Alan Sussman. "The Incidence of
    Child Abuse in the United States." <u>Child Welfare</u> 54
    (1975): 432-43.

A typical entry for a journal article (see 198–99).

de Young, Mary. "Self-Injurious Behavior in Incest
    Victims: A Research Note." <u>Child Welfare</u> 61
    (1982): 577-84.

A book entry (see 185–198).

Fontana, Vincent J. <u>Somewhere a Child Is Crying</u>.
    New York: Macmillan, 1973.

A journal entry may include the issue number (see 199).

Giarretto, Henry. "The Treatment of Father-daughter
    Incest: A Psycho-Social Approach." <u>Children</u>
    <u>Today</u> 5.4 (1976): 2-5.

Hawley, N. P., and E. L. Brown. "Use of Group Treatment
    With Children of Alcoholics." <u>Social Casework</u> 62
    (1981): 40-46.

Herman, Patricia. "Educating Children About Sexual
    Abuse: The Teacher's Responsiblity." <u>Childhood
    Education</u> 61 (1985): 169-74.

Kinard, E. Milling. "Child Abuse and Depression: Cause
    or Consequence?" <u>Child Welfare</u> 61 (1982): 403-13.

Kratcoski, Peter C. "Child Abuse and Violence
    Against the Family." <u>Child Welfare</u> 61 (1982): 435-44.

Orme, T. C., and J. Rimmer. "Alcoholism and Child Abuse:
    A Review." <u>Journal of Studies on Alcohol</u> 42
    (1981): 273-87.

Perlman, Helen H. "On the Art of Caring." <u>Child
    Welfare</u> 64 (1985): 3-11.

Steinberg, Laurence D., R. Catalano, and D. Dooley.
    "Economic Antecedents of Child Abuse and Neglect."
    <u>Child Development</u> 52 (1981): 975-85.

Walters, David R. <u>Physical and Sexual Abuse of
    Children: Causes and Treatment</u>. Bloomington:
    Indiana UP, 1975.

Wayne, Julianne L., and Nancy C. Avery. <u>Child Abuse:
    Prevention and Treatment through Social Group Work</u>.
    Charleston, MA: Rivers, 1980.

An entry with
three authors (see
190).

Note abbreviation
for a university
press (see 189).

An entry for two
authors.

Walker 18

An entry for more than three authors (see 191 for alternate form that uses *et al*).

Wolin, S. J., L. A. Bennett, D. L. Noonan, and M. A.

Teitebaum. "Disrupted Family Rituals: A

Factor in the Intergenerational Transmission of

Alcoholism." <u>Journal of Studies on Alcohol</u> 41

(1980): 199-214.

Include any subtitles separated from the main title by a colon.

Young, Leontine. <u>Wednesday's Children: A Study of Child</u>

<u>Neglect and Abuse</u>. New York: McGraw, 1964.

Zigler, Edward F. "The Unmet Needs of America's Children."

<u>Children Today</u> 5.3 (1976): 9-43.

6

Works Cited

After writing your paper, you should prepare a "Works Cited" page to list your reference materials. List only the ones actually used in your manuscript, including works mentioned within content endnotes or in captions of tables and illustrations.

Your heading indicates the nature of your list. "Works Cited" or "References Cited" means that your list includes only those printed works quoted and paraphrased in the paper. "Sources Cited" or "List of Sources Cited" suggests that your list includes nonprint items (e.g., interviews or speeches) as well as printed works. "References" means that you are listing all works that contributed to the study even though you did not paraphrase or quote from them all. "Bibliography" means a fairly complete listing of *all* works related to the subject, an unlikely prospect for undergraduate papers. "Selected Bibliography" suggests, like "References," that you have narrowed the list to important works but that you have not cited all of them in your paper.

If you carefully developed your early working bibliography cards (see 23–28), the preparation of a final list is relatively simple. Your bibliography cards, arranged alphabetically, provide the necessary information if, of course, you have kept the cards up-to-date during note-taking by adding new sources and by disposing of cards citing irrelevant sources.

Type your "Works Cited" page according to standards which follow. Works pertinent to the paper but not quoted or paraphrased, such as an article on related matters, can be mentioned in a content endnote (138–41) and then listed within the "Works Cited." On this point see especially the "Notes" page of the sample paper, 179.

FORMAT FOR "WORKS CITED" PAGE

Arrange items in alphabetical order by the surname of the author. When no author is listed, alphabetize by the first important word of the title. Imagine lettered spelling for unusual items, such as "#2 Red Dye" (entered as though "Number 2 Red Dye"). Place the first line of each entry flush with the left margin and indent succeeding lines five spaces. Double-space each entry and double-space between entries. Set the title "Works Cited" one inch down from the top of the sheet and double-space between it and the first entry. A sample page follows (see also the sample Works Cited page on 180–82):

```
                                              Robertson 12

                          Works Cited
        The Bible.  Revised Standard Version.
        Bulfinch, Thomas.  Bulfinch's Mythology.  2 vols.
             New York: Mentor, 1962.
        Campbell, Joseph.  The Hero With a Thousand Faces.
             Cleveland: Meridian, 1956.
        ---.  The Masks of God.  4 vols.  New York: Viking,
             1970.
        Henderson, Joseph L., and Maud Oakes.  The Wisdom of
             the Serpent: The Myths of Death, Rebirth, and
             Resurrection.  New York: Collier, 1971.
        Homer.  The Iliad.  Trans. Richmond Lattimore.
             Chicago: U of Chicago P, 1951.
        Laird, Charlton.  "A Nonhuman Being Can Learn Lan-
             guage."  College Composition and Communication
             23 (1972): 142-54.
        Levi-Strauss, Claude.  "The Structural Study of Myth."
             Myth: A Symposium.  Ed. A. Sebeok.
             Bloomington: Indiana UP, 1958.
        McFadden, George.  "'Life Studies'--Robert Lowell's
             Comic Breakthrough."  PMLA 90 (1975): 96-106.
        Robinson, Lillian S.  "Criticism--and Self-Criticism."
             College English 36 (1974): 436-45.
```

Bibliography Form—Books

When entering references to books, you should use the following order, omitting unnecessary items (1, 3, and 8 are required):

1. Author(s)	6. Number of volumes
2. Chapter or part of book	7. Name of the series
3. Title of the book	8. Place, publisher, and date
4. Editor, translator, or compiler	9. Volume number of this book
5. Edition	10. Page numbers

Name of the Author(s)

The author's name, surname first, followed by given name or initials, followed by a period:

```
Baxter, John.  The Bidders.  New York: Lippincott, 1979.
```

Always give authors' names in the fullest possible form; for example, "Cosbey, Robert C." rather than "Cosbey, R. C." unless, as indicated on the title page of the book, the author prefers initials.

When an author has two or more works, do not repeat the name with each entry. Rather, insert a continuous three-dash line flush with the left margin, followed by a period:

```
Hansberry, Lorraine.  A Raisin in the Sun.  New York:

    Random, 1959.

---.  To Be Young, Gifted and Black.  Ed. Robert Nemiroff.

    Englewood Cliffs: Prentice, 1969.
```

Order the works by the first important word of the title, in this case "R" precedes "T." Remember: the hyphens stand for exactly the same name(s) as in the preceding entry.

Do not substitute three hyphens for an author who has two or more works in the bibliography when one is written in collaboration with someone else:

```
Lagarsfeld, Paul F., et al., eds.  Continuities in the

    Language of Social Research.  Rev. ed.  New York:

    Free, 1972.

Lagarsfeld, Paul F., and E. Katz.  Language of Social

    Research: A Reader in the Methodology of Social

    Research.  New York: Free, 1965.
```

A Chapter or Part of a Book

List the chapter or part of a book in "Works Cited" only when it is separately edited, translated, or written, or when it demands special attention. For
example, if you quote from a specific chapter of a book, let's say Lewis
Thomas's chapter entitled "The Music of This Sphere" from his book *The Lives
of a Cell,* the entry should read:

```
Thomas, Lewis. The Lives of a Cell. New York: Viking, 1974.
```

Your in-text citation should list specific page numbers, so there is no reason to
mention a specific chapter even though it's the only portion of Thomas's book
that you read.

Anthologies, however, contain works by many authors or different works
by the same author. Because readers will search your list for the person cited
in the text, not an editor, you need specifics in the "Works Cited," as follows:

1. A textual reference to Elder's essay would require:

```
Elder, Lonne. "Ceremonies in Dark Old Men." New Black
    Playwrights: An Anthology. Ed. William Couch, Jr.
    Baton Rouge: Louisiana State UP, 1968. 55-72.
```

2. A textual reference to Aristophanes's drama *The Birds* would
require:

```
Aristophanes. The Birds. Five Comedies of Aristophanes.
    Trans. Benjamin B. Rogers. Garden City: Doubleday,
    1955. 110-154.
```

3. A textual reference to Child's essay on Jane Austen would require:

```
Child, Harold. "Jane Austen." The Cambridge History of
    English Literature. Ed. A. W. Ward and A. R. Waller.
    London: Cambridge UP, 1927. 12:231-44.
```

The Title of the Book

Show the title of the work, underlined, followed by a period. Separate any
subtitle from the primary title by a colon and one space even though the title
page has no mark of punctuation or the card catalog entry has a semicolon:

```
Lagercrantz, Olof. From Hell to Paradise: Dante and His
    Comedy. Trans. Alan Blair. New York: Washington
    Square P, 1966.
```

When a title of a book includes the title of another book, do not underline the latter:

```
Schilling, Bernard N. Dryden and the Conservative Myth: A
    Reading of Absalom and Achitophel. New Haven: Yale UP,
    1961.
```

Name of the Editor or Translator
List the editor or translator, preceded by "Ed." or "Trans.":

```
Dante. The Purgatorio. Trans. John Ciardi. New York:
    New American, 1961.
```

However, if your in-text citation refers to the work of the editor or translator (e.g., "The Ciardi edition caused debate among Dante scholars") use this form:

```
Ciardi, John, trans. The Purgatorio. By Dante. New
    York: New American, 1961.
```

Edition of the Book
Indicate the edition used, whenever it is not the first, in Arabic numerals (for example, "3rd ed."), without further punctuation:

```
Beyer, Robert, and Donald J. Trawicki. Profitability
    Accounting: For Planning and Control. 2nd ed.
    New York: Ronald, 1972.
```

Name of a Series
Show the name of the series, without quotation marks and not underlined, with the series number (for example, "vol. 3," "no. 3" or simply "3"), followed by a period:

```
Brown, J. R., and Bernard Harris. Restoration Theatre.
    Stratford-upon-Avon Studies 6. London: Arnold, 1965.
```

Number of Volumes with This Title
Show the number of volumes with this particular title, if more than one, in Arabic numerals (for example, "6 vols."):

> Horecek, Leo, and Gerald Lefkoss. <u>Programmed Ear</u>
>
> <u>Training</u>. 4 vols. New York: Harcourt, 1970.

Place, Publisher, and Date
Indicate the place, publisher, and date of publication:

> Steinbeck, John. <u>The Grapes of Wrath</u>. New York:
>
> Viking, 1939.

If more than one place of publication appears on the title page, the first city mentioned is sufficient. If successive dates of copyright are given, use the most recent (unless your study is specifically concerned with an earlier, perhaps definitive, edition). Note: a new printing is merely a press run, but a new edition is a textual revision. A new printing does not constitute a new edition nor demand usage of its corresponding date. For example, if the text has a 1940 copyright date but a 1975 printing, use 1940 unless you have other information, such as: "facsimile printing" or "1975 third printing rev." (see immediately below):

> Bell, Charles Bailey, and Harriett P. Miller. <u>The Bell Witch:</u>
>
> <u>A Mysterious Spirit</u>. 1934; facsim. ed. Nashville:
>
> Elder, 1972.
>
> Weaver, Raymond. Introduction. <u>The Shorter Novels of</u>
>
> <u>Herman Melville</u>. 1928; New York: Premier-Fawcett,
>
> 1960. v-xxi.
>
> Lewes, George Henry. <u>The Life and Works of Geothe</u> (1855).
>
> 2 vols. Rpt. as vols. 13 and 14 of <u>The Works of</u>
>
> <u>J. W. von Goethe</u>. Ed. Nathan Haskell Dole. 14 vols.
>
> London: Nicolls, n.d.

If the place, publisher, or date of publication is not provided, insert either "n.p." or "n.d." as shown above. Include the abbreviation for the state only if necessary for clarity:

> Forliti, John E. <u>Program Planning for Youth Ministry</u>.
>
> Winona, MN: St. Mary's College P, 1975.

Provide the publisher's name in a shortened form, as suggested by the following: Allyn (Allyn and Bacon, Inc.), Bobbs (Bobbs-Merrill Co., Inc.), Cambridge UP (Cambridge University Press), GPO (Government Printing Office), McGraw (McGraw-Hill, Inc.), Scott (Scott, Foresman and Co.), and U of Chicago P (University of Chicago Press).

A publisher's special imprint name should be joined with the official name: Anchor-Doubleday, Jove-Berkley, Ace-Grossett, Del Rey-Ballantine, Mentor-NAL.

```
Faulkner, William.  "Spotted Horses."  Three Famous Short

    Stories.  New York: Vintage-Random, 1963.
```

Volume Number of the Book Used
When citing one entire volume of a multivolumed work, use the following form:

```
Durant, Will.  The Age of Faith.  Vol. 4 of The

    Story of Civilization.  7 vols.  New York: Simon, 1950.
```

If you cite from part of one volume in a multivolume work, show the volume number, in Arabic numerals, followed by a colon and page numbers:

```
Child, Harold.  "Jane Austen."  The Cambridge History

    of English Literature.  Ed. A. W. Ward and A. R.

    Waller.  London: Cambridge UP, 1927.  12: 231-44.
```

Page Numbers to a Section of a Book
Cite pages as shown immediately above if the work has more than one volume; otherwise, conform to the following for anthologies and collections:

```
Knoepflmacher, U. C.  "Fusing Fact and Myth:  The New

    Reality of Middlemarch."  This Particular Web:

    Essays on Middlemarch.  Ed. Ian Adam.  Toronto:

    U of Toronto P, 1975.  55-65.
```

Sample Bibliography Entries—Books
Author

```
Baxter, John.  The Bidders.  New York: Lippincott, 1979.
```

Author, anonymous

The Song of Roland. Trans. Frederick B. Luquines.
New York: Macmillan, 1960.

Author, anonymous but name supplied

[Madison, James.] All Impressments Unlawful and
Inadmissible. Boston: William Pelham, 1804.

Author, pseudonymous but name supplied

Slender, Robert [Freneau, Philip]. Letters on Various and
Important Subjects. Philadelphia: D. Hogan, 1799.

Author, listed by initials with name supplied

A[lden], E[dmund] K. "Alden, John." Dictionary of
American Biography. 1928 ed.

Author, more than one work by the same author

Hansberry, Lorraine. A Raisin in the Sun. New York:
Random, 1959.
---. To Be Young, Gifted and Black. Ed. Robert
Nemiroff. Englewood Cliffs: Prentice, 1969.

Authors, two

Hooper, Henry O., and Peter Gwynne. Physics and the
Physical Perspective. New York: Harper, 1977.

Authors, three

Richardson, Charles E., Fred V. Hein, and Dana L.
Farnsworth. Living: Health, Behavior, and
Environment. 6th ed. Glenview: Scott, 1975.

Authors, more than three

```
Lewis, Laurel J., et al. Linear Systems Analysis.
   New York: McGraw, 1969.
```

Author, corporation or institution

```
Committee on Telecommunications. Reports on Selected
   Topics in Telecommunications. New York: Nat. Acad.
   of Sciences, 1970.
```

List the work by corporate author even when the institution is also the publisher:

```
American Council on Education. Annual Report, 1970.
   Washington: American Council on Educ., 1971.
```

Alphabetized Works, Encyclopedias, and Biographical Dictionaries

```
Dickinson, Robert E. "Norman Conquest." The World
   Book Encyclopedia. 1976 ed.
```

Familiar works, as shown above, need only edition date, but less familiar works need a full citation:

```
Perrin, Porter G. "Puns." Writer's Guide and
   Index to English. 4th ed. Glenview: Scott, 1968.
```

The Bible

```
The Bible. [Denotes King James version]
The Bible. Revised Standard Version.
The Geneva Bible. 1560; facsim. rpt. Madison:
   U of Wisconsin P, 1961.
The Four Translation New Testament. Minneapolis:
   World Wide, 1966.
```

Classical Works

> Homer. <u>The Iliad</u>. Trans. Richmond Lattimore.
>
>   Chicago: U of Chicago P, 1951.

Committee Report, published as a book

> National Committee on Careers for Older Americans.
>
>   <u>Older Americans: An Untapped Resource</u>.
>
>   Washington, DC: Acad. for Educ. Dev., 1979.

See also "Author, corporation or institution," 191.

Component Part of an Anthology or Collection

In general, works in an anthology have been published previously, but the prior publication data may not be readily available; therefore, use this form:

> Updike, John. "A & P." <u>Fiction 100</u>. Ed. James E. Pickering.
>
>   4th ed. New York: Macmillan, 1982. 1086-1089.

But use the following if you can quickly identify original publication information:

> Updike, John. "A & P." <u>Pigeon Feathers and Other Stories</u>. New
>
>   York: Knopf, 1962. Rpt. in <u>Fiction 100</u>. Ed. James H.
>
>   Pickering. 4th ed. New York: Macmillan, 1982. 1086-1089.

Note also the following sample entries:

> Hoy, Cyrus. "Fathers and Daughters in Shakespeare's
>
>   Romances." <u>Shakespeare's Romances Reconsidered</u>.
>
>   Ed. Carol McGinnis Kay and Henry E. Jacobs. Lincoln:
>
>   U of Nebraska P, 1978. 77-90.
>
> Hawthorne, Nathaniel. <u>The Scarlet Letter</u>. The Scarlet
>
>   Letter <u>and Other Writings by Nathaniel Hawthorne</u>. Ed.
>
>   H. Bruce Franklin. Philadelphia: Lippincott, 1967. 22-233.
>
> Scott, Nathan, Jr. "Society and the Self in Recent American
>
>   Literature." <u>The Broken Center</u>. New Haven: Yale UP,

```
1966.  Rpt. in Dark Symphony: Negro Literature in
America.  Ed. James A. Emanuel and Theodore L. Gross.
New York: Free, 1968.  539-54.
```

Cross-References

If you are citing several selections from one anthology or collection, cite the main work and then cite individual pieces from it with cross-references to the editor(s) of the main collection:

```
Emanuel, James A., and Theodore L. Gross, eds. Dark Symphony:
     Negro Literature in America.  New York: Free, 1968.
Hughes, Langston.  "Mulatto."  Emanuel and Gross, 204-06.
Scott, Nathan, Jr.  "Society and the Self in Recent American
     Literature."  Emanuel and Gross, 539-54.
```

Note also the following in which the first entry refers to the one that follows:

```
Eliot, George.  "Art and Belles Lettres."  Westminster
     Review.  U. S. A. ed.  April 1856.  Partly rpt. Eliot,
     A Writer's Notebook.
---.  A Writer's Notebook, 1854-1879, and Uncollected
     Writings.  Ed. Joseph Wiesenfarth.  Charlottesville:
     UP of Virginia, 1981.
```

Edition

Note any edition beyond the first, as shown below:

```
Keith, Harold.  Sports and Games.  6th ed.  Scranton:
     Crowell, 1976.
Stone, Lawrence.  The Crisis of the Aristocracy: 1558-1660.
     Abridged ed.  London: Oxford UP, 1971.
```

Indicate that a work has been prepared by an editor, not the original author:

```
Melville, Herman.  Moby Dick.  Ed. with Intro. by
     Alfred Kazin.  Riverside ed.  Boston: Houghton, 1956.
```

Editor

List the editor first only if your in-text citation is to the work of the editor (for example, the editor's introduction or notes):

Bevington, David, ed. The Complete Works of Shakespeare.

   3rd ed. Glenview: Scott, 1980.

Newlin, Claude M., ed. Modern Chivalry. By Hugh Henry

   Brackenridge. New York: American, 1962.

Encyclopedia

"Thomas Jefferson." Encyclopedia Americana. 1980 ed.

Introduction, Preface, Foreword, or Afterword

If you are citing the person who has written the introduction to a work by another author, use the following form:

Lowell, Robert. Foreword. Ariel. By Sylvia Plath.

   New York: Harper & Row, 1966. vii-ix.

If the author has also written the prefatory matter, use only the last name after "By," but use this form only if you cite from the prologue and not from the main text:

Vonnegut, Kurt. Prologue. Jailbird. By Vonnegut.

   New York: Delacorte, 1979.

Manuscript collections in book form

Cotton Vitellius. A. XV. British Museum.

See also "Manuscripts and Typescripts, Unpublished."

Play, classical

Shakespeare, William. Macbeth. Shakespeare: Twenty-Three

   Plays and the Sonnets. Ed. T. M. Parrott. New York:

   Scribner's, 1953.

Racine, Jean. Phaedra. Trans. Robert Lowell. World

   Masterpieces. Continental edition. 2 vols.

   Ed. Maynard Mack, et al. New York: Norton, 1956. 2: 102-46.

Play, modern

Greene, Graham. <u>The Complaisant Lover</u>. New York:

    Viking, 1959.

Eliot, T. S. <u>The Cocktail Party</u>. <u>The Complete Poems</u>

    <u>and Plays: 1909-1950</u>. New York: Harcourt, 1952. 295-387.

Poem, classical

Dante. <u>The Divine Comedy</u>. Trans. Lawrence G. White.

    New York: Pantheon, 1948.

Ciardi, John, trans. <u>The Purgatorio</u>. By Dante. New

    York: New Amer. Library, 1961.

    Note: use this form only if citation is to Ciardi's prefatory matter or notes to the text.

Poem, modern collection
Use this form if you cite one short poem:

Eliot, T. S. "The Love Song of J. Alfred Prufrock."

    <u>The Complete Poems and Plays 1909-1950</u>. New York:

    Harcourt, 1952. 3-7.

Use this form if you cite a book-length poem:

Eliot, T. S. <u>Four Quartets</u>. <u>The Complete Poems and</u>

    <u>Plays 1909-1950</u>. New York: Harcourt, 1952. 115-45.

Use this form if you cite several different poems of the collection:

Eliot, T. S. <u>The Complete Poems and Plays 1909-1950</u>.

    New York: Harcourt, 1952.

Republished book

Lowes, John Livingston. <u>The Road to Xanadu: A Study in the</u>

    <u>Ways of the Imagination</u>. 1930. New York: Vintage-

    Knopf, 1959.

Use this form in citing a republished book, such as a paperback version of a cloth-bound edition.

Hooker, Richard. <u>Of the Lawes of Ecclesiasticall Politie</u>.

    1594. Fascim. rpt. Amsterdam: Teatrum Orbis Terrarum, 1971.

Arnold, Matthew. "The Study of Poetry." <u>Essays: English</u>

    <u>and American</u>. Ed. Charles W. Eliot. 1886. New York:

    Collier, 1910. Originally published as the General

    Introduction to <u>The English Poets</u>. Ed. T. H. Ward. 1880.

Series, numbered and unnumbered

Jefferson, D. W. "'All, all of a piece throughout':

    Thoughts on Dryden's Dramatic Poetry." <u>Restoration</u>

    <u>Theatre</u>. Ed. J. R. Brown and Bernard Harris.

    Stratford-upon-Avon Studies 6. London: Arnold, 1965. 159–76.

Commager, Henry Steele. <u>The Nature and the Study of History</u>.

    Social Science Seminar Series. Columbus, OH: Bobbs,

    1965.

Wallerstein, Ruth C. <u>Richard Crashaw: A Study in Style and</u>

    <u>Poetic Development</u>. University of Wisconsin Studies in

    Language and Literature 37. Madison: U of Wisconsin P, 1935.

Sourcebooks and Casebooks

Ellmann, Richard. "Reality." <u>Yeats: A Collection of</u>

    <u>Critical Essays</u>. Ed. John Unterecker. Twentieth

    Century Views. Englewood Cliffs: Prentice, 1963. 163–74.

But use the following if you can identify original facts of publication:

Ellmann, Richard. "Reality." <u>Yeats: The Man and the Masks</u>.

    New York: Macmillan, 1948. Rpt. in <u>Yeats: A Collection of</u>

    <u>Critical Essays</u>. Ed. John Unterecker. Twentieth

    Century Views. Englewood Cliffs: Prentice, 1963. 163–74.

Title, foreign

Use lowercase letters for foreign titles except for the first major word and proper names. Provide a translation in brackets if you think it necessary (for example, *Étranger* [*The Stranger*] or Praha [Prague]).

Brombert, Victor. <u>Stendhal et la voie oblique</u>. New

    Haven: Yale UP, 1954.

Levowitz-treu, Micheline. <u>L'Amour et la mort chez Standhal</u>.

    Aran: Editions due Grand Chêne, 1978.

Castex, P-G. <u>Le Rouge et le noir de Stendhal</u>. Paris:

    Sedes, 1967.

    Compare with journal entry (see "Title, foreign," 196).

Translator

Eliade, Mircea. <u>The Sacred and the Profane</u>. Trans.

    Willard R. Trask. New York: Harcourt, 1959.

Use the translator's name first only if the translator's work is the focus of your study:

Shorey, Paul, trans. <u>The Republic</u>. By Plato. Cambridge:

    Harvard UP, 1937.

Volumes, a work of several volumes

Ruskin, John. <u>The Works of Ruskin</u>. Ed. E. T. Cook and

    Alexander Wedderburn. 39 vols. London: Allen; New York:

    Longmans, 1903.

Parrington, Vernon L. <u>Main Currents in American Thought</u>.

    3 vols. New York: Harcourt, 1927-32.

Volumes, one of several volumes

Dryden, John. <u>Poems 1649-1680</u>. Vol. 1 of <u>The Works of John</u>

    <u>Dryden</u>. Ed. Edward Niles Hooker et al. 4 vols. Berkeley:

    U of California P, 1956.

Volumes, component part of one of several volumes

Daiches, David. <u>A Critical History of English Literature</u>.

    2nd ed. 2 vols. New York: Ronald, 1970. 2: 117-186.

Hawthorne, Nathaniel. "My Kinsman, Major Molineaux." <u>The</u>

American Tradition in Literature. Ed. Sculley Bradley,

    R. C. Beatty, and E. Hudson Long. 3rd ed. 2 vols.

    New York: Norton, 1967. 1: 507-22.

Bibliography Form—Periodicals

For journals or magazine articles, use the following order, omitting unnecessary items:

1. Author   3. Name of the periodical
2. Title of the article   4. Volume, issue, and page numbers

Name of the Author(s)

Show the author's name flush with the left margin, without a numeral and with succeeding lines indented five spaces. Enter the surname first, followed by a comma, followed by a given name or initials, followed by a period:

Shade, B. J. "Social-Psychological Traits of Achieving

    Black Children." Education Digest 44 (1978): 38-40.

Title of the Article

Show the title within quotation marks followed by a period inside the closing quotation marks:

Chiasson, Elias J. "Dryden's Apparent Skepticism."

    Harvard Theological Review 54 (1961): 207-21.

Name of the Periodical

Give the name of the journal or magazine, underlined, and with no following punctuation:

Boose, Lynda E. "Othello's Handkerchief: 'The Recognizance

    and Pledge of Love.'" English Literary Renaissance 5

    (1975): 360-74.

Volume, Issue, and Page Numbers

In general, magazines are paged anew with each issue, but journals are paged continuously through all issues of an entire year. Thus the volume number, year, and pages (34 (1985): 789–96) will locate the journal article. With magazines the volume number offers little help, but an exact date is better. Thus magazine citations omit the volume number and provide a month (Apr. 1982: 22–24) and even a specific day in the case of weekly publications (6 Sept. 1985: 45–48).

For a journal include volume number, year within parentheses and followed by a colon, and inclusive page numbers (see sample immediately above). If a journal has separate pagination for each issue, add an issue number following the volume number, separated by a period:

```
Frey, John R.  "America and Her Literature Reviewed by

    Post-War Germany."  American-German Review 20.5 (1954):

    4-6.
```

Bib. Form—Periodicals

Add the month if more information would ease the search for the article: "20.5 (Nov. 1954): 4–6."

Weekly magazines require the day, month, and year without a volume number listed:

```
"Chaos in Television."  Time 12 Mar. 1979: 60-61.
```

Note: Some libraries now store newspapers and magazines on microfilm, which may be noted in your entry:

```
"Chaos in Television."  Microfilm.  Time 12 Mar. 1974: 60-

    61.
```

Monthly magazines require the month and year without a volume number listed:

```
"New Systems Abound at the National Computer Conference."

    Byte July 1983: 7.
```

Give the pages for the complete article, not just the pages that you use. Write inclusive numbers (202–09, 85–115, or 1112–24). If an article is paged here and there throughout the issue (for example, pages 74, 78, and 81–88), write only the first page number and a plus sign with no intervening space:

```
Sontag, Susan.  "Baby."  Playboy Feb. 1974: 74+.
```

Sample Bibliography Entries—Periodicals

Address, published

```
Humphries, Alfred.  "Computers and Banking."  Address to

    Downtown Kiwanis Club, Nashville, TN 30 Aug. 1981.

    Rpt. in part Tennessee Monthly 31 Aug. 1985: 33-34.

U. S.  President.  "Address to Veterans of Foreign Wars."

    19 Aug. 1974.  Rpt. in Weekly Compilation of Presidential

    Documents 10 (26 Aug. 1974): 1045-50.
```

Author, anonymous

"Commodities: Sweet and Sour." <u>Time</u> 16 Dec. 1974: 32.

Interview, published

Hanks, Nancy. Chairperson, National Endowment of the Arts.

   Interview. <u>U.S. News and World Report</u> 7 Oct. 1974: 58-60.

Journal, with all issues for a year paged continuously

Dyke, Vernon Van. "Human Rights and the Rights of Groups."

   <u>American Journal of Political Science</u> 18 (1974): 725-41.

Journal, with each issue paged anew

Mangan, Doreen. "Henry Casselli: Superb Contradictions."

   <u>American Artist</u> 38.2 (1974): 39-43.

Use the issue number after the volume number because page numbers alone cannot locate the article within a volume of six or twelve issues when one issue has separate pagination. An alternative is the use of month or season to locate the one issue:

Stuart, Jesse. "Love Affair at the Pasture Gate." <u>Ball</u>

   <u>State University Forum</u> 15 (Winter 1974): 306.

Should a journal use only issue numbers, treat the issue number as you would a volume number:

Wilson, Katharina M. "Tertullian's <u>De cultu foeminarum</u>

   and Utopia." <u>Moreana</u> 73 (1982): 69-74.

Journal, volume numbers embracing two years

Brooks, Peter. "Freud's Masterplot." <u>Yale French</u>

   <u>Studies</u> 55-56 (1977-78): 280-300.

Magazine, monthly

Crickmer, Barry. "Can We Control Spending?" <u>Nation's</u>

   <u>Business</u> Apr. 1982: 22-24.

Magazine, weekly

von Hoffman, Nicholas. "The White House News Hole."

The New Republic 6 Sept. 1982: 19-23.

Monograph

LeClercq, R. V. "Crashaw's 'Epithalamium': Pattern and

Vision." Literary Monographs 6. Madison:

U of Wisconsin P, 1975. 73-108.

Notes, Queries, Reports, Comments, Letters

"Professional Notes and Comment." PMLA 97 (1982): 724+.

Robinson, Ken. "Does Otway Ascribe Sodom to Rochester? A

Reply." Notes and Queries ns 29 (1982): 50-51.

Indicate old series "os" or new series "ns" when necessary.

Seymour, Thom. "Faulkner's The Sound and the Fury."

The Explicator 39.1 (1980): 24-25.

Stoppelmann, Ron. "Letters." New York 23 Aug. 1982: 8.

Reprint of a journal article

Hope, A. D. "Anne Killigrew: or, The Art of Modulating."

Southern Review: An Australian Journal of Literary

Studies 1 (1963): 4-14. Rpt. in Hope, The Cave and

the Spring: Essays on Poetry. Adelaide, Australia:

Rigby, 1965. 129-43.

Review, in a magazine or journal

Clignet, Remi. Rev. of Urban Poverty in a Cross-Cultural

Context, by Edwin Eames and Judith Granich Goode.

American Journal of Sociology 80 (1974): 589-90.

Steck, Richard. "The Next Best Thing to Being There."

Rev. of Remote Access [Computer software], by

Custom Software. PC World 1.5 n.d.: 97-99.

Series

> Hill, Christopher. "Sex, Marriage and the Family in
>   England." <u>Economic History Review</u> 2nd ser. 31 (1978):
>   450-63.

See also "Notes, Queries, Comments, Letters," 201.

Title, omitted

> Berkowitz, David. <u>Renaissance Quarterly</u> 32 (1979): 396-493.

Title, quotation within the article's title

> Ranald, Margaret Loftus. "'As Marriage Binds, and Blood
>   Breaks': English Marriage and Shakespeare."
>   <u>Shakespeare Quarterly</u> 30 (1979): 68-81.

Title, within the article's title

> Dundes, Alan. "'To Love My Father All': A Psychoanalytic
>   Study of the Folktale Source of <u>King Lear</u>." <u>Southern</u>
>   <u>Folklore Quarterly</u> 40 (1976): 353-66.

Title, foreign

> Stivale, Charles J. "Le Vraisemblable temporel dans <u>Le Rouge</u>
>   <u>et le noir</u>." <u>Stendhal Club</u> 84 (1979): 299-313.

Bibliography Form—Newspapers

> Clayton, Beth. "U.N. Agency Eyes Health Center Here."
>   <u>Nashville Banner</u>. 24 Aug. 1985, early ed.: A6+.

The standard form for a newspaper article. Note that it includes which edition of the day is cited; in other cases use "late ed." or "natl. ed."

> Bryant, Alice Franklin. "U.N. Role." Letter to the Editor.
>   <u>Chattanooga Times</u> 15 Dec. 1974: B7, cols. 6-7.

Use this form to cite special newspaper articles, such as editorials, letters to the editor, cartoons, and so on.

"Eygpt Demands that Israel Put Limit on Population Growth."

    <u>Los Angeles Times</u> 14 Dec. 1974: 1.

Use this form for unsigned articles.

Fletcher, C. B. "Bonnie and Clyde--Two-Bit Heroes?"

    Rev. of <u>The Strange History of Bonnie and Clyde</u>.

    By John Treherne. <u>Nashville Banner</u> 24 Aug. 1985: A-5.

Note: you may need special designations for sections of newspapers. Use merely a page number (e.g., 23) if the newspaper is paged continuously throughout. Use a capital letter with parts so designated (e.g., B-3 or D-6+). Use a section designation if necessary (e.g., "late ed., sec. 2: 5–6.").

Bibliography Form—Government Documents

Since the nature of public documents is so varied, the form of the entry cannot be standardized. Therefore, you should provide sufficient information so that the reader can easily locate the reference. As a general rule, place information in the bibliography entry in this order: Government. Body. Subsidiary body. Title of document. Identifying numbers. Publication facts.

Congressional papers

United States. Cong. <u>Cong. Rec</u>. 6 Mar. 1974:

    S2916-28.

United States. Cong. Senate. <u>Transportation System</u>

    <u>for Alaskan Natural Gas</u>. 95th Cong., 1st sess.

    S. 2411. Washington: GPO, 1977.

United States. Cong. House. Committee on Interstate and

    Foreign Commerce. <u>Federal Cigarette Labeling and</u>

    <u>Advertising Act</u>. 89th Cong., 1st sess. H. Rept. 449

    to accompany H.R. 3014. Washington: GPO, 1965.

Executive branch documents

United States. President. <u>Public Papers of the</u>

    <u>Presidents of the United States</u>. Washington:

    Office of the Federal Registrar, 1978.

```
---. ---. Alternative to Drugs: A New Approach to
     Drug Education. Pr Ex 13.2:D84/3/1972. Washington:
     GPO, 1972.
```

The hyphens signal repetition of "United States" and "President."

```
United States. Dept. of State. Foreign Relations of the
     United States: Diplomatic Papers, 1943. 5 vols.
     Washington: GPO, 1943-44.
```

Legal citations

```
U. S. Const. Art 2, sec. 1.
California. Const. Art. 2, sec. 4.
15 US Code. Sec. 78h. 1964.
Noise Control Act of 1972. Statutes at Large. 86. Public
     Law 92-574. 1972.
Environmental Protection Agency et al. v. Mink et al.
     U. S. Reports, CDX. 1972.
Illinois. Revised Statutes Annotated. Sec. 16-7-81. 1980.
People v. McIntosh. California 321 P.3d 876, 2001-6. 1970.
State v. Lane. Minnesota 263 N. W. 608. 1935.
```

Bibliography Form—Other Sources

Art Work

```
Raphael. School of Athens. The Vatican, Rome. Illus.
     in The World Book Encyclopedia. 1976 ed.
Wyeth, Andrew. Hay Ledge. [1957]. Illustrated in
     The Art of Andrew Wyeth. Ed. Wanda M. Corn.
     San Francisco: The Fine Arts Museum, 1973. 31.
```

Use the form shown above for reproductions in books and journals. If you actually experience the work itself, use the form shown by the next two entries:

```
Wyeth, Andrew. Hay Ledge. Private Collection of Mr.
     and Mrs. Joseph E. Levine.
Remington, Frederic. Mountain Man. Metropolitan
     Museum of Art, New York.
```

Bulletin

Economic Research Service. <u>Demand and Price Situation</u>.
    Bulletin DPS-141, 14 pp. Washington, DC: Department of
    Agriculture, Aug. 1974.

French, Earl. <u>Personal Problems in Industrial Research and</u>
    <u>Development</u>. Bulletin No. 51. Ithaca, NY: New York
    State School of Industrial and Labor Relations, 1963.

Computer Data

<u>Statistics on Child Abuse--Montgomery County, Tennessee</u>.
    Computer software. Clarksville, TN: Harriett Cohn
    Mental Health Center, 1983. Apple IIe, Diskette 12.

Sears, Robert O. <u>Trends in Women's Sports: Factual Data on</u>
    <u>Participation and Revenue</u>. Computer software. Bowling
    Green: Western Kentucky State U, 1983. VAX-1419.

<u>Scipax</u>. Series 3 computer software. Cleveland: Hunt
    Information Services, 1982.

<u>Purchase Ledger</u>. Computer software. Chamberley, England:
    Graham Doreian Software, 1982. CPM C-Basic for Apple II.

Data Base Sources

"Alexander Hamilton." <u>Academic American Encyclopedia</u>. 1981
    ed. CompuServe, 1983, record no. 1816.

Nevin, John J. "Doorstop to Free Trade." <u>Harvard Business</u>
    <u>Review</u> 61 (1983): 88-95. DIALOG Information Services,
    1983, record no. 83-N43.

Dissertation, published

Nykrog, Per. <u>Les Fabliaux: Etude d'histoire littéraire</u>
    <u>et de stylistique mediévale</u>. Diss. Aarhus U, 1957.
    Copenhagen: Munksgaard, 1957.

Dissertation, unpublished

Havens, Nancy Bergstrom. "Verbalized Symbolic Play of
    Pre-School Children in Two Types of Play Environments."
    Diss. Temple U, 1982.

Dissertation, abstract only

```
Havens, Nancy Bergstrom.  "Verbalized Symbolic Play of

    Pre-School Children in Two Types of Play Environments."

    DAI 42 (1982): 5058A.  Temple U.
```

Use this form when you cite from *Dissertation Abstracts International (DAI)*. The page number features A, B, or C to designate the series used: A Humanities, B Sciences, C European dissertations.

Film

```
Last Tango in Paris.  United Artists, 1972.
```

Add specific information if you suspect the film might be difficult for others to locate:

```
Wilets, Bernard.  Environment.  Santa Monica, Calif.:

    BFA Educational Media, 1971.  (16 mm., 29 min., color.)
```

Interview, unpublished

```
Turrentine, Robert.  President, Acme Boot Co.  Personal

    interview.  11 Feb. 1985.
```

For a published interview see 200.

Letter, personal

```
Weathers, Winston.  Letter to the author.  5 Mar. 1985.
```

Letter, published

```
Eisenhower, Dwight.  Letter to Richard Nixon.  20 April

    1968.  Memoirs of Richard Nixon.  By Richard

    Nixon.  New York: Grosset & Dunlap, 1978.
```

Manuscripts (ms) and typescripts (ts)

```
Glass, Malcolm.  Journal 3, ms.  M. Glass Private Papers,

    Clarksville, TN.

Tanner.  ms 346.  Bodleian Library, Oxford.

Williams, Ralph.  Notebook 15, ts.  Williams Papers.

    Vanderbilt U, Nashville.
```

Microfilm or microfiche

Tuckerman, H. T. "James Fenimore Cooper." Microfilm.
North American Review 89 (1859): 298-316.

Mimeographed material

Smith, Jane L. "Terms for the Study of Fiction."
Mimeographed. Cleveland, 1975.

Monograph

NEA Research Division. Kindergarten Practices, 1961.
Monograph 1962-M2. Washington, DC: 1962.

See 201 for monograph published in a journal.

Musical composition

Mozart, Wolfgang A. Jupiter. Symphony No. 41.
Wagner, Richard. Lohengrin.

Pamphlet

U.S. Civil Service Commission. The Human Equation:
Working in Personnel for the Federal Government.
Pamphlet 76. Washington: GPO, 1970.

Treat pamphlets as you would books.

Public address or lecture

Sarnoff, David. "Television: A Channel for Freedom."
Address. U of Detroit Academic Convocation.
Detroit, 1961.

Recording on record or tape

John, Elton. "This Song Has No Title." Goodbye Yellow
Brick Road. MCA, MCA 2-10003, 1974.
Berlioz, Hecter. Symphonie fantastique, op. 14.
Cond. Georg Solti. Chicago Symphony Orch.
London, CS 6790, 1968.

"Chaucer: The Nun's Priest's Tale." <u>Canterbury Tales</u>.
   Narrated in Middle English by Robert Ross. Caedmon,
   TC 1008, 1971.

Report

Linden, Fabian. "Women: A Demographic, Social and Economic
   Presentation." Report. The Conference Board. New
   York: CBS/Broadcast Group, 1973.

Unbound reports are placed within quotation marks; bound reports are
treated as books:

Panama Canal Company. <u>Annual Report: Fiscal Year Ended</u>
   <u>June 30, 1968</u>. Panama: Canal Zone Government, 1968.

Reproductions and photographs

Blake, William. <u>Comus</u>. Plate 4.   Photograph in Irene
   Taylor. "Blake's <u>Comus</u> Designs." <u>Blake Studies</u>
   4 (Spring 1972): 61.
Michener, James A. "Structure of Earth at Centennial,
   Colorado." Line drawing in <u>Centennial</u>. By
   Michener. New York: Random, 1974. 26.

Table, illustration, map, chart

<u>Mexico</u>. Map. St. Louis: Western Publ., 1976.
<u>Alphabet</u>. Chart. Columbus: Scholastic, 1984.

Tables or graphs published within works need detailed citation:

Corbett, Edward P. J. Syllogism graph. <u>Classical Rhetoric</u>
   <u>for the Modern Student</u>. New York: Oxford UP, 1965.

Because the graph has no title, the descriptive heading should not be
placed within quotation marks.

Television or radio program

<u>The Commanders: Douglas MacArthur</u>. NBC-TV, New York.

    17 Mar. 1975.

Shakespeare, William. <u>As You Like It</u>. Nashville

    Theatre Academy. WDCN-TV, Nashville. 11 Mar. 1975.

Thesis

See "Dissertation, unpublished," 205.

Transparency

Sharp, La Vaughn, and William E. Loeche. <u>The Patient</u>

    <u>and Circulatory Disorders: A Guide for Instructors</u>.

    54 transparencies, 99 overlays. Philadelphia:

    Lippincott, 1969.

Unpublished paper

Elkins, William R. "The Dream World and the Dream Vision:

    Meaning and Structure in Poe's Art." Unpublished

    paper, 1981.

Videotape

Thompson, Paul. "W. B. Yeats." Lecture on Videotape.

    VHS-MSU 160. Memphis: Memphis State U, 1982.

Sevareid, Eric. <u>CBS News</u>. CBS-TV, New York.

    11 Mar. 1975; Media Services Videotape 1975-142.

    Nashville: Vanderbilt U, 1975.

7

Form and Style for Other Disciplines

The MLA research style advocated by this text, as based upon principles of the Modern Language Association, should be adequate for most undergraduate assignments in your English classes. The style focuses upon the author and the work, especially the page number, for example, "Jones 342" or "Hawthorne, *Letter* 23." However, scientists focus upon the date because scientific data change dramatically and rapidly from year to year. For instance, an essay on new findings in psychology or computer science becomes dated quickly. Therefore, the sciences call attention to the date by placing it within the textual citations and by positioning it for attention in bibliography entries.

If you learn the MLA style, you can convert your manuscript format to other systems with little difficulty. When using the author-date system, you need only alter the in-text citations to include the date, for example, "Jones, 1983, p. 342." When using the author-number system, you need only change your in-text citations to numbers, for example, "Smith (1)" or "Camp and Jones (2)."

At the same time, you must make minor variations in the "Works Cited" list, which you will now label "References," "List of References," or "References Cited." If your in-text citations are numbers, then you must number the list of references to correspond. Otherwise, alphabetize the list by the last name of the author. Also, you will usually capitalize only the first word of titles of books and articles, for example, "The biology of the algae." But some fields, such as chemistry and physics omit completely the title of a periodical article.

You will usually abbreviate and seldom underline the name of the periodical, for example, "Amer. J. Bot."

Sketched below are basic rules for handling conventions of format by discipline according to the name and year system, the number system, and the footnote system. In general, use the name and year system with papers in the social sciences, biological and earth sciences, education, linguistics, and business. Use the number system with applied sciences, such as chemistry, computer science, mathematics, or physics. Use the traditional footnote system with papers in the fine arts (art, theater, music) and humanities (history, philosophy, religion, but excluding language and literature, which use the MLA style). Find your area of study in the following list, then consult the appropriate pages for guidelines.

GUIDE TO DOCUMENTATION SYSTEMS

Agriculture, Name and Year, 224
Anthropology, Name and Year, 225
Archaeology, Name and Year, 225
Art, Footnotes, 242
Astronomy, Name and Year, 226
Biology, Name and Year, 226
Botany, Name and Year, 226
Business, Name and Year, 229
Chemistry, Number, 232
Computer Science, Number, 233
Dance, Footnotes, 242
Education, Name and Year, 222
Geology, Name and Year, 228
Health, Number, 236
History, Footnotes, 240

Home Economics, Name and Year, 223
Linguistics, Name and Year, 223
Mathematics, Number, 234
Medicine, Number, 236
Music, Footnotes, 242
Nursing, Number, 236
Philosophy, Footnotes, 240
Physical Education, Name and Year, 224
Physics, Number, 235
Political Science, Name and Year, 221
Psychology, Name and Year, 220
Religion, Footnotes, 240
Sociology, Name and Year, 221

THE NAME AND YEAR SYSTEM

The name and year system of documentation is advocated by the *Publication Manual of the American Psychological Association,* which is known as the APA style manual. It sets standards for writers in many fields who wish to emphasize the publication date of a work to stress its timeliness. In general, the APA style requires an alphabetized list of references at the end of the paper and in-text citations to name and year of each source cited within the paper. (Note: if you have specific questions not answered below, consult 132–

55, which gives you alphabetically arranged solutions for such matters as numbering, capitalization, writing dates, underlining, and so forth.)

When writing research papers by the name and year system, conform to the following:

1. Place the year within parentheses immediately after the authority's name:

```
Smith (1983) ascribes no species-specific behavior to man.

However, Adams (1984) presents data that tend to be contradictory.
```

2. If you do not mention the authority's name in your sentence, insert the name, year, and page numbers in parentheses:

```
Hopkins (1980) found some supporting evidence for a portion

of the questionable data (Marr & Brown, 1979, pp. 23-32)

through point bi-serial correlation techniques.
```

3. For two authors, employ both names: "(Torgerson & Andrews, 1979)." For three authors, name them all in the first entry, as "(Torgerson, Andrews, & Dunlap, 1979)," but thereafter use "(Torgerson et al., 1979)." For four or more authors, employ "(Fredericks et al., 1979)" in the first and all subsequent instances.

4. Use small letters (a,b,c) to identify two or more works published in the same year by the same author, for example, "Thompson (1966a)" and "Thompson (1966b)." Then use "1966a" and "1966b" in your "List of References" (see 213 for an example).

5. If necessary, specify additional information:

```
Horton (1966; cf. Thomas, 1962, p. 89) suggests an intercorrela-

tion of these testing devices.  But after multiple-group analysis,

Welston (1979, esp. p. 211) reached an opposite conclusion.
```

6. In the case of direct quotation or paraphrase to a specific page, you must include the author, year, *and* page number(s), as follows:

a. A quotation or paraphrase in the middle of the sentence:

```
He stated, "These data of psychological development

suggest that retarded adolescents are atypical in

maturational growth" (Jones, 1983, p. 215), but he failed to

clarify which data were examined.
```

b. A quotation or paraphrase that falls at the end of a sentence:

```
Jones (1984) found that "these data of psychological
development suggest that retarded adolescents are
atypical in maturational growth" (p. 215).
```

c. A long quotation is set off from the text in a block (and therefore without quotation marks):

```
Albert (1983) found the following:
    Whenever these pathogenic organisms attack the human
    body and begin to multiply, the infection is set in
    motion.  The host responds to this parasitic invasion
    with efforts to cleanse itself of the invading agents.
    When rejection efforts of the host become visible
    (fever, sneezing, congestion), the disease status
    exists.  (pp. 314-315)
```

7. Every reference used in your text should appear in your alphabetical
list of references at the end of the paper. List chronologically two or more
works by the same author, for example, Fitzgerald's 1979 publication would
precede his 1983 publication. Entries of a single author precede multiple-
author entries beginning with the same surname:

```
Fitzgerald, R. F.  (1984).
Fitzgerald, R. F., & Smithson, C. A.  (1981).
```

References with same first author and different second or third authors
should be alphabetized by the surname of the second author:

```
Fitzgerald, R. F., & Smithson, C. A.  (1981).
Fitzgerald, R. F., & Waters, W. R.  (1978).
```

References with the same author in the same year are alphabetized and
marked with lowercase letters—a, b, c—immediately after the date:

```
Fitzgerald, R. F.  (1984a).  Controlling. . . .
Fitzgerald, R. F.  (1984b).  Water samples. . . .
```

Note the APA style of these psychology entries:

```
Anderson, J. R., & Bower, G. H.   (1972).  Recognition and
    retrieval processes in free recall.  Psychological Review,
    79, 97-123.
Hall, Calvin S.   (1973).  A primer of Freudian psychology.
    Phoenix: NAL.
```

Compare those entries with two from the natural sciences, which use CBE style (see below, 226–27), in which you place the date at the end, indent only two spaces, and abbreviate the titles of journals:

```
Baldwin, K. M.   Cardiac gap junction configuration after an
    uncoupling treatment as a function of time.  J. Cell. Biol.
    82: 66-75; 1979.
Berlyn, G. P., and J. P. Mikshe.   Botanical micro-technique and
    cytochemistry.  Iowa State Univ. Press, Ames; 1976.
```

A short sample paper in APA style follows. Discussions of form and style for individual fields will be found on 220–244.

SAMPLE PAPER IN APA STYLE—
The Selected Review of Literature

The following paper conforms to the standards of the American Psychological Association. Use it as a model of page format for papers in the social sciences. In particular, this paper represents the model for a limited review of books and articles on one subject. The assignment requires the researcher to read and analyze several (or many) books and articles in order to present an up-to-date digest of the state of knowledge on a well-focused scholarly issue, especially a focus that sets reasonable limits on the numbers of works to review. A complete review would examine *all* articles and books on a subject. Most reviews are "limited" to works of one year or "limited" to articles that have appeared in one publication (for example, child abuse articles that appeared in 1985 issues of *Child Welfare*). Others are "selected" works within a limited period, which means the reviewer does not intend to review *all* works within the limited period. The review below examines selected literature for 1985. It thereby updates research on child abuse as reported in the theoretical research paper shown on pages 161–82.

A Selected Review of Literature

1985 Articles on Child Abuse

Tommy Burchett

Psychology 1120

Running Head: REVIEW

Selected Review of Literature

1985 Articles on Child Abuse

A limited overview of 1985 literature on child abuse
indicates that serious work continues. Reviews, empirical
reports, and theoretical studies are evident.

The review of Bruce Roscoe (1985) in <u>Childhood Education</u>
examines a number of reports on empirical research that compared
matching groups of abused and non-abused children. The
overwhelming evidence of work in the field demonstrates
detrimental consequences for abused children that affect their
development on emotional, social, and intellectual levels. This
review includes a 20-item bibliography.

In another review, this one in <u>Child Welfare,</u> Linda Gordon
(1985) traces the history of child abuse with a focus on the
practices of one agency, the Massachusetts Society for the
Prevention of Cruelty to Children. Gordon demonstrates how
through the years social control was imposed on the patriarchal
structure of the autonomous family, thereby giving aid to victims
of child abuse and to battered wives.

K. A. Armstrong and Yvonne L. Fraley (1985) report in
<u>Children Today</u> a follow-up empirical study on how families were
faring three years after a special program to improve
childrearing patterns of parents at high risk of child abuse. In
1978-81 the Family Support Center instructed 99 families in three
phases: family counseling in the home, Family School, which
parents and their children attended for 13 weeks, and

Peer Support Groups in which parents who had finished the Family School met monthly in various homes of participants.

Immediately following the services families had fewer incidents of abuse, fewer children were placed in foster care, parenting skills improved, and children developed more rapidly in language and motor skills. The Armstrong/Fraley study proved the hypothesis that the Family Support Center continued to affect these families: no report of child abuse had been filed on any participant families, no children were placed in foster care since the families program had ended, parenting skills were adequate, families had fewer stresses, and members were more self-supporting. Armstrong/Fraley demonstrate that prevention programs do change families who are at risk of child abuse.

A report on empirical research by Christine Adams-Tucker (1985) examines the coping strategies of sexually molested children. Methods involved psychiatric evaluations in 1978 of 27 children. Parents were interviewed alone and with their children. Narcissistic defense mechanisms were evident for 13 children; immature mechanisms for 25; neurotic for 15; and mature for 5. Four children evidenced "undefended anxiety"--constant sighing, increased motor activity, restlessness, and increased frequency of urination. The most distressed adolescents had fewer defenses and showed regression, schizoid fantasy, acting-out, and introjection. When perpetrators were peers, neighbors and distant relatives, children victimized used acting-out, denial, introjection, and schizoid fantasy as their main

defenses. The father-molested children who had family loyalty
used denial and introjection but children who blamed their
fathers for the abuse more than themselves showed little denial
and depended more on acting-out. Although defenses varied
according to age, all children dealt with sexual victimization
with a variety of coping mechanisms.

A theoretical study in <u>Childhood Education</u> by Patricia
Herman (1985) examines the role of teachers in educating their
students about sexual abuse. Herman urges teachers toward active
roles by planning personal-safety components within school
curricula. She exposes several myths (for example, that
discussions of sexual abuse will damage children, frighten them,
or scare them away from all touching). The study suggests 11
clear guidelines for teaching children about abuse and explains
helpful teaching aids. The article includes a list of sexual
abuse indicators and a nine-item bibliography.

Helen H. Perlman in <u>Child Welfare</u> advances theory about the
art of caring, especially in the "recognition and understanding
of the child as a self-hood and as a person-in-the-making" (1985,
p. 5). Yet caring is not sufficient with children who do not
respond or with parents who are opponents rather than
collaborators. Consequently, social workers need, according to
Perlman, exceptional skills, understanding and respect for
children, and self-discipline.

References

Adams-Tucker, C. (1985). Defense mechanisms used by sexually abused children. *Children Today*, 14(1), 8-12, 34.

Armstrong, K. A., & Fraley, Y. L. (1985). What happens to families after they leave the program? *Children Today*, 14(3), 17-20.

Gordon, L. (1985). Child abuse, gender, and the myth of family independence: A historical critique. *Child Welfare*, 64, 213-224.

Herman, P. (1985). Educating children about sexual abuse: The teacher's responsiblity. *Childhood Education*, 61, 169-174.

Perlman, H. H. (1985). On the art of caring. *Child Welfare*, 64, 3-11.

Roscoe, B. (1985). Intellectual, emotional and social deficits of abused children: A review. *Childhood Education*, 61, 388-392.

SOCIAL SCIENCES

Psychology   Sociology   Political Science   Education
Home Economics   Linguistics   Physical Education

The various disciplines of the social sciences employ the name and year system. Variations exist by discipline, but in general the stipulations of the APA *Publication Manual* have gained wide acceptance.

PSYCHOLOGY—APA style

In-text Citation
Use the name and year system with commas separating items and with the use of "p." or "pp." for page numbers, for example, "Shaffer, 1978" or "Shaffer, 1978, pp. 10–19." See 211–14 for additional guidelines on the author-year system.

List of References
Alphabetize the list of references at the end of your paper. Start the list on a new page entitled "References." Double-space throughout. Type the first line of each entry flush left; indent the second line and other succeeding lines three spaces. Main parts for a periodical entry are: author, date, title of the article without quotation marks and with only the first word capitalized, name of the journal underlined and with all major words capitalized, volume number underlined, and inclusive page numbers. Main parts for a book entry are: author, date, title of the book underlined and with only first word capitalized (except for proper names), place, and publisher. A sample reference list follows:

*Psychology**

```
                          References

Ahlquist, J. W.   (1980).  Communication deviance in

   hypothetical schizotypes.  Unpublished master's thesis,

   University of Wisconsin.

Anderson, J. R., & Bower, G. H.   (1972).  Recognition and

   retrieval processes in free recall.  Psychological

   Review, 79, 97-123.

Gaito, John (Ed.).   (1966).  Macromolecules and behavior.

   New York: Appleton-Century-Crofts.

Marlin, Nancy A.   (1983).  Early exposure to sugars

   influences the sugar preference of the adult rat.

   Physiology and Behavior, 31(5), 619-623.

McClelland, D. C.   (1981).  Is personality consistent?  In A. I.

   Rubin, J. Aronoff, A. M. Barclay, & R. A. Zucker (Eds.),
```

<u>Further explorations in personality</u> (pp. 622-704). New York: Wiley.

Miller, G. A. (1969, December). On turning psychology over to the unwashed. <u>Psychology Today</u>, pp. 53-54.

Winett, Richard A. (1970). Attribution of attitude and behavior change and its relevance to behavior therapy. <u>Psychological Record</u>, <u>20</u>, 17-32.

Winter, D. G. (1979). <u>Navy leadership and management competencies: Convergence among tests, interviews and performance ratings</u>. Boston: McBer.

*The form of these psychology entries conforms to *Publication Manual of the American Psychological Association,* 3rd ed. (Washington, DC: American Psychological Association, 1983.)

SOCIOLOGY AND POLITICAL SCIENCE

In-text Citation:
Use the basic name and year system as explained previously on pages 211–14.

List of references:
Label the list as "References." For a book: list author; year, *not enclosed within parentheses;* the title, underlined and *with* major words capitalized; the place of publication, followed by a colon; and the publisher. For a journal article: list author; year, *not enclosed within parentheses;* title of the article without quotation marks and with only the first word capitalized; the name of the journal, underlined and with major words capitalized; the volume number *not* underlined and *followed by a colon;* and the inclusive page numbers without "p." or "pp." A sample reference list follows:

Sociology/Political Science/Geography*

References

Adamny, David W., and George E. Agree. 1975. <u>Political Money</u>. Baltimore: Johns Hopkins University Press.

Baron, James N., and William Bielby. 1980. Bring the firms back in: Stratification, segmentation and the organization of work. <u>American Sociological Review</u> 45: 737-765.

Beck, E. M., Patrick Horan, and Charles Tolbert. 1978. Stratification in a dual economy: A sectoral model of earnings determination. <u>American Sociological Review</u> 43: 704-720.

Blalock, Hubert M. 1967. Causal inferences, closed
     populations, and measure of association. <u>American</u>
     <u>Political Science Review</u> 61: 130-136.

Epstein, Edwin M. 1980. Business and labor under the
     Federal Election Campaign Act of 1971. In Michael J.
     Malbin (ed.). <u>Parties, Interest Groups, and Campaign</u>
     <u>Finance Laws</u>, pp. 107-151. Washington, D.C.: American
     Enterprise Institute for Public Policy Research.

Illinois. 1980. Revised Statutes Annotated. Sec. 16-7-81.

People v. McIntosh. 1970. California 321 P.3d 876,2001-6.

U. S. Congress. 1978. Electing congress. <u>Congressional</u>
     <u>Quarterly</u>. Washington, D.C.: Congressional Quarterly Inc.

U. S. President. 1978. <u>Public Papers of the President</u>
     <u>of the United States</u>. Washington, D.C.: Office of the
     Federal Registrar.

Wheare, K.C. 1966. <u>Modern Constitutions</u>. 2nd ed.
     New York: Oxford University Press.

*Note: The form of these entries conforms, in general, to the form and style of numerous journals in the fields of sociology and political science, especially to *American Journal of Sociology* and *American Political Science Review.*

EDUCATION

In-text Citation

Use the name and year system as explained on 211–14.

List of References

Label the list as "References." The form for books follows the MLA standards for books (see 185–98 for additional examples). The form for periodicals follows generally that of APA style except that volume numbers are *not* underlined and the date follows the name of the journal, not the author's name. A sample list follows:

Education*

                                References

Cross, L. H., and Frary, R. B. An empirical test of Lord's
     theoretical results regarding formula scoring of
     multiple-choice tests. <u>Journal of Educational</u>
     <u>Measurement</u>, 1977, 14, 313-321.

Edelwich, J., and Brodsky, A. <u>Burn-Out</u>. New York: Human
   Services Press, 1980.

Grise, P. J. Florida's minimum competency testing program for
   handicapped students. <u>Exceptional Children</u>, 1980, 47, 186-191.

Landsman, L. Is teaching hazardous to your health? <u>Today's
   Education</u>, 1978, 67 (2), 48-50.

Maslach, D. Burned-Out. <u>Human Behavior</u>, 1976, 5 (9), 16-22.

-------. Job burnout: How people cope. <u>Public Welfare</u>,
   1978(a), 36, 56-58.

-------. The client role in staff burn-out. <u>Journal of
   Social Issues</u>, 1978(b), 34 (4), 111-124.

Warner, R. E. Enhancing teacher affective sensitivity by a
   videotape program. <u>Journal of Educational Research</u>,
   1984, 77 (6), 366-368.

*Note: the form of these entries is based in general upon the style and format of several education journals, such as *Journal of Educational Research, The Elementary School Journal,* and *Educational and Psychological Measurement.*

HOME ECONOMICS

Follow the stipulations of APA style as explained and demonstrated on 211–19.

LINGUISTICS—LSA style

In-Text Citation

In-text citations for linguistic studies almost always include a specific page reference to the work along with the date, separated by a colon, for example, "Jones 1983: 12–18" or "Gifford's recent reference (1982: 162)." Therefore, follow basic standards for the name and year system (see 211–14) with a colon to separate year and page number(s).

List of References

As shown below, label the list as "References" and alphabetize the entries. Place the year immediately after the author's name. For journal entries, a period rather than a colon or comma separates volume and page. There is *no* underlining. Some journals are abbreviated, some are not (see *LSA Bulletin* if necessary). A sample list follows:

*Linguistics**

References

Bach, Emmon, and Robin Cooper. 1978. The NP-S analysis

 of relative clauses and compositional semantics.

 Linguistics and Philosophy 2.145-50.

Bresnan, Joan. 1970. On complementizers: Toward a

 syntactic theory of complement types. Foundation of

 Language 6.297-321.

Chomsky, Noam. 1965. Aspects of the theory of syntax.

 Cambridge, MA: MIT Press.

------. 1975. Reflections on language. New York: Pantheon.

Keenan, Edward, and Bernard Comrie. 1977. Noun phrase

 accessibility and universal grammar. LI 8.63-99.

------, ------. 1979. Noun phrase accessibility revisited.

 Lg. 44.244-66.

Ross, John R. 1967. Constraints on variables in syntax.

 MIT dissertation.

*The form of these entries conforms in general to that advocated by the Linguistic Society of America, LSA Bulletin, No. 71 (December 1976), 43–45, the December issue annually, and to the form and style practiced by the journal *Language.*

PHYSICAL EDUCATION

In-Text citation
Use the name and year system discussed on pages 211–14.

List of references
Follow the stipulations of the Education format as explained and demonstrated above, 222–23.

BIOLOGICAL AND EARTH SCIENCES

Agriculture Anthropology Archaeology Astronomy Biology Botany Geology Zoology

The disciplines of this major grouping employ the name and year system. Again, stylistic variations in form and style exist among the fields of study.

AGRICULTURE

In-text citation
Use the name and year system. See the general discussion above, 211–14.

List of references

In general, the agriculture form follows that of CBE style as mentioned below, 226–27, except that the date appears after the name of the author(s) and second and succeeding lines of each entry are indented five rather than two spaces. A sample list follows:

Agriculture*

```
                    References


Corring, T., A. Aumaitre, and G. Durand.  1978.  Development

    of digestive enzymes in the piglet from birth to 8

    weeks.  Nutr. Metab.  22:231.
Cranwell, P. D.  1974.  Gastric acid secretion in newly

    born piglets.  Res. Vet. Sci.  16:105.
Cranwell, P. D.  1976.  Gastric secretion in the young

    pig.  Proc. Nutri. Soc.  35:28A (Abstr.).
Kmenta, J.  1971.  Element of econometrics.  New York: Macmillan.
```

*The form of these entries conforms, in general, to that found in numerous agriculture journals, especially *Animal Science, Journal of Animal Science,* and *Journal of the American Society for Horticultural Science.*

ANTHROPOLOGY/ARCHAEOLOGY

In-text Citation

Use the name and year system as discussed on pages 211–14.

List of References

Label the list "References Cited" and set the author's name and the date to the left, as shown next.

Anthropology/Archaeology*

```
              References Cited
Austin, James H.

    1978  Chase, Chance, and Creativity: The Lucky Art of

        Novelty.  New York: Columbia University Press.
Bastien, Joseph

    1978  Mountain of the Condor: Metaphor and Ritual

        in an Andean Ayllu.  American Ethnological Society

        Monograph 64.  St. Paul: West Publishing Co.
Binford, Louis R.

    1962  Archaeology as Anthropology.  American Antiquity

        28:217-225.
```

```
Dunnell, Robert
    1978  Style and Function: A Fundamental Dichotomy.
    American Antiquity 43:192-202
Dye, Daniel S.
    1949  A Grammar of Chinese Lattice.  2nd ed.  Harvard-
    Yenching Monograph Series VI.  Cambridge: Harvard
    University Press.
Jennings, J. D.
    1978  Origins.  In J. D. Jennings, ed.  Ancient Native
    Americans, pp. 1-41.  San Francisco: Freeman.
```

*The form of these entries is based upon the stylistic format of the journal *American Anthropologist.*

ASTRONOMY

See format of geology, below, 228–29.

BIOLOGY/BOTANY/ZOOLOGY—CBE Style

The basic system for the biological sciences is one advocated by the *CBE Style Manual,* an official guide published by the Council of Biology Editors in association with the American Institute of Biological Sciences. Use it for papers in biology, botany, zoology, physiology, anatomy, and genetics.

In-text Citation

Conform to basic standards of the name and year system, as explained on pages 211–14 and as demonstrated below:

```
    This fact would ensure their continued presence in the
cell as a screen mechanism (McClure 1976).  Kirk and Tilney-
Bassett (1976, pp. 83-84) suggest that "many of the other
plants that have these air blisters are also shade plants,
indicating that such structures may be safeguards against
loss of the shading cover and subsequent photo-oxidation of
the photosynthetic pigments" (cf. Downs et al. 1980).
```

List of References

Alphabetize the list and label it "Literature Cited." Type the first line of each entry flush left; indent the second line and other succeeding lines two spaces. However, if you both alphabetize and number the list, keep the left margin uniform, as shown below:

1. Jones, A. E. The complete history of the Tennessee Walking Horse from 1920 to the present. Nashville: Byman Press; 1983.

2. Thompson, Samuel. Pasture grasses. New York: Trammel; 1984.

For journals use name(s) of the author(s); title of the article; name of the journal; volume number; inclusive page numbers; year. For books list name(s) of author(s); title of book; city of publication followed by colon; name of publisher; year. Do not underline the title of the book, and capitalize only the first word and proper nouns. Total number of pages at the end of the entry is not required, but if included, a colon precedes the number of pages: "1970:256 p." or "1970:198–200 (Table II)." A sample list follows:

Biological Sciences*

Literature Cited

Baldwin, K. M. Cardiac gap junction configuration after an uncoupling treatment as a function of time. J. Cell. Biol. 82:66-75; 1979.

Berlyn, G. P., and Mikshe, J. P. Botanical microtechnique and cytochemistry. Ames, IA: Iowa State Univ. Press; 1976.

Gardner, J. D.; Jensen, R. T. Regulation of pancreatic enzyme secretion in vitro. In: L. R. Johnson, ed. Physiology of the gastrointestinal tract. New York: Raven Press; 1981:p. 831-871.

Hodson, P. H., and Foster, J. W. Dipicolinic acid synthesis in Penicillium citreoviride. J. Bacteriol. 91:562-69; 1966.

Klein, R. M.; Klein, D. T. Research methods in plant science. Garden City, NY: Natural History Press; 1970.

Olive, L. S. The genus Protostelium. Amer. J. Bot. 49: 297-303; 1962.

Starkey, J. E.; Karr, P. R. Effect of low dissolved oxygen concentration on effluent turbidity. J. Water Pollution Control Fed. 56:837-843; 1984.

*The form of these botany entries conforms to the *CBE Style Manual.* 5th ed. Bethesda, MD: Council of Biology Editors, Inc., 1983.

GEOLOGY

The United States Geological Survey sets the standards for geological papers, as explained below.

In-text Citation

Use the name and year system as explained above, 211–14, and as demonstrated with this example:

> In view of Niue's position as a former volcanic island rising from a submarine plateau (Schofield, 1959), it might be further speculated that it has a late-stage, silicic, peralkaline phase (Baker, 1974, pp. 344-45). Such melts readily lose significant amounts of uranium and other elements on crystallization (Rosholt et al., 1971; Haffty and Nobel, 1972; Dayvault, 1980), which are available to contemporary or later hydrothermal systems (Wallace, 1980, p. 61).

List of References

Label the bibliography as "Literature Cited," and list only those works mentioned in the paper. If listing references not used in the paper, label it "Selected Bibliography." Alphabetize the list. For books list author, followed by a comma; year, followed by a comma; title of the work with only first word and proper names capitalized, followed by a colon; the place of publication, followed by a comma; publisher, followed by a comma; total pages, followed by a period. For journals list author, followed by comma; date, followed by comma; title of the article with only first word and proper nouns capitalized, followed by a colon; name of the journal, abbreviated but not underlined, followed by a comma; the volume number with lower case "v." as in "v. 23," followed by a comma; the inclusive page numbers preceded by one "p." Add other notations for issue number, maps, illustrations, plates, and so forth (see the Mattson entry below). A sample list follows:

Geology*

> Literature Cited
>
> Donath, F. A., 1963, Strength variation and deformational behavior in anisotropic rock, p. 281-197 in Judd, Wm. R., Editor, State of stress in the earth's crust: New York, American Elsevier Publishing Co., Inc., 732 p.

Friedlander, G., Kennedy, J. W., and Miller, J. M., 1964,
Nuclear and radiochemistry: New York, John Wiley and
Sons, 585 p.

Heard, H. C., Turner, F. J., and Weiss, L. E., 1965, Studies
of heterogeneous strain in experimentally deformed
calcite, marble, and phyllite: Univ. Calif. Pub. Geol.
Sci., v. 46, p. 81-152.

Hill, M. L., and Troxel, B. W., 1966, Tectonics of Death
Valley region, California: Geol. Soc. America Bull.,
v. 77, p. 435-438.

Mattson, Peter H., 1979, Subduction, buoyant braking, flipping,
and strike-slip faulting in the northern Caribbean: J. of
Geology, v. 87, no. 3, p. 293-304, 3 figs., map.

Thorpe, R. S., 1974, Aspects of magnetism and plate
tectonics in the precambrian of England Wales: Geol.
J., v. 9, p. 115-136.

*Note: The form of these geology entries conforms to *Suggestions to Authors of the Reports of the United States Geological Survey,* 6th ed. (Washington, D.C.: Dept. of the Interior, 1978).

BUSINESS AND ECONOMICS

In-text Citation

Use the basic form of name and year system as explained on 211–14.

List of References

Label the list "References." For books list author followed by a period; the year of publication enclosed in parentheses and followed by a period; the title capitalized and underlined and followed by a period; place of publication, followed by a colon, and the publisher, followed by a period. For journals list author, followed by a period; the year of publication enclosed in parentheses and followed by a period; the title of the article within quotation marks and followed by a comma inside the final quotation mark; the name of the journal underlined and followed by a comma; the volume number underlined and followed by a comma; and the inclusive page numbers. For magazines and reports, include the month with the year and omit the volume number. For a newspaper or weekly news magazine include the day, month, and year (22 May 1985) and omit the volume number. Note: when volume number is omitted, use "p." or "pp." with the page numbers to clarify that the number refers to page, not volume. A sample follows:

Business/Economics*

References

Anderson, James E. (1981). "Cross-Section Tests of the Heckscher-Ohlin Theorem: Comment," <u>American Economic Review</u>, <u>71</u>, 1037-39.

Carter, A. (1970). <u>Structural Change in the American Economy</u>. Cambridge: Harvard University Press.

Deardorff, Alan V. (1979). "Weak Links in the Chain of Comparative Advantage," <u>Journal of International Economics</u>, <u>9</u>, 197-209.

--------. (1980). "The General Validity of the Law of Comparative Advantage," <u>Journal of Political Economy</u>, <u>88</u>, 941-57.

Note: use eight hyphens in lieu of repeating the name of the author who has two or more works in the list, in this case Alan Deardorff.

Dooley, Michael, and Peter Isard. (May 1979). "The Portfolio-Balance Model of Exchange Rates," International Finance Discussion Paper No. 141, Federal Reserve Board.

Doti, James. (Jan. 1978). "An Economic Theory of Shopping Behavior." Center for Economic Research Report No. 3, Chapman College.

Ellis, Junius. (June 1985). "Starting a Small Business Inside a Big One," <u>Money</u>, pp. 85-86, 88, 90.

Gunderson, M. (1974a). "Retention of Trainees: A Study of Dichotomous Dependent Variables," <u>Journal of Econometrics</u>, <u>2</u>, 212-14.

--------. (1974b). "Training Subsidies and Disadvantaged Workers: Regression with a Limited Dependent Variable," <u>Canadian Journal of Economics</u>, <u>7</u>, 35-48.

*The form of these economics entries is based in general upon the style and format of *Applied Economics* and *The Economics Journal.*

THE NUMBER SYSTEM

The number system is used in the applied sciences (chemistry, computer science, mathematics, and physics) and in the medical sciences (medicine, nursing, and general health). In simple terms, it requires an in-text *number,* rather than the year, and a list of "Works Cited" to correspond by numbers to the in-text citations. Writers in these fields conform to several general regulations that apply to all five disciplines.

After completing a list of references, assign a number to each entry. Use one of two methods for numbering the list: (1) arrange references in alphabetical order and number them consecutively (in which case, of course, the numbers will not appear in consecutive order in the text), or (2) forego an alphabetical arrangement and number the references consecutively as they appear in the text, interrupting that order when entering references cited earlier. The "Works Cited" entries are similar to those for the name and year system except that each is preceded by a numeral. When writing a rough draft, use such numbers alone as in-text citations or join the number with the name of the authority. In both cases the number serves as a key reference to the source, as listed at the end of the paper. Add page numbers to in-text citations when using quotations and paraphrases. Conform to the following regulations:

1. Place the number within parentheses (1) or brackets [2] immediately after the authority's name:

> In particular the recent paper by Hershel, Hobbs, and
> Thomason (1) raises many interesting questions related to
> photosynthesis, some of which were answered by Skelton (2).

However, several fields use a raised superscript number:

> In particular the recent paper by Hershel, Hobbs, and
> Thomason[1] raises many interesting questions related to
> photosynthesis, some of which were answered by Skelton.[2]

2. If the sentence construction does not require the use of the authority's name, employ one of the following three methods:

a. Insert the number only, enclosing it within parentheses (or brackets):

> It is known (1) that the DNA concentration of a nucleus
> doubles during interphase.

b. Insert both name and number within parentheses:

```
Additional observations include alterations in carbonhydrate
metabolism (Evans, 3), changes in ascorbic acid incorporation
into the cell (Dodd and Williams, 11) and in adjoining
membranes (Holt and Zimmer, 7).
```

3. If necessary, add specific data to the entry:

```
The results of the respiration experiment published by
Jones (3, p. 412) had been predicted earlier by Smith (5,
Proposition 8).
```

APPLIED SCIENCES

Chemistry   Computer Science   Mathematics   Physics

The disciplines of the applied sciences employ the number system, but variations by field exist in both textual citations and the form of entries in the list of references.

CHEMISTRY—ACS Style

In-text Citation

Use raised superscript numerals as references occur and number your references in consecutive order as used, *not* in alphabetical order:

```
The stereochemical features of arene molecules chemisorbed
on metal surfaces cannot be assessed precisely.[3] However,
composite statistics from theoretical calculations[4] and
chemical studies[5-7] indicate that benzene is often
chemisorbed.
```

List of References

Label the list "References." List entries as they occur in the text, not in alphabetical order; therefore, number your bibliography cards one at a time as each source is used in the text and thereafter employ that same number for citing that source. For example, item (1) might appear as your first citation and then appear several times throughout the research paper. The basic forms for chemical entries are demonstrated below. Note that titles of books are placed within quotation marks, *not* underlined. Titles of journal articles are not listed at all, and dates are marked for boldface (wavy underline) with no space after the date or after the volume number. A sample list follows:

Chemistry*

> ### References
>
> (1) Bowen, J. M.; Crone, T. A.; Head, V. L.; McMorrow, H. A.; Kennedy, P. K.; Purdie, N. J. Forensic Sci. 1981, 26(4),664-70.
>
> (2) "Selected Values of Chemical and Thermodynamic Properties". Natl.Bur.Stand.(U.S.)Circ. 1950, No.500.
>
> (3) Humphries, R. B. In "High School Chemistry", 3rd ed.; Lamm, Nancy, Ed.; Lumar Press: New York, 1984; Vol. III, Chapter 6.
>
> Use the above form for contribution to a book.
>
> (4) Terrel, L. J. Chem. 1960,34,256; Chem. Abstr. 1961, 54,110a.
>
> Use the above form for reference to an abstract.
>
> (5) Cotton, F. A. J. Am. Chem. Soc. 1968,90,6230.
>
> (6) (a) Sievert, A. C.; Muetterties, E. L. Inorg. Chem. 1981,20,489. (b) Albright, T. A., unpublished data, 1984.
>
> The in-text citation may refer to 6, 6a, or 6b.
>
> *The form of these chemistry entries conforms to the *Handbook for Authors of Papers in American Chemical Society Publications* (Washington, D.C.: American Chemical Society, 1978).

COMPUTER SCIENCE

In-text Citation

Use raised superscript numerals (as above for chemistry, like this[12]), and then number them in consecutive order by appearance in the paper, not by alphabetical order.

List of References

Label the list "Works Cited." Number the references according to their appearance in the text, not by alphabetical order. For books, titles are underlined, publisher precedes city of publication, and specific page(s) of books need not be listed, but in-text citation should specify pages for paraphrases and direct quotations. For journals, the title of the article is provided within quotation marks and with first word only of the title capitalized; title of the journal is underlined; volume number is underlined; issue number is provided whenever available, preceding the date and page number(s). A sample follows:

Computer Science

```
                        Works Cited

1.  Aho, A. V.; Hopcroft, J. E.; and Ullman, J. D.  The
    Design and Analysis of Computer Algorithms.  Addison-
    Wesley, Reading, Mass., 1974.

2.  Gligor, V.D., and Shattuck, S. H.  "On deadlock
    detection in distributed systems."  IEEE Trans.
    Softw. Eng. SE-6, 5 (Sept. 1980), 435-40.

3.  Sklansky, J.; Wassel, G. N.  Pattern Classifiers and
    Trainable Machines.  Springer-Verlag, New York, 1981.

4.  Holt, R. C.  Some deadlock properties of computer
    systems."  Computer Surv. 4, 3 (Sept. 1972), 179-96.
```

MATHEMATICS—AMS style

In-text Citation

First alphabetize and then number the list of references. Label the list "References." All in-text citations are then made to the reference number, which you should place in your text within brackets and marked for boldface (wavy line), as in the following example:

```
In addition to the obvious implications it is already

known from [5] that every d-regular Lindelof space is D-

normal.  Further results on D-normal spaces will appear in

[8], which is in preparation.  The results obtained here and

in [2], [3], and [5] encourage further research.
```

List of References

For books the titles are underlined, publisher precedes city of publication, and specific page(s) of books need not be listed. For journals, title of the article is underlined, journal title is *not* underlined, volume is marked for boldface (wavy line), followed by year of publication within parentheses, followed by complete pagination of the article. A sample list follows:

Mathematics*

References

1. M. Artin, <u>On the joins of Hensel rings</u>, Advances in Math. **7** (1971), 282–86.

2. R. Artzy, <u>Linear geometry</u>, Addison-Wesley, Reading, Mass., 1965.

3. I. M. Isaacs and D. S. Passman, <u>Groups with representations of bounded degree</u>, Canad. J. Math. **16** (1964), 299–309.

4. ———, <u>Characterization of groups in terms of the degrees of their characters</u>, Pacific J. Math. **15** (1965), 877–903.

5. O. Solbrig, <u>Evolution and systematics</u>. Macmillan, New York, 1966.

*The form of these entries conforms to *A Manual for Authors of Mathematical Papers,* 4th ed. (Providence: American Mathematical Society, 1973).

PHYSICS—AIP style

In-text Citation

Use raised superscript numerals, like this.[12] Number the list of references in consecutive order of in-text usage, not in alphabetical order.

List of References

For books, titles are underlined, publisher precedes place of publication, and specific page references *should* be provided. For journals the title of the article is omitted entirely, the title of the journal is abbreviated and *not* underlined, the volume is marked for boldface (wavy line), and the year within parentheses follows the pagination. A sample list follows:

Physics*

References

[1]T. Poorter and H. Tolner, Infrared Phys. 19, 317 (1979).

[2]C. D. Motchenbacher and F. C. Fitchen, Low-Noise Electronic Design (Wiley, New York, 1973), p. 16.

[3]L. Monchick, S. Chem. Phys. 71, 576 (1979).

[4]F. Riesz and Bela Nagy, Functional Analysis (Ungar, New York, 1955), Secs. 121 and 123.

[5]G. E. Brown and M. Rho, Phys. Letters 82B, 177 (1979); G. E. Brown, M. Rho, V. Vento, Phys. Letters 84B, 383 (1979); Phys. Rev. D 22, 2838 (1980; Phys. Rev. D 24, 216 (1981).

[7]Marc D. Levenson, Phys. Today 30(5), 44–49 (1977).

*The form of these entries conforms to *Style Manual for Guidance in the Preparation of Papers for Journals Published by the American Institute of Physics,* 3rd ed. (New York: American Institute of Physics, 1978).

MEDICAL SCIENCES—AMA style

Health   Medicine   Nursing

Like other applied sciences, the medical sciences, as a general rule, employ the number system. Variations among medical journals do exist, but the style and format demonstrated below is standard.

In-text Citation

Number your citations as they occur in the text, like this (1). Use the system explained and demonstrated previously on pages 231–32.

List of References

Label the list "References." Do not alphabetize the list; rather, number it to correspond to sources as you cite them in the text. For books, list author, title underlined and with all major words capitalized, the place, publisher, and year. For journals, list author, title without quotation marks and with only the first word capitalized, the name of the journal abbreviated *without* periods and underlined, the year followed by a semicolon, the volume followed by a colon, and page number(s). A sample list follows:

Medical Sciences*

References

1. Crane, C. W., Neuberger, A.   The digestion and absorption of protein by normal man.   Biochem 1960;74:313–323.

2. Angell, M. Juggling the personal and professional life. J Am Med Wom Assoc 1982;37:64-68.

3. Antonovsky, A. Health, Stress, and Coping. San Francisco, Jossey-Bass, 1979.

4. Ayman, D. The personality type of patients with arteriolar essential hypertension. Am J Med Sci 1933;186:213-233.

5. Nash, Paul. Authority and Freedom in Education. New York, Wiley, 1966.

6. Green, M. I., Haggery, R. J. (eds). Ambulatory Pediatrics. Philadelphia, W. B. Saunders, 1968.

*The form of these entries represents a standard as established by the American Medical Association, *Style Book: Editorial Manual,* 6th ed. (Acton, MA: Publishing Sciences Group, Inc., 1976) and as used in numerous medical journals, such as *JAMA, Nutrition Reviews, Journal of American College Health,* and others.

THE FOOTNOTE SYSTEM

The fine arts and some fields in the humanities (but not literature) employ traditional footnotes, which should conform to standards set by the *Chicago Manual of Style,* 13th ed., 1982. With this system, you must employ superscript numerals within the text, (like this[15]) and place documentary footnotes on corresponding pages. Usually, no "Works Cited" will be necessary; however, some instructors will ask for one at the end of your paper; if so, see below (243). The discussion below assumes that notes will appear as footnotes; however, some instructors accept endnotes, that is, all notes appear together at the end of the paper, not at the bottom of individual pages (see 240).

In-text Citation: Superscript Numerals

Use Arabic numerals typed slightly above the line (like this[12]). Place this superscript numeral at the end of quotations or paraphrases, with the number following immediately without a space after the final word or mark of punctuation, as in this sample:

Colonel Warner soon rejoined his troops despite severe pain. He wrote in September of 1864: "I was obliged to ride at all times on a walk and to mount my horse from some steps or be helped on. My cains [sic] with which I walked when on foot were strapped to my saddle."[6] Such heroic dedication

```
did not go unnoticed, for the Washington Chronicle cited

Warner as "an example worthy of imitation."⁷ At Gettysburg

Warner's troops did not engage in heavy fighting and suf-

fered only limited casualties of two dead and five wounded.⁸
```

The superscript numbers go outside the marks of punctuation. The use of "[sic]" indicates exact quotation, even to the point of typing an apparent error. Avoid placing one superscript at the end of a long paragraph because readers will not know if it refers to the final sentence only or to the entire paragraph. If you introduce borrowed materials with an authority's name and then place a superscript numeral at the end, you direct the reader to the full extent of the borrowed material..

Footnotes

Citations appear as footnotes at the bottom of pages to correspond with superscript numerals (see immediately above). Some papers will require footnotes on almost every page. Follow these conventions:

1. *Spacing.* Single space footnotes, but double space between notes.

2. *Indention.* Indent the first line five spaces, use a raised superscript numeral with no space between it and the first word of the note.

3. *Numbering.* Number the notes consecutively throughout the entire paper.

4. *Placement.* Collect at the bottom of each page all footnotes to citations made on that page.

5. *Distinguish footnotes from text.* Separate footnotes from text by triple spacing or, if preferred, by a twelve-space bar line from the left margin.

6. *Footnote form.* Basic forms of notes as stipulated by the *Chicago Manual of Style* should conform to the following:

For a book:

```
      ¹W. V. Quine, Word and Object (Cambridge,
MA: MIT Press, 1966), 8.
```

For a journal article:

```
      ²G. S. Boolos, "On Second-Order Logic,"
Journal of Philosophy 72 (1975): 590-610.
```

For a collection:

[3]Lonne Elder, "Ceremonies in Dark Old Men," in
New Black Playwrights: An Anthology, ed. William Couch,
Jr. (Baton Rouge: Louisiana State University Press, 1968),
62-63.

For an edition with multiple authors:

[4]Albert C. Baugh, et al. A Literary History of
England. 2nd ed. (New York: Appleton, 1967), 602-11.

For a magazine article:

[5]von Hoffman, Nicholas, "The White House News
Hole," The New Republic, 6 September 1982, 19-23.

For a newspaper article:

[6]Malcolm G. Scully, "National Concern Over Educational
Quality Seen Spreading from Schools to Colleges,"
The Chronicle of Higher Education, 12 September
1984, 1, 20.

For a review article:

[7]John Gardner, review of Falconer, by John
Cheever, Saturday Review, 2 April 1977, 20.

7. **Subsequent footnote references,** according to the *Chicago Manual of Style,* after a first full reference should be shortened to author's name and page number. When an author has two works mentioned, employ a shortened version of the title, "[3]Jones, *Paine,* 25." In general, avoid latinate abbreviations such as *loc. cit.* or *op. cit.;* however, whenever a note refers to the source in the immediately preceding note, you may use *"Ibid."* with a page number as follows (note especially the difference between notes 4 and 6):

[3]S. C. Kleene, Introduction to Metamathematics
(Princeton, N. J.: Van Nostrand, 1964), 24.

[4]Ibid., 27.

[5]Abraham J. Heschel, Man Is Not Alone: A Philosophy
of Religion (New York: Farrar, Straus, and Young, 1951),
221.

[6]Kleene, 24.

[7]Ibid., 27.

8. **Endnotes.** Write footnotes as a single group of endnotes with permission of the instructor to lessen the burden of typing the paper. Follow these conventions:

Begin notes on a new page at the end of the text.
Entitle the page "Notes," centered, and placed two inches from
  the top of the page. This page is unnumbered, but number all
  other pages of endnotes.
Indent the first line of each note five spaces, type the note number slightly above the line, begin the note, and use the left margin for succeeding lines.
Double-space the notes and double-space between the notes.
Triple-space between the heading and the first note.

Conform to the following sample:

                              Notes

   ^{1}W. V. Quine, <u>Word and Object</u> (Cambridge, MA: MIT

Press, 1966), 8.

   ^{2}G. S. Boolos, "On Second-Order Logic," <u>Journal of</u>

<u>Philosophy</u>, 72 (1975): 509-510.

   ^{3}S. C. Kleene, <u>Introduction to Metamathematics</u>

(Princeton, N. J.: Van Nostrand, 1964), 24.

   ^{4}<u>Ibid.</u>, 27.

   ^{5}Abraham J. Heschel, <u>Man Is Not Alone: A Philosophy</u>

<u>of Religion</u> (New York: Farrar, Straus, and Young, 1951), 221.

   ^{6}Kleene, 24.

   ^{7}<u>Ibid.</u>, 27.

   ^{8}Heschel, 222.

   ^{9}Boolos, 509.

HUMANITIES

History   Philosophy   Religion and Theology

In-text Citation
Use the form of raised superscript numerals as explained on 237.

List of References
Place the references at the bottom of each page on which a citation occurs. See explanation above, 237–38, and duplicate the form and style of the following footnotes:

Lower portion of a religious paper*

In some cases, the attempts of anthropologists to explain certain religious phenomena have only resulted in confusion.

¹E. E. Evans-Pritchard, Nuer Religion (Oxford: Clarendon Press, 1956), 84.

²Claude Levi-Strauss, The Savage Mind (Chicago: University of Chicago Press, 1966), chap. 9, esp. p. 312.

Note: use "p." for clarity, if necessary.

³Ibid., 314.

⁴Ibid.

⁵E. E. Evans-Pritchard, Theories of Primitive Religion (Oxford: Clarendon Press, 1965), chap. 2.

⁶Evans-Pritchard, Nuer, 85.

⁷Evans-Pritchard, Primitive Religion, 46.

⁸Humphries, P. T., "Salvation Today, Not Tomorrow," Sermon (Bowling Green, KY: First Methodist Church, 1984).

⁹Romans 6:2.

¹⁰1 Cor. 13:1-3.

¹¹The Church and the Law of Nullity of Marriage, Report of a Commission Appointed by the Archbishops of Canterbury and York in 1949 (London: Society for Promoting Christian Knowledge, 1955), 12-16.

*Notes conform to the standards of the *Chicago Manual of Style,* 13th ed., 1982.

Lower portion of a history paper*

Such heroic dedication did not go unnoticed, for the Washington Chronicle cited Warner as "an example worthy of imitation."¹¹

¹G. E. Thomas, "Puritans, Indians, and the Concept of Race," New England Quarterly 48 (1975): 3-27.

²Thomas Jefferson, Notes on the State of Virginia (1784), ed. William Peden (Chapel Hill, N.C.: Univ. of North Carolina Press, 1955), 59.

³Harold Child, "Jane Austen," in The Cambridge History of English Literature, ed. A. W. Ward and A. R. Waller (London: Cambridge Univ. Press, 1927), 12:231-44.

⁴Encyclopaedia Britannica: Macropaedia, 1974 ed., s.v. "Heidegger, Martin."

Note: "s.v." means *sub verbo,* "under the word(s)."

⁵Henry Steele Commager, <u>The Nature and Study of History</u>, Social Science Seminar Series (Columbus, Ohio: Merrill, 1965), 10.

⁶Dept. of the Treasury, "Financial Operations of Government Agencies and Funds," <u>Treasury Bulletin</u> (Washington, D. C.: GPO, June 1974), 134-41.

⁷<u>Constitution</u>, Art. 1, sec. 4.

⁸Great Britain, <u>Coroner's Act, 1954</u>, 2 & 3 Eliz. 2, ch. 31.

⁹State v. Lane, Minnesota 263 N. W. 608 (1935).

¹⁰Papers of Gen. A. J. Warner (P-973, Service Record and Short Autobiography), Western Reserve Historical Society.

¹¹<u>Ibid</u>., clipping from the <u>Washington Chronicle</u>.

*Notes conform to the standards of the *Chicago Manual of Style,* 13th ed., 1982.

FINE ARTS

Art   Dance   Music   Speech   Theater

Documentation for a research paper in the fine arts uses superscript numerals in the text and footnotes or endnotes. Examples of *endnote* entries are shown:*

Notes

¹Suzanne G. Cusick, "Valerio Dorico: Music Printer in Sixteenth Century Rome," <u>Studies in Musicology</u> 43 (1981): 214.

²There are three copies of the papal brief in the archives of the German College, now situated on Via S. Nicola da Tolentino. The document is printed in Thomas D. Culley, <u>Jesuits and Music,</u> (Rome and St. Louis, 1979), 1: 358-59.

³Cusick, 214.

⁴Denys Hay, ed., <u>The Age of the Renaissance</u> (New York, 1967), 286.

⁵Aristophanes, <u>The Birds,</u> in <u>Five Comedies of Aristophanes,</u> trans. Benjamin B. Rogers (Garden City, N.Y.: Doubleday, 1955), 1.2.12-14.

⁶Jean Bouret, <u>The Life and Work of Toulouse Lautrec,</u> trans. Daphne Woodward (New York: Abrams, n.d.), 5.

Carol McGinnis Kay and Henry E. Jacobs (Lincoln: Univ. of
Nebraska Press, 1978), 77-78.

    [8]Lionello Venturi, <u>Botticelli</u> (Greenwich, Conn.:
Fawcett, n.d.), plate 32, p. 214.

    Note: Add "p." for page only if needed for clarity.

    [9]Cotton Vitellius MSS, A., 15. British Museum.

    [10]<u>Ham</u>. 2.3.2.

    [11]George Henry Lewes, Review of "Letters on Christian
Art," by Friedrich von Schlegel, <u>Athenaeum</u> No. 1117 (1849):
296.

    [12]Ron Stoppelmann, "Letters," <u>New York</u>, 23 August
1982, 8.

    [13]<u>The World Book Encyclopedia</u>, 1976 ed., s.v.
"Raphael."

    [14]<u>The Last Tango in Paris</u>, United Artists, 1972.

    [15]Wolfgang A. Mozart, <u>Jupiter</u>, Symphony No. 41.

    [16]William Blake, <u>Comus</u>, Photographic reproduction in
Irene Taylor, "Blake's <u>Comus</u> Designs," <u>Blake Studies</u> 4
(Spring, 1972): 61, plate 4.

    [17]Lawrence Topp, <u>The Artistry of Van Gogh</u> (New York:
Matson, 1983), transparency 21.

    [18]Eric Sevareid, <u>CBS News</u> (New York: CBS-TV, 11 March
1975); Media Services Videotape 1975-142 (Nashville:
Vanderbilt Univ., 1975).

    *Notes conform to the standards of the *Chicago Manual of Style,* 13th
ed., 1982.

Bibliography Page for a Humanities Research Paper

    In addition to footnotes or endnotes, you may need to supply a separate
bibliography page that lists sources used in developing the paper. Use a heading that represents its contents, such as "Selected Bibliography," "Sources
Consulted," or "Works Cited." Note: if you write completely documented
footnotes, the bibliography is redundant. Check with your instructor before
preparing one because it may not be required. Separate the title from the first

entry with a triple space. Type the first line of each entry flush left; indent the second line and other succeeding lines five spaces. Alphabetize the list by last names of authors. List alphabetically by title two or more works by one author. The basic forms are:

For a book:

```
Quine, W. V. Word and Object. Cambridge, MA:
    MIT Press, 1966.
```

For a journal article:

```
Boolos, G. S. "On Second-Order Logic." Journal
    of Philosophy 72 (1975): 509-510.
```

See also bibliographies that accompany the sample papers, 160, 180–82.

APPENDIX

List of Reference Sources by Discipline

ART

General Guides to Art Literature

American Art Dictionary. New York: Bowker, 1952–present.

Art Education: A Guide to Information Sources. Detroit: Gale, 1977.

Art Library Manual: A Guide to Resources and Practice. Ed. Philip Pacey. New York: Bowker, 1977.

Art Research Methods and Resources: A Guide to Finding Art Information. Ed. L. S. Jones. Dubuque: Kendall/Hunt, 1978.

Britannica Encyclopedia of American Art. Ed. M. Rugoff. Chicago: Encyclopaedia Britannica, 1973.

Contemporary Architects. New York: St. Martin's, 1980.

Contemporary Artists. New York: St. Martin's, 1983.

De La Croix, Horst, and Richard G. Tansey. *Art Through the Ages.* 2 vols. 7th ed. New York: Harcourt, 1980.

Dictionary of American Painters, Sculptors, and Engravers. Ed. Mantle Fielding. N. p.: Apollo, 1983.

Encyclopedia of American Art. New York: Dutton, 1981.

Encyclopedia of World Art. 15 vols. New York: McGraw-Hill, 1959–1968. Supplement, 1983.

Fine and Applied Arts Terms Index. Detroit: Gale, 1983.

Guide to Art Reference Books. Chicago: ALA, 1959.

Guide to Basic Information Sources in the Visual Arts. Ed. Gerd Muehsam. Santa Barbara: ABC/Clio, 1978.

Guide to the Literature of Art History. Chicago: ALA, 1980.

Fletcher, Bannister. *A History of Architecture.* 17th ed. New York: Scribner's, 1967. [Lists vital information on every important building.]

How to Find Out in Architecture and Building: A Guide to Sources of Information. Pergamon, 1967.

Larousse Dictionary of Painters. New York: Larousse, 1981.

Macmillan Encyclopedia of Architects. 4 vols. New York: Free Press, 1982.

The New International Illustrated Encyclopedia of Art. 24 vols. New York: Greystone, 1967.

Oxford Companion to Twentieth Century Art. Oxford: Oxford UP, 1981.

Pelican History of Art. 50 vols. in progress. Baltimore: Pelican, 1953–present.

Print Index: A Guide to Reproductions. Comp. P. J. Parry and Kathe Chipman. Westport: Greenwood, 1983.

Random House Library of Painting and Sculpture. 4 vols. New York: Beazley, 1981.

Research Guide to the History of Western Art. Chicago: ALA, 1982.

Who's Who in American Art. New York: Bowker, 1984.

Bibliographies to Art Books and Other Sources

Annotated Bibliography of Fine Art. 1897; rpt. Boston: Longwood, 1976.
Applied and Decorative Arts: A Bibliographic Guide. Ed. D. L. Ehresmann. Littleton: Libraries Unlimited, 1977.
Art Books. New York: Bowker, 1950–85.
Arts in America: A Bibliography. Ed. Bernard Karpel. 4 vols. Washington: Smithsonian, 1979–1980.
Bibliographic Guide to Art and Architecture. Boston: Hall, 1977–85.
Fine Arts: A Bibliographic Guide. Ed. D. L. Ehresmann. 2nd ed. Littleton: Libraries Unlimited, 1979.

Data Bases to Art Information

ART BIBLIOGRAPHIES MODERN
RILA (Repetoire Internationale the Literature of Art)

Indexes to Journal Articles

Art Index. New York: Bowker, 1929–present.

  Indexes most art journals, such as *American Art Journal, Art Bulletin, Artforum, Design, Sculpture Review,* and many others.

Index to Art Periodicals. 11 vols. Boston: G. K. Hall, 1962. With supplements.
Humanities Index. New York: Bowker, 1974–present.
RILA. Repetoire International de la Litterature de'Art. Williamstown, MA: RILA, 1975–date.

BIOLOGICAL SCIENCES

General Guides to the Literature

Dictionary of Biology. 6th ed. Baltimore: Penguin, 1978.
Biology Data Book. Ed. P. L. Altman and Dorothy S. Dittmer. 2nd ed. 3 vols. Madison: FASEB, 1972–74.
Encyclopedia of Bioethics. 2 vols. New York: Macmillan, 1982.
Encyclopedia of the Biological Sciences. Ed. Peter Gray. 2nd ed. New York: Reinhold, 1970.

Guide to the Taxonomic Literature of Vertebrates. Ed. Richard E. Blackwelder. Ames: Iowa State UP, 1972.
Guide to Sources for Agricultural and Biological Research. Berkeley: U of California P, 1981.
Guide to the Literature for the Industrial Microbiologist. Comp. Peter A. Hahn. New York: Plenum, 1973.
Guide to the Literature of the Life Sciences. Ed. R. C. Smith and W. M. Reid. 9th ed. Minneapolis: Burgess, 1980.
Library Research Guide to Biology: Illustrated Search Strategy and Sources. Ann Arbor: Pierian, 1978.
Science Reference Sources. Ed. F. B. Jenkins. 5th ed. Cambridge: MIT Press, 1969.

Bibliographies to Books and Other Sources in the Biological Sciences

Biological Abstracts. Philadelphia: Biological Abstracts, 1926–date.
Bibliography of Bioethics. 8 vols. New York: Macmillan, 1982.
Botanical Bibliographies: A Guide to Bibliographical Materials Applicable to Botany. Monticello: Lubrecht & Cramer, 1974.

Data Bases for the Biological Sciences

AQUACULTURE
AQUALINE
BIOSIS PREVIEWS
ENVIRONMENTAL BIBLIOGRAPHY
SCISEARCH
ZOOLOGICAL RECORD

Indexes to Journal Articles in the Biological Sciences

Biological Abstracts. Philadelphia: Biological Abstracts, 1926–present.

  Indexes and gives brief descriptions of books and journal articles, especially to journals such as *American Journal of Anatomy, American Zoologist, Biochemistry, Journal of Animal Behavior, Quarterly Review of Biology, Social Biology,* and many others.

Biological and Agricultural Index. New York: Wilson, 1947–date.

BUSINESS

(see also ECONOMICS)

General Guides to the Literature

AMA Management Handbook. Ed. William K. Fallo. 2nd ed. New York: American Management Association, 1983.
American Economic and Business History: Information Sources. Detroit: Gale, 1971.
Basic Business Library: Core Resources. Ed. Bernard S. Schlessinger. Phoenix: Oryx, 1983.
Business Firms Master Index. Ed. Donna Wood. Detroit: Gale, 1983–present.
A Business Information Guidebook. Ed. O. Figueroa and C. Winkler. New York: American Mgmt., 1980.
Encyclopedia of Banking and Finance. 7th ed. Boston: Bankers, 1973.
Encyclopedia of Business Information Sources. 5th ed. Ed. Paul Wasserman et al. Detroit: Gale, 1983.
Encyclopedia of Management. Ed. Carl Heyel. 3rd ed. New York: Van Nostrand, 1982.
International Dictionary of Business. Ed. H. Johannsen and G. T. Page. Englewood Cliffs: Prentice, 1981.
Use of Management and Business Literature. Ed. K. D. C. Vernon. New York: Butterworths, 1975.
Where to Find Business Information. New York: Wiley, 1979.

Bibliographies to Business Books and Other Sources

Business Reference Sources: An Annotated Guide for Harvard Business School Students. Rev. Ed. Cambridge: Harvard, 1979.
Bibliographic Guide to Business and Economics. 3 vols. Boston: Hall, annually.
Business and Economics Books and Serials in Print. New York: Bowker, 1983.
Business Publications Index and Abstracts. Detroit: Gale, annually.
Historial Bibliography of Administration, Business, and Management. Ed. D. D. Van Fleet. Monticello: Vance Biblios., 1978.

Data Bases to Business Information

ABI / INFORM
PAIS
HARVARD BUSINESS REVIEW
ECONOMIC LITERATURE INDEX
TRADE AND INDUSTRY INDEX
MANAGEMENT CONTENTS
PTS F&S INDEXES
STANDARD & POOR'S NEWS
FINIS (Financial Industry National Information Service)

Indexes to Business Journal Articles

Business Periodicals Index. New York: Wilson, 1958–date.

> Indexes journals such as *Business Quarterly, Business Week, Fortune, Journal of Business, Journal of Marketing, Personnel Journal,* and many others.

Accountants' Index. New York: AICPA, 1921–present.

> Indexes accounting and tax subjects in journals such as *Accountants' Digest, Accounting Review, Banker's Magazine, CA Magazine, Journal of Finance, Tax Adviser,* and many others.

The Wall Street Journal Index. New York: Dow Jones, annually.

> Indexes contemporary issues.

Personnel Literature. Washington: OPM Library, 1942–present.

> Indexes issues of personnel management.

CHEMISTRY AND CHEMICAL ENGINEERING

General Guides to the Literature

Annual Reviews of Industrial and Engineering Chemistry. Washington: ACS, 1972–present.
Chemical Engineers' Handbook. 6th ed. New York: McGraw, 1984.
Chemical Industries Information Sources. Ed. T. P. Peck. Detroit: Gale, 1979.
The Chemist's Companion: A Handbook. Ed. A. J. Gordon and R. A. Ford. New York: Wiley, 1972.
Dictionary of Chemistry. 2 vols. New York: International, 1969.

Encyclopedia of Chemistry. 3rd ed. New York: Reinhold, 1973.

Guide to Basic Information Sources in Chemistry. Ed. Arthur Antony. New York: Wiley, 1979.

Handbook for Authors. Washington: American Chemical Society, 1977.

Literature of Chemical Technology. Ed. T. E. Singer and J. F. Smith. Washington: ACS, 1968.

How to Find Chemical Information: A Guide for Practicing Chemists, Teachers, and Students. Ed. R. E. Maizell. New York: Wiley, 1979.

How to Find Out in Chemistry. Ed. C. R. Burman. 2nd ed. Elmsford: Pergamon, 1967.

Research in the Chemical Industry. Ed. A. Baines. Englewood: Burgess, 1969.

Riegel's Handbook of Industrial Chemistry. 8th ed. New York: Reinhold, 1983.

Searching the Chemical Literature. Washington, ACS, 1977.

Use of Chemical Literature. Ed. R. T. Bottle. 3rd ed. London: Butterworths, 1979.

Using the Chemical Literature: A Practical Guide. New York: Dekker, 1974.

Bibliographies to Chemistry Books and Other Sources

Chemical Abstracts. Easton: ACS, 1907–present. Weekly.

Chemical Publications: Their Nature and Use. 5th ed. New York: McGraw, 1982.

Chemical Titles. Easton: ACS, 1960. Biweekly.

Selected Titles in Chemistry. 4th ed. Washington: ACS, 1968.

Data Bases to Chemical Literature

CA SEARCH
CHEMSEARCH
CHEMNAME
CHEMSIS
CHEMICAL EXPOSURE
CHEMICAL INDUSTRY NOTES
COMPENDEX

Indexes of Journal Articles to Chemistry and Chemical Engineering

Chemical Abstracts: Key to the World's Chemical Literature. Easton: American Chemical Society, 1907–present. Weekly.

Indexes such journals as *Applied Chemical News, American Chemical Society Journal, Chemical Bulletin, Chemist, Journal of the Chemical Society,* and many more.

COMPUTER SCIENCE

General Guides to the Literature

Computer Dictionary for Everyone. Ed. Donald Spencer. New York: Scribner, 1981.

Encyclopedia of Computer Science and Technology. Ed. Jack Belzer. 14 vols. New York: Dekker, 1980.

Guide to Reference Sources in the Computer Sciences. New York: Macmillan, 1974.

Bibliographies to Computer Books and Other Sources on Data Processing

Annotated Bibliography of Files in Automation, Data Processing, and Computer Science. Lexington: UP of Kentucky, 1967.

Annotated Bibliography on the History of Data Processing. Ed. J. W. Cortada. Greenwood: 1983.

Computer-Readable Bibliographic Data Bases: A Directory and Data Sourcebook. Washington: ASIS, 1976–present.

Data Bases to Computer Information

COMPUTER DATABASE
BUSINESS SOFTWARE DATABASE

Indexes to Computer Journal Articles

Applied Science and Technology Index. New York: Wilson, 1958–date.

Indexes articles in *Byte, Computer Design, Computers in Industry, The Computer Journal, Computer Methods, Computer, Data Processing,* and *Microcomputing.*

Computer Literature Index. Phoenix: ACR, 1971–present.

Computer Abstracts. Great Britain: Technical Information, 1957–date.

ECONOMICS

General Guides to the Literature

American Dictionary of Economics. Ed. Douglas Auld et al. New York: Facts on File, 1983.

Dictionary of Banking and Finance. Ed. J. M. Rosenberg. New York: Wiley, 1982.

Economic Education: A Guide to Information Sources. Detroit: Gale, 1977.

Economic Handbook of the World. Ed. A. S. Banks et al. New York: McGraw, 1981.

Economics Information Resources Directory. Detroit: Gale, 1984–present.

Emory, C. William. *Business Research Methods.* Rev. ed. Homewood: Irwin, 1982.

Encyclopedia of Economics. New York: McGraw, 1982.

Studies in Economics and Economic History. Ed. Marcelle Kooy. Durham: Duke UP, 1972.

Use of Economics Literature. Ed. John Fletcher. New York: Archon Books, 1971.

Who's Who in Hard Money Economics. Mill Valley, CA: Matlock-Silber, 1981.

Bibliographies to Economics Books and Other Sources

Bibliographic Guide to Business and Economics. Boston: Hall, annually.

Bibliography on Methods of Social and Business Research. Ed. W. A. Belson and B. A. Thompson. New York: Halsted, 1973.

Business and Economics Book Guide. 2 vols. Boston: Hall, 1974. Supplements.

Business and Economics Books and Serials in Print. New York: Bowker, annually.

Economics: Bibliographic Guide to Reference Books and Information Resources. Ed. Peter Melnyk. Libraries Unlimited, 1971.

Select Bibliography of Modern Economic Theory: 1870–1929. Ed. Harold E. Batson. Clifton, NJ: Kelley, 1930.

Special Bibliography in Monetary Economics and Finance. Ed. J. Cohen. New York: Gordon, 1976.

Data Bases to Economics Literature

ECONOMICS ABSTRACTS INTERNATIONAL
ECONOMIC LITERATURE INDEX
FOREIGN TRADE AND ECONOMIC ABSTRACTS

Indexes to Economic Journal Articles

Journal of Economic Literature

Indexes such journals as *American Economist, Applied Economics, Business Economics, Economic History Review, Economic Journal, Federal Reserve Bulletin, Journal of Economic Issues,* and many more.

Index of Economic Articles

The Wall Street Journal Index

ECOLOGY

General Guides to Environmental Literature

Environment Information Access. New York: EIC, 1971–present.

Encyclopedia of Community Planning and Environmental Protection. Ed. Marilyn Schultz and Vivian Kasen. New York: Facts on File, 1983.

Energy Information Guide. Ed. David R. Weber. Santa Barbara: ABC:Clio, 1982–83.

Bibliographies to Environmental Books and Other Sources

Air Pollution Abstracts. Washington: EPA, 1970–present.

Energy Bibliography and Index. 4 vols. Houston: Gulf, 1979–81.

Environmental Abstracts. New York: Environment Information Center, 1971–present.

Pollution Abstracts. Washington: Cambridge Scientific Abstracts, 1970–present.

Data Bases to Environmental Literature

BIOSIS PREVIEWS
COMPENDEX
ENVIRONLINE
POLLUTION ABSTRACTS
ENVIRONMENTAL BIBLIOGRAPHY

Indexes to Journal Articles on Environmental Issues

Biological Abstracts.

Indexes articles on environmental issues in journals such as *American Forests, The Conservationist, Florida*

Naturalist, Journal of Soil and Water Conservation, The Living Wilderness, Sierra, Ambio, Ecology, Environmental Pollution, and others.

Environmental Index. New York: EIC, 1971– present.

Gives additional indexing of other journals, such as *Environment, Environmental Ethics, Journal of Applied Ecology, Solar Age,* and others.

EDUCATION

General Guides to the Literature

Encyclopedia of Educational Research. 4th ed. London: Macmillan, 1969.
Encyclopedia of Education. 10 vols. New York: Macmillan, 1971.
Encyclopedia of Eduation. New York: Philosophical Library, 1970.
Guide to Periodicals in Education and Its Academic Disciplines. Ed. W. L. Camp and B. L. Schwark. 2nd ed. Metuchen: Scarecrow, 1975.
A Guide to Sources of Educational Information. Ed. M. L. Woodbury. 2nd ed. Arlington: Information Resources, 1982.
Handbook of Research in Teaching. Chicago: Rand McNally, 1963.
International Yearbook of Education. Paris: UNESCO, 1948–present.
Library Research Guide to Education. Ed. J. R. Kennedy. Ann Arbor: Pierian, 1979.
Philosophy of Education: A Guide to Information Sources. Ed. C. A. Baatz. Detroit: Gale, 1980.
Research Methods in Education. Ed. L. Cohen and L. Manion. Totowa: Biblio Dist., 1980.
Sources in Educational Research. Detroit: Wayne State UP, 1969.

Bibliographies to Education Books and Other Sources

Bibliographic Guide to Educational Research. Ed. D. M. Berry. 2nd ed. Metuchen: Scarecrow, 1980.
Bibliographic Guide to Education. Boston: Hall, 1978–date.
Early Childhood Education: An ERIC Bibliography. New York: ERIC, 1973.
Education Documents Abstracts. New York: ERIC, 1968–date.

Education Abstracts. Fulton: ECH, 1936– · present.
Subject Bibliography of the History of American Higher Education. Westport: 1984.

Data Bases to Education Literature

ERIC
AIM / ARM (vocational and technical education sources)
A-V ONLINE (non-print educational materials)

Indexes to Journal Articles

Education Index. New York: Wilson, 1929– date.

Indexes articles in such journals as *Childhood Education, Comparative Education, Education Digest, Educational Forum, Educational Review, Educational Studies, Journal of Educational Psychology, Review of Education,* and many more.

Current Index to Journals in Education. Phoenix: Oryx, 1969–present.
Education Documents Index. New York: ERIC 1966–present.
Exceptional Child Education Resources. Reston: CEC, 1968–present.
Resources in Education (formerly *Research in Education*). Washington: ERIC, 1956– present.

ELECTRONICS

General Guides to the Literature

Buchsbaum's Complete Handbook of Practical Electronics Reference Data. 2nd ed. Englewood Cliffs: Prentice, 1978.
Dictionary of Electronics. Ed. S. W. Amos. Woburn: Butterworth, 1981.
Electronic Industries Information Sources. Ed. Chester Morrill. Detroit: Gale, 1969.
Electronic Properties Research Literature Retrieval Guide. 4 vols. New York: IFI Plenum, 1979.
Electronic Properties of Materials: A Guide to Literature. 3 vols. New York: Plenum, 1967– 68.
Electronics Style Manual. Ed. John Markus. New York: McGraw, 1978.

Encyclopedia of Computer Science and Technology. Ed. Jack Belzer, A. G. Holzman, and Allen Kent. New York: Dekker, 1975–present.

Bibliographies to Electronics Books and Other Sources

Annotated Bibliography of Electronic Data Processing. Gainesville: U of Florida P, 1968.

Bibliography of the History of Electronics. Ed. George Shiers. Metuchen: Scarecrow, 1972.

Electronics: A Bibliographical Guide. Ed. C. K. Moore and K. J. Spencer. 2 vols. New York: Plenum, 1965.

Data Base for Electronics Literature

SCISEARCH

Index to Journal Articles

Applied Science and Technology Index. New York: H. W. Wilson, 1958–date.

  Indexes economics articles in journals such as Bell System Technical Journal, Electrical Communication, Electrical Engineer, Electrical Review, Electronic News, Electronics, Electronics Letters and many more.

ETHNIC STUDIES

Guides and Bibliographies to American Indian Literature

American Indian Novelists: An Annotated Critical Bibliography. New York: Garland, 1982.

An Annotated Bibliography of American Indian and Eskimo Autobiographies. Lincoln: U of Nebraska P, 1981.

Guide to Research on North American Indians. Ed. Arlene Hirschfelder. Chicago: ALA, 1983.

Studies in American Indian Literature: Critical Essays and Course Designs. New York: MLA, 1983.

Guides to Asian American Studies

Chen, Jack. The Chinese of America. New York: Harper, 1980.

Melendy, Henry Brett. Asians in America: Filipinos, Koreans, and East Indians. New York: Hippocrene, 1981.

Montero, Darrel. Vietnamese Americans: Patterns of Resettlement and Socioeconomic Adaptation in the United States. Boulder: Westview, 1979.

Wilson, Robert A., and Bill Hosokawa. East to America: A History of the Japanese in the United States. New York: Quill, 1980.

Guides and Bibliographies to Black American Studies
(See also Black Literature, 256)

Bibliographic Guide to Black Studies. Boston: Hall, 1975–present.

A Bibliography of the Negro in Africa and America. Ed. M. N. Work. New York: Octagon, 1966.

Black Index: Afro-Americans in Selected Periodicals 1907–1949. New York: Garland, 1981.

Dictionary of American Negro Biography. Ed. R. W. Logan and M. R. Winton. New York: Norton, 1982.

Encyclopedia of Black America. Ed. W. A. Low. New York: McGraw, 1981.

Hughes, Langston, et al. A Pictorial History of Black Americans. 5th rev. ed. New York: Crown, 1983.

Index to Periodical Articles By and About Negroes. Boston: Hall, 1971.

The Negro Almanac. 4th ed. New York: Wiley, 1983.

Negro in the United States: A Research Guide. Ed. E. K. Welsch. Bloomington: Indiana UP, 1965.

Who's Who Among Black Americans. Northbrook: WWABA, 1976–present.

Guides and Bibliographies to Hispanic American Studies

Chicano Literature: A Reference Guide. Ed. J. A. Martinez and F. A. Lomeli. Westport: Greenwood, 1985.

Chicano Literature. Ed. C. M. Tatum. New York: Hall, 1982.

Hispanic American Periodicals Index. Los Angeles: UCLA Latin American Center, 1974–present.

Hispanics in the United States: A New Social Agenda. Ed. P. S. J. Cafferty and W. McCready. New Brunswick: Transaction, 1984.

Literaturea Chicana. Comp R. G. Trujillo. Floricanto Press, 1985.

Manual of Hispanic Bibliography. 2nd ed. Ed. D. W. Foster and V. R. Foster. New York: Garland, 1976.

Pablo Neruda: An Annotated Bibliography of Criticism. Ed. D. S. Zubatsky and H. C. Woodbridge. New York: Garland, 1984.

¿Quien Sabe?: A Preliminary List of Chicano Reference Materials. Los Angeles: U of California Chicano Studies Research Center, 1981.

Sourcebook of Hispanic Culture in the United States. Chicago: ALA, 1983.

Spanish-American Women Writers: A Bibliographical Research Checklist. Ed. L. E. R. Cortina. New York: Garland, 1982.

Data Bases for Ethnic Studies

SOCIAL SCISEARCH
AMERICA: LIFE AND HISTORY
POPULATION BIBLIOGRAPHY
SOCIOLOGICAL ABSTRACTS

Indexes to Journal Articles on Ethnic Issues

Social Sciences Index.

Indexes articles on many ethnic topics in journals such as *American Journal of Physical Anthropology, Aztlan, Black Scholar, Ethnic Groups, Ethnic and Racial Studies, Ethnohistory, Ethnology, Journal of Black Studies, Journal of Ethnic Studies, Japan Quarterly, Modern Asian Studies,* and others.

MLA International Bibliography.

Indexes ethnic languages and ethnic literature.

GEOGRAPHY

General Guides to the Literature

Aids to Geographical Research. Ed. J. K. Wright and E. T. Platt. 2nd ed. Greenwood, 1971.

Encyclopedia of Geographic Information Sources. Ed. Paul Wasserman et al. 3rd ed. Detroit: Gale, 1978.

Geography and Cartography: A Reference Handbook. 3rd ed. Hamden, CT: Shoe String, 1976.

Goode's World Atlas. Ed. E. B. Espenshade. 17th ed. Chicago: Rand McNally, 1985.

How to Find Out in Geography: A Guide to Current Books in English. Ed. Charles S. Minto. New York: Pergamon, 1966.

The Literature of Geography: A Guide to Its Organization and Use. Hamden: Shoe String, 1978.

Research Catalogue of the American Geographical Society. 15 vols. Boston: Hall, 1962.

Source Book in Geography. Ed. George Kish. Cambridge: Harvard UP, 1978.

The Times Atlas of the World. Rev. ed. New York: Times Books, 1980.

Bibliographies to Geography Books and Other Sources

Geographers: Bibliographical Studies. Ed. T. W. Freeman et al. Lawrence: Merrimack, 1980.

Geography and Local Administration: A Bibliography. Ed. Keith Hoggart. Monticello, IL: Vance, 1980.

Geologic Reference Sources: A Subject and Regional Bibliography. Ed. D. C. Ward, M. Wheeler, and R. Bier. 2nd ed. Metuchen: Scarecrow, 1981.

International List of Geographical Serials. 3rd ed. Chicago: U of Chicago, 1980.

Data Bases to Geography Information

ERIC
GEOARCHIVE
GEOREF
SOCIAL SCISEARCH
SPIN

Index to Geography Journal Articles

Social Sciences Index

Indexes articles in such journals as *American Cartographer, Cartographic Journals, Cartography, Economic Geography, Geographical Analysis, Geographical Journal, Geographical Magazine, Geographical Review, Geography, Journal of Geography, Journal of Historical Geography,* and others.

Serial Bibliographies in the Humanities and Social Sciences. Ann Arbor: Pierian, annually.

GEOLOGY

General Guides to the Literature

Dictionary of Geology. 5th ed. New York: Oxford, 1978.

Glossary of Geology. Ed. R. L. Bates and J. A. Jackson. Falls Church: AGI, 1980.

Guide to Information Sources in Mining, Minerals, and Geosciences. Ed. S. R. Kaplan. New York: McGraw, 1978.

McGraw-Hill Encyclopedia of the Geological Sciences. New York: McGraw, 1978.

Sourcebook in Geology: Fourteen Hundred to Nineteen Hundred. Ed. K. F. Mather. Cambridge: Harvard UP, 1970.

Use of Earth Sciences Literature. Ed. D. N. Wood. New York: Archon, 1973.

Bibliographies to Books and Other Sources

Bibliography and Index of Geology. Boulder: GSA, monthly with annual indexes.

Bibliography of North American Geology. 49 vols. Washington: Geological Survey, 1923–1971.

Catalog of the U. S. Geological Survey Library. Boston: Hall, 1964. Supplements.

Geological Reference Sources: A Subject and Regional Bibliography. Ed. D. Ward and M. Wheeler. Metuchen: Scarecrow, 1972.

New Publications of the Geological Survey. Washington: Geological Survey, 1971–present, monthly.

Data Bases to Geology Literature

GEOARCHIVE
GEOREF

Indexes to Geology Journal Articles

Bibliography and Index of Geology. Boulder: GSA, monthly.

Indexes geology journals, such as *American Journal of Science, American Mineralogist, Chemical Geology, Earth Science, Geological Magazine, Geological Society of America Bulletin, Geology, Journal of Geology,* and others.

HEALTH AND PHYSICAL EDUCATION

(see also EDUCATION and MEDICINE)

General Guides to the Literature

Author's Guide to Journals in the Health Field. New York: Haworth, 1980.

Completed Research in Health, Physical Education, and Recreation. Washington: AAHPER, 1980.

Consumer Health Information Source Book. New York: Bowker, 1981.

The Dance Encyclopedia. Ed. A. Chujoy and P. W. Manchester. New York: Simon and Schuster, 1978.

Encyclopedia of Sports. New York: Barnes and Noble, 1978. Supplements.

Foundations of Physical Education. Ed. C. A. Bucher. 8th ed. Philadelphia: Lea & Febiger, 1979.

Health Maintenance Through Food and Nutrition: A Guide to Information Sources. Ed. H. D. Ullrich. Detroit: Gale, 1981.

Health Statistics: A Guide to Information Sources. Detroit: Gale, 1980.

Introduction to Reference Sources in Health Sciences. Ed. F. Roper and J. Boorkman. Chicago: Medical Library, 1980.

Research in Dance. Washington: AAHPER, 1973.

Research Processes in Physical Education, Recreation, and Health. Englewood Cliffs: Prentice, 1970.

Bibliographies to Books and Other Sources

Annotated Bibliography of Health Economics. Ed. A. J. Culyer et al. New York: St. Martin's, 1977.

Bibliography of Research Involving Female Subjects. Washington: AAHPER, 1975.

Data Bases

ERIC
SOCIAL SCISEARCH

Indexes to Journal Articles
(see also EDUCATION and MEDICINE)

Current Index to Journals in Education. Phoenix: Oryx, 1969–present.

> Indexes articles on physical education and health education in such journals as *Journal of Physical Education and Recreation, Journal of School Health, Physical Educator, Research Quarterly for Exercise and Sport,* plus many others.

Education Index

HISTORY

General Guides to Historical Literature

Britannica Book of the Year. Chicago: Encyclopaedia Britannica, 1938–present.

Dictionary of American History. Ed. M. Martin and L. Gelber. Rev. ed. Totowa: Littlefield, 1978.

Encyclopedia of American History. Ed. Richard Morris. 6th ed. New York: Harper, 1982.

Encyclopedia of World History. 5th ed. Boston: Houghton, 1972.

Facts on File Yearbook. New York: Facts on File, 1946–present.

Guide to American Foreign Relations Since 1700. Ed. R. D. Burns. Santa Barbara: ABC-Clio, 1983.

Guide to Historical Method. Ed. R. J. Shafer. 3rd ed. Dorsey, 1980.

Harvard Guide to American History. Ed. F. Freidel. Cambridge: Harvard UP, 1974.

Goldentree Bibliographies in History. Northbrook: AHM, n.d.

Library Research Guide to History. Ed. E. Frick. New York: Pierian, 1980.

McCoy, F. N. *Researching and Writing in History: A Practical Handbook for Students.* Berkeley: U of California P, 1974.

Narrative and Critical History of America. Ed. Justin Winso. 8 vols. 1889; New York: AMS, 1978.

Pulton, H. J. and M. S. Howland. *The Historian's Handbook.* Norman: U of Oklahoma P, 1977.

Research in Archives: The Use of Unpublished Primary Sources. Ed. P. C. Brooks. Chicago: U of Chicago P, 1968.

Writing History Papers. Ed. J. D. Bennett and L. H. Harrison. St. Louis: Forum, 1979.

Bibliographies to History Books and Other Sources

Bibliography of English History. Oxford: Clarendon, 1928–present.

Bibliographer's Manual of American History. 5 vols. New York: Gordon, n.d.

Combined Retrospective Indexes to Journals in History: 1838–1974. 11 vols. Arlington: Carrollton, 1977.

English Historical Reviews. (This journal regularly features valuable bibliographies.)

Facts on File Master Indexes. New York: Facts on File, 1946–date.

Historical Abstracts. Santa Barbara: ABC-Clio, 1955–present.

Historical Bibliography. Ed. D. Williamson. Hamden: Shoe String, 1967.

International Bibliography of Historical Sciences. New York: Wilson, 1930–present.

Writings on American History, 1981–82: A Subject Bibliography of Articles. Ed. C. H. Dadian. Washington: AHA, 1983.

Data Bases to History Literature

AMERICA: HISTORY AND LIFE
HISTORICAL ABSTRACTS

Indexes to Journal Articles

America: History and Life: Abstracts, Citations, Bibliographies, and Indexes.

American Historical Association. *Recently Published Articles.*

> Both works above index articles on American history in journals such as *American Historical Review, Civil War History, Journal of American History, Journal of the West, Reviews in American History,* and many others.

Humanities Index.

Indexes general world history in such journals as *Canadian Journal of History, English Historical Review, European Historical Quarterly, Journal of Modern History,* and many others.

JOURNALISM/MASS COMMUNICATIONS

General Guides to the Literature

The Associated Press Stylebook. New York: AP, 1977.

Encyclopedia of Twentieth-Century Journalists. Ed. William H. Taft. New York: Garland, 1984.

Galvin, Kathy. *Media Law: A Legal Handbook for the Working Journalist.* Berkeley: Nolo Press, 1984.

Journalist's Bookshelf. Ed. R. E. Wolseley and Isabel Wolseley. 8th ed. Atlanta: Berg, 1985.

Media Research: An Introduction. Ed. R. D. Wimmer and J. R. Dominick. Belmont: Wadsworth, 1982.

Nelson, Harold L., and Dwight L. Teeter, Jr. *Law of Mass Communications.* 4th ed. Mineola, NY: Foundation, 1981.

U.S. Television Network News: A Guide to Sources in English. Comp. M. J. Smith, Jr. Jefferson, NC: McFarland, 1984.

Bibliographies to Journalism Books and Other Sources

Annotated Media Bibliography. Ed. B. Congdon. Washington: ACC, 1985.

An Annotated Journalism Bibliography: 1958–1968. Minneapolis: U of Minnesota P, 1970.

Basic Books in the Mass Media. Ed. Eleanor Blum. Champaign: U of Illinois P, 1980.

Journalism Biographies: Master Index. Detroit: Gale, 1979. Supplements.

The Literature of Journalism: An Annotated Bibliography. Ed. Warren C. Price. Minneapolis: U of Minnesota P, 1959.

Multi-Media Reviews Index. Ed. C. W. Wall and P. B. Northern. Ann Arbor: Pierian, 1972.

News Media and Public Policy: An Annotated Bibliography. Ed. J. P. McKerns. 2 vols. New York: Garland, 1985.

Data Bases

AP NEWS
NATIONAL NEWSPAPER INDEX
MAGAZINE INDEX
NEWSEARCH
UPI NEWS

Indexes to Journalism Articles

Humanities Index.

Indexes journalism articles in such journals as *Journalism History, Journalism Quarterly, Columbia Journalism Review, Commentary, Quill, Encounter, Communications Quarterly, Journal of Broadcasting,* and others.

Readers' Guide to Periodical Literature.

Indexes news magazines, such as *Nation, Newsweek, New York Review of Books, New Republic, Saturday Review, U.S. News and World Report,* and others.

Resources in Education. Washington: ERIC, monthly.

Indexes articles on journalism education.

LANGUAGE AND LITERATURE

General Guides and Bibliographies to the Literature

Abstracts of English Studies. Urbana: NCTE, 1958–present.

Book Review Digest. New York: Wilson, 1905–present.

Book Review Index. Detroit: Gale, 1965–present.

Concise Bibliography for Students of English. Stanford: Stanford UP, 1972.

Contemporary Authors. Detroit: Gale, 1962–present.

Contemporary Literary Criticism. 14 vols. Detroit: Gale, 1973–present.

Essay and General Literature Index. New York: Wilson, 1934–present.

Fiction Catalog. New York: Wilson, 1980. Supplements annually.

McGill's Bibliography of Literary Criticism. Ed.
Frank McGill. 4 vols. Englewood Cliffs:
Salem Press, 1979.
*Selective Bibliography for the Study of English
and American Literature.* Ed. R. D. Altick
and A. Wright. 6th ed. New York: Macmillan,
1979.

American Literature

American Bibliography. Ed. Charles Evans. 14
vols. Magnolia, MA: Smith, 1967.
American Literary Scholarship. Durham: Duke
UP, 1963–present.
American Literature: Poe Through Garland.
Comp. H. H. Clark. New York: AHM, 1971.
American Novel: 1789 to 1968. Ed. D. Ger-
stenberger and George Hendrick. Chicago:
Swallow, 1961 & 1970.
American Writers. 4 vols. 5 suppl. New York:
Scribner's, 1961–81.
Backgrounds of American Literary Thought.
Ed. R. W. Horton and H. W. Edwards. 2nd ed.
New York: Meredith, 1967.
*Bibliographical Guide to the Study of Litera-
ture of the USA.* Ed. C. Gohdes. 4th ed. Dur-
ham: Duke UP, 1976.
*A Bibliographical Guide to the Study of West-
ern American Literature.* Ed. R. W. Etulain.
Lincoln: U of Nebraska P, 1982.
Bibliography of American Literature. New Ha-
ven; Yale UP, 1955–present.
*Bibliography of Bibliographies in American
Literature.* Ed. Charles H. Nilon. New York:
Bowker, 1970.
*Eight American Authors: A Survey of Research
and Criticism.* Ed. James Woodress. Rev. ed.
New York: Norton, 1971.
*Guide to American Literature and Its Back-
grounds Since 1890.* Ed. J. M. Jones and R. M.
Ludwig. 4th ed. Cambridge: Harvard UP,
1972.
Kazin, Alfred. *An American Procession.* New
York: Random House, 1984.
Literary History of the United States. Ed. R. E.
Spiller et al. 4th ed. 2 vols. New York: Mac-
millan, 1974.
Mathiessen, F. O. *American Renaissance.* Lon-
don: Oxford UP, 1941.
Modern American Literature. Ed. D. Nyren. 4th
ed. New York: Unger, 1969–76.
Oxford Companion to American Literature.
Ed. J. D. Hart. 5th ed. New York: Oxford UP,
1983.
*Sixteen Modern American Authors: A Survey of
Research and Criticism.* Ed. J. R. Bryer. New
York: Norton, 1969.
*The Transcendentalists: A Review of Research
and Criticism.* Ed. Joel Myerson. New York:
MLA, 1984.

Black Literature

Bibliographic Guide to Black Studies. New
York: Hall, 1980. Supplements.
*A Bibliography of Neo-African Literature from
Africa, America, and the Caribbean.* New
York: Grove Press, 1966.
*Black American Fiction Since 1952: A Prelim-
inary Checklist.* Ed. F. Deodene and W. P.
French. Metuchen: Scarecrow, 1970.
Black American Fiction: A Bibliography. Ed. C.
Fairbanks and E. A. Engeldinger. Metuchen:
Scarecrow, 1978.
Black American Writers: Bibliographic Essays.
2 vols. New York: St. Martin's, 1978.
*Black American Writers Past and Present: A
Biographical and Bibliographical Dictio-
nary.* Ed. T. G. Rush et al. Metuchen: Scare-
crow, 1975.
*Black Americans in Autobiography: An Anno-
tated Bibliography of Autobiographies and
Autobiographical Books Written Since the
Civil War.* Durham: Duke UP, 1974.
Black Literature Resources. New York: Dekker,
1975.
Blacks in America: Bibliographic Essays. Ed.
James P. McPherson, et al. New York: Dou-
bleday, 1971.
*Conjuring: Black Women, Fiction, and Liter-
ary Tradition.* Bloomington: Indiana UP,
1985.
Davis, Arthur. *From the Dark Tower: Afro-
American Writers from 1900 to 1960.* Wash-
ington: Howard UP, 1974.
*The Negro in American Literature and a Bibli-
ography of Literature by and about Negro
Americans.* Ed. Abraham Chapman. Osh-
kosh: Wisconsin Council of Teachers of
English, 1966.
Poetry of the Negro: 1746–1970. Ed. Langston
Hughes and Arna Bontempts. New York:
Doubleday, 1970.
Whitlow, Roger. *Black American Literature: A
Critical History.* Totowa: NJ: Littlefield,
1974.

British Literature

Anglo-Irish Literature: A Review of Research.
Ed. Richard J. Finneran. New York: MLA,
1976. Supplement, 1983.
Baker, Ernest A. *History of the English Novel.* 11
vols. 1967. New York: Barnes, 1975.
*Bibliographical Resources for the Study of
Nineteenth Century English Fiction.* Ed. G.
N. Ray. Folcroft, PA: Folcroft, 1964.
British Writers. Ed. Ian Scott-Kilvert. 8 vols.
New York: Scribner's, 1979–83.
British Writers and Their Works. 10 vols. Lin-
coln: U of Nebraska P, 1964–70.

Cambridge Bibliography of English Literature. Ed. G. Wilson. 5 vols. New York: Cambridge UP, 1965.

Cambridge History of English Literature. 15 vols. Cambridge: Cambridge UP, 1961.

A Descriptive Catalogue of the Bibliographies of Twentieth Century British Poets, Novelists, and Dramatists. Ed. E. W. Mellown. 2nd ed. Troy, NU: Whitston, 1978.

Directory of Literary Biography. Detroit: Gale, 1983–85.

Encyclopedia of Victorian Britain. Ed. Sally Mitchell. New York: Garland, 1987 forthcoming.

The English Romantic Poets: A Review of Research and Criticism. 3rd ed. New York: MLA, 1972.

Evans, Gareth L., and Barbara Evans. *The Shakespeare Companion.* New York: Scribner's, 1978.

Garland Shakespeare Bibliographies. 18 vols. New York: Garland, 1980–present. Work in progress.

McGraw-Hill Guide to English Literature. 2 vols. Ed. K. Lawrence, B. Seifter, and L. Ratner. New York: McGraw, 1985.

Modern British Literature. 4 vols. Literary Criticism Series. New York: Ungar, 1966–75.

Oxford History of English Literature. Oxford: Clarendon, 1945–present.

Romantic Movement Bibliographies. New York: MLA, 1980–present.

Victorian Fiction: A Guide to Research. New York: MLA, 1980. [Covers research through 1962.]

Victorian Fiction: A Second Guide to Research. Ed. G. H. Ford. New York: MLA, 1978. [Covers research 1963–74.]

Victorian Prose: A Guide to Research. Ed. David J. DeLaura. New York: MLA, 1973.

Drama and Theater

American Drama Criticism: Interpretations, 1890–1977. Ed. F. E. Eddleman. Hamden: Shoe String, 1979. Supplement 1984.

Bailey, J. *A Guide to Reference and Bibliography for Theatre Research.* 2nd ed. Columbus: Ohio State U, 1983.

Catalog of the Theatre and Drama Collections. Boston: Hall, 1967. Supplements.

Cheshire, David F. *Theatre: History, Criticism, and Reference.* Archon, 1967.

Chicorel Theater Index to Drama Books and Periodicals. Ed. M. Chicorel. New York: Chicorel Library, 1975.

Contemporary Dramatists. Ed. J. Vinson. 3rd ed. New York: St. Martin's, 1982.

Cumulated Dramatic Index: 1909–1949. 2 vols. Boston: Hall, 1965.

Cumulated Dramatic Index. 2 vols. Westwood: Faxon, 1965.

Drama Criticism. 2 vols. Denver: Swallow, 1970.

Dramatic Criticism Index. Ed. P. F. Breed and F. M. Sniderman. Detroit: Gale, 1972.

Index to Full Length Plays. 3 vols. Westwood: Faxon, 1956–1965.

Index to Plays in Periodicals. Metuchen: Scarecrow, 1979.

McGraw-Hill Encyclopedia of World Drama. 5 vols. New York: McGraw, 1984.

Modern Drama: A Checklist. Metuchen: Scarecrow, 1967.

Oxford Companion to the Theatre. 4th ed. Fair Lawn: Oxford UP, 1984.

Play Index. 6 Vols. New York: H. W. Wilson, 1953–present.

A Survey and Bibliography of Renaissance Drama. 4 vols. Lincoln: U of Nebraska P, 1975–78.

Language Studies

American Literature and Language: A Guide to Information Sources. Detroit: Gale, 1982.

A Concise Bibliography for Students of English. 5th ed. Stanford: Stanford UP, 1972.

A Dictionary of American English on Historical Principals. Ed. W. Craigie and J. R. Hulbert. 4 vols. Chicago: U of Chicago P, 1938–1944.

Oxford English Dictionary. Ed. J. A. H. Murray, et al. 13 vols. New York: Oxford UP, 1933.

Mythology and Folklore

American Folklore: A Bibliography. Metuchen: Scarecrow, 1977.

The Arthurian Encyclopedia. Ed. N. J. Lacy. New York: Garland, 1984.

Arthurian Legend and Literature: An Annotated Bibliography. 2 vols. New York: Garland, 1983.

Bibliography of Greek Myth in English Poetry. Ed. H. H. Law. Folcroft, 1955.

Dictionary of Classical Mythology. Ed. R. S. Bell. Santa Barbara: ABC-Clio, 1982.

Bullfinch's Mythology. New York: Avenel, 1978.

Campbell, Joseph. *Historical Atlas of World Mythology.* San Francisco: Harper, 1983–in progress.

Fable Scholarship: An Annotated Bibliography. Ed. Pack Carnes. New York: Garland, 1982.

Folklore and Literature in the United States: An Annotated Bibliography. Ed. S. S. Jones. New York: Garland, 1984.

Frazer, Sir James. *The Golden Bough.* New York: Avenel, 1981.

Index to Fairy Tales, Myths, and Legends. Ed. M. H. Eastman. 2nd ed. Westwood: Faxon, 1926. Supplements.

Index to Fairy Tales, 1949–1972. Ed. N. O. Ireland. Westwood: Faxon, 1973.

Storyteller's Sourcebook. Detroit: Gale, 1982.

Novel

American Fiction: A Contribution Toward a Bibliography. Ed. Lyle H. Wright. 3 vols. San Marino: Huntington Library, 1969, 1979.

American Fiction 1900–1950: A Guide to Information Service. Ed. James Woodress. Detroit: Gale, 1974.

The American Novel. Ed. Christof Wegelin. New York: Macmillan, 1977.

The American Novel 1789–1959: A Checklist of Twentieth Century Criticism. Denver: Swallow, 1961.

The American Novel: A Checklist. Volume 2: Criticism Written 1960–68. Ed. D. Gerstenberger and G. Hendrick. Chicago: Swallow, 1970.

Chase, Richard. *American Novel and Its Tradition.* Baltimore: Johns Hopkins, 1980.

The Contemporary Novel: A Checklist of Critical Literature on the British and American Novel Since 1945. Ed. I. Adelman and R. Dworkin. Metuchen: Scarecrow, 1972.

The Contemporary English Novel: An Annotated Bibliography of Secondary Sources. Ed. H. W. Drescher and Bernd Kahrmann. New York: IPS, 1973.

The Continental Novel: A Checklist of Criticism in English, 1900–1960. Metuchen: Scarecrow, 1968. Supplements 1967–83.

English Novel: 1578–1956: A Checklist of Twentieth Century Criticism. Ed. J. F. Bell and D. Baird. Denver: Swallow, 1958.

English Novel Explication: Criticism to 1972. Ed. Helen Palmer and Jane Dyson. Hamden: Shoe String, 1973. Supplement: 1976–present.

Holman, C. Hugh. *American Novel Through Henry James.* Arlington Heights: Harlan Davidson, 1973.

Watt, Ian. *British Novel: Scott through Hardy.* Arlington Heights: Harlan Davidson, 1973.

Wiley, Paul L. *British Novel: Conrad to the Present.* Arlington Heights: Harlan Davidson, 1973.

Poetry

American and British Poetry: A Guide to the Criticism. Athens, OH: Swallow, 1984.

English Poetry: Select Bibliographical Guides.

Ed. A. E. Dyson. New York: Oxford UP, 1971.

Granger's Index to Poetry. Ed. W. J. Smith. 7th ed. New York: Columbia UP, 1982.

Pearce, Roy Harvey. *The Continuity of American Poetry.* Princeton: Princeton UP, 1961.

Poetry Explication: A Checklist of Interpretations since 1925 of British and American Poems Past and Present. Boston: Hall, 1980.

Subject Index to Poetry for Children and Young People. Ed. D. B. Frizzell-Smith and Eva L. Andrews. Chicago: ALA, 1977.

Waggoner, Hyatt H. *American Poetry: From the Puritans to the Present.* Boston: Houghton, 1968.

Short Story

American Short-Fiction Criticism and Scholarship, 1959–1977: A Checklist. Ed. Joe Weixlmann. Athens: Ohio UP, 1982.

Short Story Index. Ed. D. E. Cook and I. S. Monro. New York: Wilson, 1953. Supplements.

Short Story Index: Collections Indexed 1900–1978. New York: Wilson, 1979.

Twentieth-Century Short Story Explication. Ed. W. S. Walker. 3rd ed. Hamden, CT: Shoe String, 1977.

World Literature

Columbia Dictionary of Modern European Literature. Ed. Jean-Albert Bede and William Edgerton. Columbia UP, 1980.

A Critical Bibliography of German Literature in English Translation: 1481–1927. Ed. B. Q. Morgan. Metuchen: Scarecrow, 1965.

Directory of World Literary Terms. Ed. J. T. Shipley. Boston: Writer, n.d.

The Oxford Companion to Classical Literature. Ed. Paul Harvey. 2nd ed. New York: Oxford UP, 1937.

The Oxford Companion to French Literature. Ed. P. Harvey and J. E. Heseltine. Oxford: Clarendon, 1959.

Reader's Companion to World Literature. Ed. L. H. Horstein. Rev. ed. New York: NAL, 1973.

Data Bases for Literature and Language Studies

BOOK REVIEW INDEX
LLBA (Language and Language Behavior Abstracts)
MLA BIBLIOGRAPHY

Indexes to Articles in Literary Journals

MLA International Bibliography of Books and Articles on the Modern Language and Literatures. New York: Modern Language Association, 1921–present. Annually.

> The best overall index to major literary figures and language topics.

Abstracts of English Studies. Urbana: NCTE, 1958–date.

> Provides abstracts to monographs and journal articles. 10th issue each year features a subject index.

Abstracts of Folklore Studies. Austin: U of Texas P, 1962–date.

> Indexes folklore journals, such as *Dovetail, Kentucky Folklore Record, Relics,* and others.

Book Review Digest
Book Review Index
Current Book Review Citations
Index to Book Reviews in the Humanities

> Consult one of the four indexes above for reviews of novels and other literary works.

Humanities Index.

> Provides general indexing to literary and language topics.

FOREIGN LANGUAGES
French

An Annotated Bibliography of French Language and Literature. Ed. F. Bassan, et al. New York: Garland, 1975.

Concise Bibliography of French Literature. Ed. Denis Mahaffey. New York: Bowker, 1976.

Critical Bibliography of French Literature: The Eighteenth Century Supplement. Ed. R. A. Brooks. Syracuse: Syracuse UP, 1968.

Critical Bibliography of French Literature: Twentieth Century. Ed. D. W. Alden and R. A. Brooks. Syracuse: Syracuse UP, 1979.

Dictionnaire étymologiquede la langue française. New York: French and European, 1975.

Dictionnaire de litterature française contemporaine. New York: French and European, 1977.

French Literature: An Annotated Guide to Selected Bibliographies. Ed. R. Kempton. New York: MLA, 1981.

French Twenty Bibliography: Critical and Biographical References for the Study of French Literature Since 1885. Ed. D. W. Alden. New York: French Institute, 1981.

Grand larousse encyclopedique. 24 vols. Elmsford, NY: Maxwell, 1973. Supplements.

Modern French Literature and Language: A Bibliography of Homage Studies. Ed. L. Griffin. Ann Arbor: University Microfils, 1976.

Oxford Companion to French Literature. Ed. Paul Harvey and Janet Heseltine. Oxford: Clarendon, 1959.

German

Bibliography of German Plays on Microcards. Ed. Norman Binger. Hamden, CT: Shoe String, 1970.

Critical Bibliography of German Literature in English Translation: 1481–1927. 1938; rpt. Metuchen: Scarecrow, 1965.

Der Grosse Duden. Ed. R. Duden. 10 vols. New York: Adler's, 1971.

Deutsches Woerterbuch. Ed. Jacob Grimm and Wilhelm Grimm. 32 vols. New York: Adler's, 1973.

German Periodical Publications. Ed. G. Erdelyi and A. F. Peterson. Stanford: Hoover, 1967.

Lese der Deutschen Lyrik: Von Klopstock bis Rilke. Ed. Friedrich Burns. New York: Irvington, 1961.

A Reference Guide to German Literature. Ed. U. K. Faulhaver and P. B. Goff. New York: Garland, 1979.

Reallexikon der deutschen Literaturgeschichte. Ed. W. Kohlschmidt and W. Mohr. 3 vols. New York: DeGruyter, 1958–1977.

Selected Bibliography of German Literature in English Translation: 1956–1960. Ed. M. F. Smith. Metuchen: Scarecrow, 1972.

Wer Ist Wer. 20th ed. New York: IPS, 1973. Supplements.

Who's Who in Germany: A Biographical Dictionary. 2 vols. New York: IPS, 1978. Supplements.

Latin

The Classical World Bibliography of Roman Drama and Poetry and Ancient Fiction. New York: Garland, n.d.

Mackail, John W. *Latin Literature.* New York: Ungar, 1966.

McGuire, Martin R., and Hermigild Dressler. *Introduction to Medieval Latin Studies: A Syllabus and Bibliographical Guide.* 2nd ed. Washington: Catholic UP, 1977.

Oxford Latin Dictionary. Ed. P. G. Glare. New York: Oxford UP, 1968–1980.

Repertoire des index et lexiques d'auteurs latins. Ed. Paul Faider. 1926; rpt. New York: Burt Franklin, 1971.

Wagenvoort, Henrik. *Studies in Roman Literature, Culture and Religion.* New York: Garland, 1978.

Russian Language

Basic Russian Publications: A Bibliographic Guide to Western-Language Publications. Ed. P. L. Horecky. Chicago: U of Chicago P, 1965.

Basic Russian Publications: A Selected and Annotated Bibliography on Russia and the Soviet Union. Ed. P. L. Horecky. Chicago: U of Chicago P, 1962.

Bibliography of Russian Literature in English Translation to 1945. Ed. M. B. Line. 1963; rpt. Totowa: Rowman, 1972.

Bibliography of Russian Word Formation. Ed. D. S. Worth. Columbus: Slavica, 1977.

Dictionary of Russian Literature. Ed. W. E. Harkins. 1956; rpt. Westport: Greenwood, 1971.

Encyclopedia of Russian and Soviet Literature. Gulf Breeze, FL: Academic International, 1979.

Guide to Bibliographies of Russian Literature. Ed. S. A. Zenkovsky and D. L. Armbruster. Nashville: Vanderbilt UP, 1970.

Guide to Russian Reference Books. Ed. Korol Maichel. 5 vols. Stanford: Hoover, 1962–1967.

Literature of the Soviet Peoples: A Historical and Biographical Survey. Ed. Harri Junger. New York: Ungar, 1971.

Who Was Who in the U.S.S.R. Metuchen: Scarecrow, 1972.

Spanish

Anderson, I. E. *Historia de la literatura hispanoamericans.* 2 vols. Mexico: Fondo, 1974.

Bibliography of Old Spanish Texts. Ed. Anthony Cardenas, et al. 2nd ed. Madison: Hispanic Seminary, 1977.

Bleznick, Donald W. *A Sourcebook for Hispanic Literature and Language.* Philadelphia: Temple UP, 1974.

Diccionario de la literatura latinoamerica. Washington: OAS, 1958.

Dissertations in Hispanic Languages and Literatures: An Index of Dissertations Completed in the United States and Canada. Ed. J. R. Chatham and Carmen C. McClendon. Lexington: UP of Kentucky, 1981.

Handbook of Latin American Studies. New York: Octagon, 1935–date.

Historia de la literatura espanola and hispanoamerica. Spain: Aguilar, 1983.

Index to Latin American Periodical Literature. New York: Hall, 1929–date.

The Literature of Spain in English Translation: A Bibliography. Comp. Robert S. Rudder. New York: Ungar, 1975.

Manual of Hispanic Bibliography. Seattle: U of Washington P, 1970.

Spanish Literature in English Translation: A Bibliographical Syllabus. Ed. A. Flores. New York: Gordon, n.d.

Spanish and Spanish-American Literature: An Annotated Guide to Selected Bibliographies. Ed. H. C. Woodbridge. New York: MLA, 1983.

Zimmerman, Irene. *Guide to Current Latin American Periodicals: Humanities and Social Sciences.* Gainesville: Kallman, 1961.

Data Base for Foreign Language Studies

MLA Bibliography

Index to Articles in Foreign Language Journals

MLA International Bibliography.

Indexes articles in journals such as *Yale French Studies, German Quarterly, Philological Quarterly, Journal of Spanish Studies,* and many others. It features special indexes to foreign language studies of the literature of the foreign country.

MATHEMATICS

General Guides to Mathematics Literature

How to Find Out in Mathematics. Ed. J. E. Pemberton. 2nd ed. Elmsford, NY: Pergamon, 1970.

International Catalogue of Scientific Literature: 1901–1914. Section A: Mathematics. Metuchen: Scarecrow, 1974.

Mathematics Encyclopedia: A Made Simple Book. Garden City: Doubleday, 1977.

NCTM Yearbook. Annually.

Use of Mathematical Literature. Ed. A. R. Darling. Boston: Butterworths, 1977.

Using Mathematical Literature: A Practical Guide. Ed. B. K. Schaefer. New York: Marcel Dekker, 1979.

The VNR Concise Encyclopedia of Mathematics. Ed. W. Gellert, et al. Florence, KY: Reinhold, 1977.

Bibliographies to Books and Other Sources

Annotated Bibliography of Expository Writing in the Mathematical Sciences. Ed. M. P. Gaffney and L. A. Steen. Washington: Mathematics Association, 1976.

Bibliography and Research Manual of the History of Mathematics. Ed. K. L. May. Toronto: U of Toronto P, 1973.

Current Information Sources in Mathematics: An Annotated Guide to Books and Periodicals: 1960–1971. Ed. E. M. Dick. Littleton: Libraries Unlimited, 1973.

Fifty-Year Index of the Mathematics Magazine. Ed. L. Steen and J. A. Seebach. Washington: Mathematics Association, 1979.

Schaaf, William L. *A Bibliography of Recreational Mathematics.* Washington: NCTM, 1970.

Schaaf, William L. *The High School Math Library.* Reston, VA: NCTM, 1982.

Vestpocket Bibliographies. Ed. William L. Schaaf. See miscellaneous issues of the *Journal of Recreational Mathematics,* 1983–present.

Data Base to Mathematics Literature

MATHFILE

Index to Journal Articles

Cumulative Index: The Mathematics Teacher, 1908–1965. Reston, VA: NCTM, 1967.

Classified indexes appear in each volume of *Mathematics Teacher.*

Index to *American Mathematical Monthly.* Montpelier: Mathematical Association of America, annually.

Mathematical Reviews. Providence: AMS, 1940–present.

MEDICAL STUDIES

General Guides to the Literature

Author's Guide to Journals in the Health Field. Ed. D. Ardell and J. James. New York: Haworth, 1980.

A Dictionary of Abbreviations in Medicine and in Health Sciences. Ed. H. K. Hughes. Lexington, MA: Lexington Books, 1977.

Guide to Library Resources for Nursing. Ed. K. P. Strauch and D. J. Brundage. New York: Appleton, 1980.

Health Maintenance Through Food and Nutrition: A Guide to Information Sources. Ed. H. D. Ullrich. Detroit: Gale, 1981.

Health Statistics: A Guide to Information Sources. Ed. F. O. Weise. Detroit: Gale, 1980.

Introduction to Reference Sources in Health Sciences. Ed. Fred Roper and JoAnne Boorkman. Chicago: MLA, 1980.

Polit, Denise, and Bernadette Hungler. *Nursing Research: Principles and Methods.* 2nd ed. Philadelphia: Lippincott, 1983.

Use of Medical Literature. Ed. L. T. Morton. 2nd ed. Butterworths, 1977.

Bibliographies to Books and Other Sources

An Annotated Bibliography of Health Economics. Ed. A. J. Culyer, et al. New York: St. Martin's, 1977.

Consumer Health Information Source Book. Ed. A. M. Rees and B. A. Young. New York: Bowker, 1981.

Health: A Multimedia Source Guide. New York: Bowker, 1976.

Medical Reference Works, 1679–1966. Ed. J. Blake and C. Roos. Medical Library Association, 1967. Supplements 1970–present.

Nursing Studies Index. Ed. Virginia Henderson. 4 vols. Philadelphia: Lippincott, 1957–72.

Resources for Third World Health Planners: A Selected Subject Bibliography. Buffalo: Conch, 1980.

Data Bases to Medical Literature

BIOSIS PREVIEWS
SCISEARCH
MEDLINE
EMBASE
NURSING AND ALLIED HEALTH

Indexes to Journal Articles

AJN International Nursing Index. New York: AJN, 1970–present.

Cumulative Index to Nursing and Allied Health Literature. Glendale: CINAHL, 1956–present.

Indexes nursing literature in journals such as *Cancer Nurse, Current Reviews for Recovery Room Nurses, Journal of Practical Nursing, Journal of Nursing Education,* and many more.

Cumulated Index Medicus. Bethesda: U. S. Department of Health and Human Services, 1959–present.

Provides general indexes to most medical journals.

MUSIC

General Guides to Music Literature

Baker's Biographical Dictionary of Musicians. 6th ed. New York: Schirmer, 1978.
Cyclopedia of Music and Musicians. 3 vols. New York: Gordon, 1974.
Dictionary of Music. Ed. Alan Isaacs and Elizabeth Martin. New York: Facts on File, 1983.
Encyclopedia of Pop, Rock, and Soul. Ed. Irwin Stambler. New York: St. Martin's, 1977.
Harvard Directory of Music. Ed. Willi Apel. 2nd rev. ed. Cambridge: Harvard UP, 1969.
Information on Music: A Handbook of Reference Sources in European Languages. 2 vols. Libraries Unlimited, 1975–1977.
International Cyclopedia of Music and Musicians. Ed. Bruce Bahle. 19th ed. New York: Dodd, 1975.
Music Reference and Research Materials. Ed. V. Duckles. 3rd ed. New York: Free Press, 1974.
New College Encyclopedia of Music. New York: Norton, 1981.
New Grove Dictionary of Music and Musicians. Ed. Stanley Sadie. New York: Macmillan, 1980.
Oxford Companion to Music. New York: Oxford UP, 1983.
Oxford History of Music. 8 vols. Totowa: Cooper Square, 1973.
World's Encyclopedia of Recorded Music. 3 vols. Westport: Greenwood, n.d.

Bibliographies to Music Books and Other Sources

Bibliographic Guide to Music. Boston: Hall, 1976. Supplements.
General Index to Modern Musical Literature in the English Language Including Periodicals for the Years 1915–1926. 1927; rpt. New York: DaCapo, 1970.
General Bibliography for Music Research. Ed. K. E. Mixter. 2nd ed. Detroit: Information Coordinators, 1975.
Muscia: Sources of Information in Music. Ed. J. H. Davies. 2nd ed. Elmsford, NY: Pergamon, 1969.

Popular Music: An Annotated Index of American Popular Songs. 6 vols. New York: Adrian, 1964–present.
Source Readings in Music History. Ed. Oliver Strunk. 5 vols. New York: Norton, 1950.

Data Base to Music Literature

RILM ABSTRACTS (Repertoire Internationale de Litterata Musicale)

Indexes to Journal Articles

Music Index. Detroit: Information Services, 1949–present.

Indexes music journals such as *American Music Teacher, Choral Journal, Journal of Band Research, Journal of Music Therapy, Music Journal, Musical Quarterly,* and many others.

Music Article Guide. Philadelphia: Information Services, 1966–present.

Indexes music education and instrumentation in such journals as *Brass and Wind News, Keyboard, Flute Journal, Piano Quarterly,* and many more.

RILM (Repertoire International de Litterature Musicale) New York: City U of New York, 1967–present.

Indexes international music information.

PHILOSOPHY

General Guides to the Literature

A Dictionary of Philosophy. Ed. P. A. Angeles. New York: Harper, 1981.
Dictionary of Philosophy. Ed. Dagobert D. Runes. Rev. ed. New York: Philosophical Library, 1981.
Encyclopedia of Philosophy. 4 vols. New York: Free Press, 1973.
A Guide to Philosophical Bibliography and Research. Ed. R. T. DeGeorge. New York: Appleton, 1971.
A History of Philosophy. 9 vols. Garden City: Doubleday, 1977.
How to Find Out in Philosophy and Psychology. Ed. D. H. Borchardt. Elmsford: Pergamon, 1968.

The Philosopher's Guide. Ed. R. T. DeGeorge. Lawrence, KS: Regents, 1980.
Research Guide to Philosophy. Ed. T. N. Tice and T. P. Slavens. Chicago: ALA, 1983.
Research in Philosophy. Ed. H. J. Koren. Atlantic Highlands, NJ: Duquesne, 1966.
Who's Who in Philosophy. 1942; rpt. Westport: Greenwood, n.d.
World Philosophy: Essay Reviews of 225 Major Works. Ed. Frank Magill. 5 vols. Englewood Cliffs: Salem, 1982.

Bibliographies to Philosophy Books and Other Sources

A Bibliography of Philosophical Bibliographies. Ed. Herbert Guerry. Westport: Greenwood, 1977.
A Bibliographical Survey for a Foundation in Philosophy. Ed. F. E. Jordack. Lanham, MD: U of America P, 1978.
The Classical World Bibliography of Philosophy, Religion, and Rhetoric. New York: Garland, n.d.
Philosophers Index. Bowling Green: Bowling Green U, 1967–present.
Philosophy and Psychology: Classification Schedule, Author and Title Listing. 2 vols. Cambridge: Harvard UP, 1973.
Philosophy: A Select, Classified Bibliography of Ethics, Economics, Law, Politics, Sociology. Ed. S. A. Matczak. Jamaica: NY: Learned Publishers, 1970.

Data Base to Philosophy Literature

PHILOSOPHER'S INDEX

Indexes to Journal Articles

Philosopher's Index. Bowling Green: Bowling Green U, 1967–present.

Indexes philosophy articles in journals such as *American Philosophical Quarterly, Humanist, Journal of the History of Ideas, Journal of Philosophy, Philosophical Review, Philosophy Today,* and many more.

Humanities Index.

Provides a general index to philosophical topics in journals such as *British Journal of Philosophy, Environmental Ethics, International Philosophy Quarter, Journal of the History of Ideas, Journal of Philosophy,* and many others.

POLITICAL SCIENCE

General Guides to the Literature

Bibliography on the American Left. Comp. L. M. Wilcox. Kansas City: ARS, 1981.
A Guide to Reference Materials in Political Science: American Government. Ed. C. E. Vose. Washington: APSA, 1975.
Guide to Reference Materials in Political Science. Ed. L. R. Wynar with Linda Fystrom. 2 vols. Denver: CBI, 1966–68.
Information Sources of Political Science. Ed. F. L. Holler. 3rd ed. Santa Barbara: ABC-Clio, 1981.
Political Handbook of the World. Ed. A. S. Banks. 6th ed. New York: McGraw, 1980.
Political Research and Political Theory. Ed. O. Garceau. Cambridge: Harvard UP, 1968.
Research in Political Science. Ed. E. S. Griffith. Port Washington, NY: Kennikat, 1969.
The Statesman's Yearbook. New York: St. Martin's Press, 1961–date.
Yearbook of the United Nations. Lake Success: United Nations, 1947–present.

Bibliographies to Political Science Books and Other Sources

Free-thought in the United States: A Descriptive Bibliography. Westport: Greenwood, 1978.
The Literature of Political Science: A Guide for Students, Librarians, and Teachers. New York: Bowker, 1969.
International Bibliography of Political Science. New York: IPS, 1979. Supplements.
Political Science: A Bibliographical Guide to the Literature. Metuchen: Scarecrow, 1965. Supplements 1966–present.

Data Bases to Political Science Literature

UNITED STATES POLITICAL SCIENCE DOCUMENTS
GPO MONTHLY CATALOG
PAIS
NATIONAL NEWSPAPER INDEX
WORLD AFFAIRS REPORT
CONGRESSIONAL RECORD ABSTRACTS

Indexes to Political Science Journal Articles

Social Sciences Index.

Indexes articles in such journals as *American Journal of Political Science, American Political Science Review,*

British Journal of Political Science,
Political Quarterly, Political Science
Quarterly, and many others.

P.A.I.S. (Public Affairs Information Service).
Indexes government-oriented articles.

ABC: Pol Sci. Santa Barbara: ABC-Clio, 1969–
present.
Indexes the tables of contents of about
300 international journals in the original language.

PHYSICS

General Guides to the Literature

American Institute of Physics Handbook. Ed.
D. E. Gray. New York: McGraw, 1972.
Annual Review of Nuclear Science. Palo Alto:
1952–date.
Encyclopedia of Physics. 2nd ed. New York:
Reinhold, 1974.
Encyclopedia of Physics. 54 vols. New York:
Springer, 1956–date.
Encyclopedia of Physics. Ed. Rita G. Lerner and
George L. Trigg. Reading: Addison, 1980.
A Guide to the Literature of Astronomy. Ed. R.
A. Seal. Libraries Unlimited, 1977.
How to Find Out About Physics. Ed. Bryan
Yates. New York: Pergamon, 1965.
An Introductory Guide to Information
Sources in Physics. Ed. L. R. A. Melton. Inst. of
Physics, 1978.
Physics Literature: A Reference Manual. Ed. R.
H. Whitford. 2nd ed. New York: Scarecrow,
1968.
Use of Physics Literature. Ed. H. Coblans.
Woburn, MA: Butterworths, 1975.

Bibliographies to Books and Other Sources

Physics Abstracts. London: IEE, 1898–present.
Bimonthly.
Solid State Physics Literature Guides. New
York: Plenum, 1972–present.
Sources of History of Quantum Physics. Ed. T.
S. Kuhn et al. Philadelphia: APS. 1967.

Data Bases to Physics Literature

SCISEARCH
SPIN (Searchable Physics Information
Notices)

Indexes to Journal Articles in Physics

Current Papers in Physics. London: IEE, 1966–
date. Bimonthly.
Current Physics Index. New York: American
Institute of Physics, 1975–date. Quarterly.
Consult both works above for indexing
to most articles in physics journals such
as *Applied Physics, Journal of Chem-*
ical Physics, Nuclear Physics, Physical
Review, Physics Letters, and many more.

Applied Science and Technology Index.
Indexes general physics topics in *Laser*
Focus, Monthly Weather Review, Physics
Today, and others.

PSYCHOLOGY

General Guides to the Literature

Alsip, J. E., and D. D. Chezik. *Research Guide in*
Psychology. General Learning Press, 1974.
Bachrach, A. J. *Psychological Research: An In-*
troduction. 4th ed. New York: Random,
1981.
Borchardt, D. H. *How to Find Out in Philoso-*
phy and Psychology. Elmsford, NY: Perga-
mon, 1968.
Encyclopedia of Human Behavior. Ed. R. M.
Goldenson. 2 vols. Garden City: Doubleday,
1974.
Encyclopedia of Psychology. 3 vols. New York:
Seaburg, 1979.
Research Guide for Psychology. Ed. R. G. McIn-
nis. Westport: Greenwood, 1982.

Bibliographies to Books and Other Sources

Annual Reviews of Psychology. Palo Alto:
Annual Reviews, 1950–date.
Bibliographical Guide to Psychology. Boston:
Hall, 1982. Supplements.
Bibliography of Aggressive Behavior: A Read-
er's Guide to the Research Literature. Ed. J. M.
Crabtree and K. E. Mayer. New York: Liss,
1977.
Coping and Adapting: A Behavioral Science
Bibliography. New York: Basic, 1974.
Counseling: A Bibliography with Annotations.
Ed. R. S. J. Freeman and H. A. Freeman. New
York: Scarecrow, 1964.

Cumulated Subject Index to Psychological Abstracts: 1927–1960. 2 vols. Boston: Hall, 1966. Supplements.

The Index of Psychoanalytic Writings. Ed. A. Grinstein. 14 vols. New York: International Universities, 1956–71.

Psychoanalysis, Psychology, and Literature: A Bibliography. Ed. Norman Kiell. 2nd ed. 2 vols. Metuchen: Scarecrow, 1982.

Psychological Abstracts. Lancaster, PA: APA, 1927–present.

Psychological Index. 42 vols. Princeton: Psychological Review, 1895–1936. Superseded by *Psychological Abstracts.*

Data Bases for Psychology Studies

CHILD ABUSE AND NEGLECT
ERIC
MENTAL HEALTH ABSTRACTS
PSYCHOLOGICAL ABSTRACTS
SOCIAL SCISEARCH
SOCIOLOGICAL ABSTRACTS

Indexes to Journal Articles

Psychological Abstracts.

Indexes and provides brief abstracts to psychology journals such as *American Journal of Psychology, Behavioral Science, Journal of Abnormal and Social Psychology, Psychological Review,* and many more.

Sociological Index.

Indexes socio-psychological issues.

Child Development Abstracts and Bibliography. Chicago: U of Chicago P, 1927–present.

Mental Retardation and Developmental Disabilities Abstracts. Washington: U. S. Department of Health, Education, and Welfare, 1964–present.

Indexes mental health topics.

RELIGION

General Guides to the Literature

Catholic Encyclopedia. Appleton, WI: Nelson, 1981.

Encyclopedia of American Religions. Ed. Gordon J. Melton. 2 vols. Wilmington, NC: McGrath, 1978.

Guide to Hindu Religion. Ed. David J. Dell. Boston: Hall, 1981.

The Interpreter's Bible. 12 vols. New York: Abingdon, 1951–57.

The Interpreter's Dictionary of the Bible. 5 vols. New York: Abingdon, 1976.

The International Standard Bible Encyclopedia. Ed. Geoffrey W. Bromley. Grand Rapids: Eerdmans, 1979–present.

Introduction to Theological Research. Ed. Cyril J. Barber. Moody, 1982.

Library Research Guide to Religion and Theology. Ed. James Kennedy. Ann Arbor: Pierian, 1973.

Lives of the Saints. Ed. Thurston Attwater. 4 vols. Westminster: Christian Classics, 1976.

Nelson's Complete Concordance to the Revised Standard Version of the Bible. Ed. John W. Ellison. New York: Nelson, 1978.

New Catholic Encyclopedia. 17 vols. New York: McGraw, 1977–79.

Oxford Dictionary of the Christian Church. New York: Oxford UP, 1974.

Philosophy of Religion: A Guide to Information Sources. Ed. Donald Capps et al. Detroit: Gale, 1976.

Research Guide to Religious Studies. Ed. J. F. Wilson and Thomas Slavens. Chicago: ALA, 1982.

A Reader's Guide to the Great Religions. Ed. C. J. Adams. 2nd ed. Riverside, NJ: Free Press, 1977.

Who's Who in Religion. Chicago: Marquis, 1975/76–present.

Yearbook of American and Canadian Churches. New York: Abingdon, annually.

Bibliographies to Books and Other Sources

Guide to Indexed Periodicals in Religion. Metuchen; Scarecrow, 1975.

Reference Works for Theological Research: An Annotated Selective Bibliographical Guide. Ed. Robert Kepple. 2nd ed. UP of America, 1981.

Religious Books and Serials in Print. New York: Bowker, annually.

Religions: A Select, Classified Bibliography. Ed. J. F. Mitros. New York: Learned, 1973.

Religion and Society in North America; An Annotated Bibliography. Ed. R. Brunkow. Santa Barbara: ABC-Clio, 1983.

A Theological Book List. Ed. R. P. Morris. Cambridge: Hadden, 1971.

Warden, Jacques. *Classical Approaches to the Study of Religion: Aims, Methods, and Theories of Research.* Part 2: *Bibliography.* Hawthorne, NY: Mouton, 1974.

Wiersbe, Warren W. *A Basic Library for Bible Students.* Grand Rapids, MI: Baker, 1981.

Data Base for Religious Studies

RELIGION INDEX

Indexes to Journal Articles

Religion: Index One: Periodicals, Religion and Theological Abstracts. (Formerly *Index to Religious Periodicals Literature*). Chicago: ATLA, 1949–present.

Indexes religious articles in journals such as *Biblical Research, Christian Scholar, Commonweal, Harvard Theological Review, Journal of Biblical Literature,* and many others.

The Catholic Periodical and Literature Index. New York: Catholic Library Assoc., 1934–present.

Indexes religious articles on Catholic issues.

Humanities Index.

Indexes general religious issues.

SOCIOLOGY and SOCIAL WORK

General Guides to the Literature

Encyclopedia of Sociology. Ed. Gayle Johnson. Guilford, CT: Dushkin, 1974.
Encyclopedia of Social Work. Ed. John Turner. 2 vols. New York: NASW, 1977.
Library Research Guide to Sociology: Illustrated Search Strategy and Sources. Ed. P. McMillan and J. R. Kennedy. Ann Arbor: Pierian, 1981.
Student Sociologist's Handbook. Ed. P. B. Bart and L. Frankel. 3rd ed. Glenview: Scott, 1981.

Bibliographies to Books and Other Sources

Index to Sociology Readers: 1960–1965. Ed. H. J. Abramson and Nicholas Sofios. 2 vols. Metuchen: Scarecrow, 1973.
Reference Sources in Social Work: An Annotated Bibliography. Ed. James H. Conrad. Metuchen: Scarecrow, 1982.
Sociological Aspects of Poverty: A Bibliography. Ed. H. P. Chalfant. Monticello, IL: Vance, 1890.

Sociology: Classification Schedule, Author and Title Listing, Chronological Listings. 2 vols. Cambridge: Harvard UP, n.d.

Data Bases to Sociological Literature

CHILD ABUSE AND NEGLECT
FAMILY RESOURCES
NCJRS (National Criminal Justice Reference Service)
SOCIAL SCISEARCH
SOCIOLOGICAL ABSTRACTS

Indexes to Journal Articles

Sociological Abstracts. New York: Sociological Abstracts, 1952–present.

Indexes and provides brief descriptions of articles in journals such as *American Journal of Sociology, Environment and Behavior, Journal of Applied Social Psychology, Journal of Marriage and the Family, Social Education, Social Research, Sociological Inquiry, Sociology,* and many others.

Humanities Index.

Provides a general index to sociological articles.

Social Work Research and Abstracts. New York: NASW, 1964, present.

Indexes social work articles.

Popular Periodical Index. Roslyn, PA: PPI, 1973–present.

Indexes contemporary and regional issues in magazines such as *GEO, Life, Ohio Magazine, Playboy, Rolling Stone, Texas Monthly,* and others.

SPEECH

(see also Drama and Theater, 257)

General Guides to the Literature

Index to Speech, Language, and Hearing: Journal Titles, 1954–78. San Diego: College Hill, n.d.
Research Guide in Speech. Ed. Gerilyn Tandberg. General Learning Press, 1974.

Bibliographies to Speech Books and Other Sources

Bibliography of Speech and Allied Areas, 1950–1960. Westport: Greenwood, 1972.
Rhetoric and Public Address: A Bibliography: 1947–1961. Madison: U of Wisconsin P, 1964. (Continued annually in *Speech Monographs*)
Radio and Television: A Selected Annotated Bibliography. Metuchen: Scarecrow, 1978.
Table of Contents of The Quarterly Journal of Speech, Speech Monographs, and Speech Teacher. Ed. John McPhee. New York: Farrar (in association with the Speech Association of America), 1985.

Data Bases to Speech Literature

MLA BIBLIOGRAPHIES
LLBA (Language and Language Behavior Abstracts)
ERIC
SOCIAL SCISEARCH

Indexes to Journal Articles

Humanities Index

Indexes such speech journals as *Communication, Journal of Communication, Quarterly Journal of Speech, Speech Monographs, and Studies in Public Communication.*

MLA International Bibliography.

Indexes rhetorical subjects.

WOMEN'S STUDIES

General Guides to the Literature

Fishburn, Katherine. *Women in Popular Culture: A Reference Guide.* Westport: Greenwood, 1982.
Guide to Social Science Resources in Women's Studies. Ed. E. H. Oakes and K. E. Sheldon. Santa Barbara, CA: ABC-Clio, 1978.
Lerner, Gerda. *Black Women in White America.* New York: Pantheon, 1972.
Index-Directory of Women's Media. Washington: Women's Institute for Freedom of the Press, 1975–present.

Index to Women of the World from Ancient to Modern Times: Biographies and Portraits. Westwood: Faxon, 1970.
Who's Who of American Women. Chicago: Marquis, 1958–present.
Womanhood Media: Current Resources About Women. Chicago, Marquis, 1958–date.
Women Today: A Multidisciplinary Approach to Women's Studies. Ed. M. A. Baker et al. Monterey: Brooks/Cole, 1979.
Women's Action Almanac: A Complete Resource Guide. Ed. J. Williamson et al. New York: Morrow, 1979.

Bibliographies to Books and Other Sources

American Women Writers: An Annotated Bibliography. Ed. B. A. White. New York: Garland, 1976.
Annotated Bibliography of Twentieth Century Critical Studies of Women and Literature; 1660–1800. New York: Garland, 1977.
Bibliography on Women Workers: 1961–1965. 2nd ed. Washington: International Labor Office, 1974.
New Feminist Scholarship: A Guide to Bibliographies. Ed. Jane Williamson. Westbury: Feminist Press, 1979.
Older Women in 20th-Century America: A Selected Annotated Bibliography. New York: Garland, 1982.
Women's Studies: A Recommended Core Bibliography. Ed. E. Stineman and C. Loeb. Littleton: Libraries Unlimited, 1979.
The Status of Women: A Selected Bibliography. New York: United Nations, n.d.
Women's Studies Abstracts. Honeoye: Rush, 1972–present.

Data Bases for Women's Studies

ERIC
SOCIAL SCISEARCH
SOCIOLOGICAL ABSTRACTS

Indexes to Journal Articles

Social Sciences Index

Indexes such journals as *Feminist Studies, Ms., Signs, Womanpower, Woman Activist, Woman's Journal, Women and Literature, Women's Studies, and Women's World.*

INDEX

Abbreviations, 132–33
  of biblical references, 136; for editor or
  translator, 187; of journal titles in CBE
  style, 214; parentheses for first use of,
  152; postal, 149; of Shakespearean plays,
  152–53
Abstracts
  bibliography form for, 206; to evaluate
  sources, 60, 64; in final paper format,
  130; to narrow topic, 21; in preliminary
  library search, 21; psychology, 44–45;
  quotation from, 45
Acknowledgments, in content endnote, 133,
  140
ACS style, 232–33
AD, 132
Address, published, bibliography form for,
  199
Afterword, bibliography form for, 194
Agriculture
  in-text citation form, 224; name and year
  system, 224–25; reference form, 225
AIP style, 235–36
Alphabetized works, bibliography form for,
  191
AMA style, 236–37
American Indians, reference sources, 251
American literature, reference sources, 256
American Psychological Association, 214
Ampersand, 133
Analysis
  of artistic works, 91–92; of historical
  events, 92–93
Analytical categories, 19
Analytical paper, 2
  audience for, 16
Anatomy. See Biological sciences
Annotated bibliography, 133–34
  in literature review paper, 2–3; summary
  notes for, 69
Annual Reviews of Psychology, 44
Anon., 132
Anonymous author, 190, 200
Anthology, bibliography form for, 186,
  192–93

Anthropology
  in-text citation form, 225; name and year
  system, 225–26; reference form, 225–26
APA style, 211–14
  ampersand, 133; capitalization, 137;
  headings, 143; hyphenation, 151;
  numerals, 135; running heads, 152;
  sample paper in, 214–17; spacing, 153
Apostrophe, 134
Appeal, in the introduction, 99
Appendix, book, 61
Appendix, research paper, 131, 144
Applied research, 3
Applied sciences, number system, 232–36
Applied Science and Technology Index, 42
Arabic numerals, 134–35
  content endnotes, 138; illustrations and
  tables, 144–45; in-text citations, 135;
  literature citations, 116; with monetary
  units and percentages, 148–49; number
  of volumes, 188; volume number, 189;
  Works Cited entries, 135
Archaeology
  in-text citation form, 225; name and year
  system, 225–26; reference form, 225–26
Architecture, writing strategy for, 104
Argumentative purpose, 1–2
Art., arts., 132
Art
  bibliography form for, 204; footnote
  system, 242–43; paradigm for analysis of,
  91–92; primary and secondary sources,
  65; reference sources for, 245–46;
  writing strategy for, 104
Article précis, 2–3
Articles
  encyclopedia, 8–10; evaluation of, 60. See
  also Journal articles; Magazine articles;
  Newspaper articles; Reviews
Arts and Humanities Citation Index
  (AHCI), 54
Asian Americans, reference sources, 251
Assn., 132
Assoc., 132
Asterisk, 135

Astronomy, name and year system, 226
Audience
adapting language for, 95–96; identification of, for argumentative paper, 1–2; meeting the needs of, 16; remembering while writing, 95; and writing situation, 17
Audiovisual materials, 54
Author
anonymous, 190, 200; on bibliography cards, 24; in bibliography form for books, 185, 189–91; in bibliography form for periodicals, 198, 200; citation, 108–10; corporate, 110, 191; listed by initials, 190; more than one work by, 113, 190; multiple, 113, 190–91, 239; in name and year system, 212–14; not listed, 109–10; in number system, 231–32; pseudonymous, 190; quoting another person, 114; reliability of, 50–53, 60
Author card, 30

Background, in the introduction, 98, 100
BC, 132
Bell and Howell's Index to the Christian Science Monitor, 43
Bible
bibliography form for, 191; parenthetical documentation, 135–36
BIBLIO document, 76, 125
Bibliographic Index, 15, 33–34, 36
Bibliography
annotated, 2–3, 69, 133–34; book evaluation, 61; defined, 2 , 183; general, 33–36; in preliminary library search, 21; trade, 34–36
Bibliography cards
call numbers, 24, 28–31; information included, 24; from preliminary reading, 21; samples, 24–28, 30–31, 34–35, 39; working, 23–32; for Works Cited, 108, 183; writing basic, 24–28
Bibliography form, 185–209
Bibliography form for books, 185–98
author, 185, 189–91; chapter or part, 186; edition, 187, 193; editor, 187, 194; number of volumes, 188, 197–98; page numbers, 189; publication information, 188–89; sample entries, 189–98; series name, 187; title, 186–87, 196–97; translator, 187, 197; volume number, 189, 197
Bibliography form for government documents, 203–204
Bibliography form for newspapers, 202–203
Bibliography form for periodicals, 198–202
abstracts, 45; author, 198, 200; name of

periodical, 198; sample entries, 199–202; title of article, 198, 202; volume, issue, and page numbers, 198–99
Bibliography of American Literature, 33
Bibliography page, in humanities, 243–44
Biographical dictionaries
bibliography form for, 191; for preliminary reading, 21
Biographies, indexes to, 37–39
Biography Index, 37–38
Biological Abstracts, 33, 50
Biological and Agricultural Index, 42
Biological sciences
in-text citation form, 226; name and year system, 226–27; reference form, 226–27; reference sources, 246; writing strategy for, 104
Bk., bks., 132
Black Americans, reference sources, 251
Black literature, reference sources, 256
Blanket citation, 94, 139
Body of the paper
in APA style, 216–18; editing, 122; samples, 156–59, 165–78; writing the, 103–104
Book
appendix, 61; bibliography, 33, 61; bibliography card for, 25; bibliography form, 185–98, 244; call numbers, 28–32; evaluation of, 60–61; footnote form, 238; footnotes in, 61; glossary, 61; index, 8, 61; introduction, 60; preface, 60; reviews, 61–62; subtitle, 60; table of contents, 7, 60; title, 60
Booklist, The, 62
Book review, 2–3
Book Review Digest, 60–62
Book Review Index, 61
Books in Print, 36
Botany. *See* Biological sciences
Braces, 121
Brackets
for English translation, 196; with inserts inside quotations, 120–21, 151
British literature, reference sources, 256–57
Bulletin, bibliography form for, 205
Business
conclusion of paper in, 105; decimal outline, 85; in-text citation form, 229; name and year system, 229–30; primary and secondary sources, 66; reference form, 229–30; reference sources, 247

Ca., c., 132
Call numbers, 28–32
on bibliography cards, 24, 28–31; Dewey

Decimal system, 32; Library of Congress system, 32
Capitalization, 136–38
of foreign titles, 143; in quotation, 112, 117–18
Captions, 145, 183
Card catalog, 22–23
author card, 30; call numbers, 28–31; for government documents, 48; main entry card, 30; in preliminary library search, 21; subject cards, 28–29; title card, 31
Casebooks, bibliography form for, 196
Case studies, 54
Cause and effect
in topic development, 6; as writing strategy, 104
CBE style
in agriculture, 225; in biological sciences, 226–27; headings, 143; numerals, 135
Cf., 113, 132
Ch., chs., chap., chaps., 132
Chapter, in bibliography form for books, 186
Chart, bibliography form for, 208
Chemical engineering, reference sources, 247–48
Chemistry
in-text citation form, 232; number system, 232–33; reference form, 232–33; reference sources, 247–48
Chicago Manual of Style, 237
Chronology, as writing strategy, 104
Circulation desk, 22
Citation
author, 108–10, 113; blanket, 94, 139; corporate authors, 110; extra information within, 113–14; frequent references to the same work, 115; in-text (*see* In-text citations); of multiple-edition works, 114; no author listed, 109–10; of one source quoting another, 114; page numbers, 108–11; parenthetical, 108–11; of prose and poetry quotations, 115–17; of several works in one citation, 113; shortened title, 113, 153; volume number, 113. *See also* Bibliography forms; Documentation; Works Cited
Citation Index, 54
Citation searching, 50–54
Cities, foreign spelling, 142
Classical works, bibliography form for, 192, 194–95
Classification, in topic development, 6
Coequal nouns, hyphenation of, 151
Coherence, in writing, 96
Col., cols., 132
Collection, footnote form for, 239

Colon, 150
with quotation marks, 111–12; separating title and subtitle, 186; with volume number, 113
Comma, 150
and dash, 150; in numbers, 134; and parentheses, 150; with quotation marks, 111, 150
Comments, bibliography form for, 201
Committee report, bibliography form for, 192
Common knowledge, and plagiarism, 81
Comp., 132
Comparative study, paradigm for, 93
Comparison
in conclusion, 106; in topic development, 6
Comparison topics, narrowing, 18–19
Compound modifiers, hyphenation of, 151
Computers
bibliography form for computer data, 205; computer-generated research papers, 3; data base card catalog, 28; data base searches, 49–51; library facilities, 23; note-taking on, 76–77; writing with word processors, 125–27
Computer science
in-text citation form, 233; number system, 233–34; reference form, 234; reference sources, 248
Conclusion
avoiding mistakes in, 108; editing, 122; techniques for, 105–107; writing the, 105–108
Congressional papers, bibliography form for, 203
Congressional Record, 48
Contemporary Authors, 60
Content endnotes, 94, 138–41, 183; notes page, 131; of sample paper, 179
Content footnotes, 108, 147
Controversy, in argumentative papers, 2
Copyright
dates, 188; law, 141
Corporate authors, 110, 191
Courtesy titles, 124
Criteria of judgment, as writing strategy, 104
Cross-references, in citation from anthology, 193
Cumulative Book Index, 36
Current Book Review Citations, 62
Cutter Three-Figure Author Table, 32

Dash, 150
Data
gathering, 20–54; in the introduction, 102

Data base
    card catalog, 28; library facilities, 23;
    searches, 49–51
Data base sources
    bibliography form for, 205; in
    preliminary library search, 21
Decimal outline, 85
Deductive outline, 58
Definition
    quotation marks with, 141; in topic
    development, 6
Department of State Bulletin, 48
Dewey Decimal Index, 11–12
Dewey Decimal system, 32
Dictionaries, biographical, 21, 191
Direct quotation, punctuation for, 111–13
Disciplinary topics, narrowing of, 19
Discriminatory language, editing to avoid,
    123–24
Diss., 132
Dissertation Abstracts International (DAI),
    37, 39–40, 206
Dissertations, bibliography form for
    abstract, 206; published, 205;
    unpublished, 205
Doc., 132
Documentation
    for biblical references, 135–36; with
    endnotes, 138, 141; footnotes for, 108,
    142; for illustrations and tables, 145; in
    paraphrase, 73; and plagiarism, 77–81; of
    Shakespearean plays, 152–53. *See also*
    Bibliography forms; Citation; Works
    Cited
Documentation systems other than MLA
    style, 210–44
    footnote, 237–44; guide to, by discipline,
    211; name and year, 211–30; number,
    231–37
Double reference, 114
Drafting the paper, 94–98
Drama, reference sources, 257

Earth sciences, name and year system, 224–
    29
Ecology, reference sources, 249–50
Economics
    in-text citation form, 229; name and year
    system, 229–30; reference form, 229–30;
    reference sources, 249
Ed., eds., 132
Editing the paper, 121–24, 126
Edition, in bibliography form for books,
    187
Editor, in bibliography form for books,
    187, 193
Education
    in-text citation form, 222; name and year
    system, 222–23; primary and secondary

sources, 66; reference form, 222–23;
    reference sources, 250
Education Index, 42
Educators Guide, 54
E.g., 132
Eight American Authors, 21
Electronics, reference sources, 250–51
Ellipsis points, 112, 118–20
Empirical study
    audience for, 16; conclusion, 108;
    explanatory purpose, 3; hypothesis in,
    17; methods, 140; outline order for, 87
Encyclopaedia Britannica, 9–10, 21
Encyclopedia of Psychology, 21
Encyclopedias
    bibliographies in, 33; bibliography form
    for, 191, 194; for preliminary reading, 21;
    for topic discovery, 8–10
Ending of the paper. *See* Conclusion
Endnotes
    contents, 94, 138–41, 183; for
    documentation, 141; in footnote system,
    237, 240, 242–43; notes page, 131;
    period with, 151
English, MLA style for, 210
English Historical Review, 33
Enl., 132
Enumeration of items, 141–42
Equations, 153
ERIC (Education Resources Information
    Center), 49
Esp., 132
Essay
    bibliography card for, 28; formal, in
    review paper, 2–3; index, 37–38; sample
    short research paper, 155–60
Essay and General Literature Index, 28,
    37–38
Et al., 113, 132
Etc., 142
Ethnic studies, reference sources, 251–52
Et pas., 132
Et seq., 132
Evaluation, in topic development, 6
Exclamation point, 151
    with quotation marks, 111–12
Executive branch documents, bibliography
    form for, 203–204
Experience, in empirical research, 3
Experiments
    in empirical research, 3, as information
    source, 54; and terminology, 19
Explanatory paper, 2–3
    audience for, 16

F., ff., 132
Fiction, writing strategies for, 104
Film, bibliography form for, 206
Film File, The, 54

Final manuscript format, 128–32
technicalities, 132–55
Final outline, 84–89
Final thesis sentence, 82–83
Fine arts. *See* Art
First draft, revising, 104, 121–22, 126
First person voice, 96
Fl., 132
Folklore, reference sources, 257–58
Footnotes
in a book, 61; content, 108, 147;
documentation, 108, 142; period with,
151
Footnote system, 237–44
disciplines using, 211, 237; endnotes,
237, 240, 242–43; fine arts, 242–43;
footnotes, 238–39; humanities, 240–44;
in-text citation, 237–38; religion, 241;
history, 241–42
Foreign cities, spelling of, 142
Foreign languages, 142–43
reference sources for, 259–60
Foreign titles, bibliography form for, 196–
97, 202
Foreign words, English translations of, 151
Foreword, bibliography form for, 194
Format, of final paper, 128–132
Free write, 5
French
reference sources, 259; titles, 143

Gender, avoiding discriminatory language
with, 123–24
General reference works, 21
Genetics. *See* Biological sciences
Geography
reference form, 221–22; reference
sources, 252–53; writing strategy for, 104
Geology
in-text citation form, 228; name and year
system, 228–29; paper conclusion, 105;
reference form, 228–29; reference
sources, 253; writing strategy for, 104
German
reference sources, 259; titles, 143
Glossary, 61
Government documents
bibliography card for, 26; bibliography
form, 203–204; index to, 43; in the
library, 47–48; for narrowing the topic,
21; primary and secondary sources, 54,
65
Guide to Reference Books, 33
Guide to Victorian Fiction, 21

Headings, 143, 152
Health
reference sources, 253–54. *See also*
Medical sciences

Hispanic Americans, reference sources,
251–52
Historical present tense, 98
History
footnote system, 241–42; paradigm for
analysis of historical events, 92–93;
reference sources, 254–55; writing
strategy for, 104
Home economics, APA style in, 223
Humanities
bibliography page, 243–44; book reviews
in, 61; footnote system, 240–44; in-text
citation form, 240; reference form, 240
Humanities Index, 15, 41–42
Hyphen, 151
Hypothesis
in empirical study, 16; and thesis
statement, 17; and writing situation, 17

Ibid., 132
I.e., 132
Illus., 132
Illustrations, 143–46, 183
bibliography form for, 208
Imagination, in topic development, 4–6
Importance, as writing strategy, 104
Indentation
of abstract, 130; of footnotes, 147, 238; of
long quotations, 110–11, 115–16, 147; of
paragraphs, 147; on Works Cited page,
147, 184
independent matter, parentheses for, 152
Index cards
for note-taking, 66; for working
bibliography, 23–24
Indexes, 36–54
to biographies within books, 37–39;
citation, 54; defined, 24; to determine
relevance, 61; to dissertations, 37, 39–40;
to essays, 37–38; to newspapers, 42–43;
to pamphlets, 43; to periodicals, 15, 40–
42; in preliminary library search, 21;
specialized, 21, 44–47; for topic
discovery, 8; types of, 36
Index to Book Reviews in the Humanities,
61
*Index to Book Reviews in the Social
Sciences,* 61
Index to Child Welfare, 47
Inductive procedure for outlining, 58
Infra, 132
Interlibrary loans, 23
International Index, 42
International Index to Recorded Poetry, 54
Interpretive paper, and audience, 16
Interviews
bibliography form for published, 200;
bibliography form for unpublished, 206;
as information source, 54; terminology
for, 19

In-text citations
  agriculture, 224; anthropology and
  archaeology, 225; biological sciences,
  226; business, 229; for chapter or part of
  a book, 186; chemistry, 232; computer
  science, 233; content endnote for
  frequent, 139; drafting the paper, 94;
  economics, 229; education, 222; in
  footnote system, 237–38; geology, 228;
  humanities, 240; for illustrations and
  tables, 145; linguistics, 223; mathematics,
  234; medical sciences, 236; MLA style,
  108; in name and year system, 211–13;
  in number system, 231–32; numeral
  usage in, 135; parentheses for, 152;
  physical education, 224; physics, 235;
  political science, 221; psychology, 220;
  shortening titles in, 153; sociology, 221
Intro., introd., 132
Introduction
  avoiding mistakes in, 103; editing, 121–
  22; Roman numerals for paging, 152;
  writing, 98–103
Introduction, book, 60
  bibliography form for, 194
Issue number, periodical, 198–99
Issues
  in analytical paper, 2; in argumentative
  paper, 2; in comparison topics, 18–19;
  focusing on specific, 16; listing before
  note-taking, 55; outlining for topic
  development, 5; as writing strategy, 104
Italian titles, 143
Italics, 147, 154

Journal articles
  bibliography card for, 26; bibliography
  form for, 198–202; bibliography form in
  humanities, 244; evaluation of, 60;
  footnote form for, 238
Journalism, reference sources, 255
Journals
  bibliographies in, 33; in libraries, 28;
  reliability, of, 59–60; title abbreviation in
  CBE style, 214
Judgments
  in argumentative papers, 2; supporting,
  16

Key words
  and coherence, 96; defining, 103; use in
  title, 84; in topic development, 5

Language
  adapting to purpose and audience, 95–
  96; avoiding discriminatory, 123–24;
  reference sources for, 255–59

Languages, foreign, 142–43
  English translations, 151; reference
  sources, 259–60; titles in, 196–97, 202
Latin, reference sources, 259–60
LC system, 13–15
Lectures
  bibliography form for, 207; as
  information source, 54
Legal citations, bibliography form for, 204
Letters
  bibliography form for personal, 206;
  bibliography form for published, 201,
  206; as information source, 54
Letters, alphabet, plural form, 134
Librarian, 20
Library
  call numbers, 28–32; card catalog, 22–
  23, 28–32; circulation desk, 22; computer
  facilities, 23; gathering data in, 20–54;
  interlibrary loans, 23; nonprint materials,
  23; photocopiers, 23; reference room,
  22; reserve desk, 22
*Library of Congress Catalog: Books,
  Subjects,* 36
Library of Congress system, 13–15, 32
Linguistics
  in-text citation form, 223; LSA style, 223–
  24; quotation marks and underlining,
  151, 155; reference form, 223–24
List of Sources Cited, 183
Literature
  conclusion in, 105–106; fictional
  characters' names, 148; frequent
  references to the same work, 115;
  indexes, 45–46; long quotations from,
  115–17; paradigm for analysis of, 91–92;
  primary and secondary sources, 65;
  reference sources, 255–59; writing
  strategies for, 104
Literature review paper, 2–3
Location, as writing strategy, 104
Loc. cit., 133
Long quotations, 110–11, 115–17, 147
LSA style, 223–24

McGill's Bibliography of Literary Criticism,
  45
Magazine articles
  bibliography card for, 25; bibliography
  form for, 200–201; evaluation of, 60;
  footnote form for, 239; indexes to, 40–42
Magazines, reliability of, 59–60
Main entry card, 30
Manuscript, final
  format, 128–32; technicalities, 152–55
Manuscripts
  bibliography form for, 206; collections in
  book form, 194
Map, bibliography form for, 208

Margins, 147–48
Market research, 3
Mass communication, reference sources, 255
Mathematics
  equation form, 153; in-text citation form, 234; number system, 234–35; reference form, 235; reference sources, 260–61; underlining algebraic variables, 155
Media Review Digest, 54
Medical sciences
  in-text citation form, 236; number system, 236–37; reference form, 236–37; reference sources, 261–62
Methods, in empirical study, 3, 16
Microfilm and microfiche, 48
  bibliography form for, 207
Mimeographed material
  bibliography form for, 207
MLA International Bibliography, 21, 45–46
MLA style
  Arabic numerals, 134–35; bibliography card samples, 23–28; documentation, 78, 108; headings, 143; hyphenation, 151; in-text citation form, 108; margins, 147–48; and other styles, 210–11; running heads, 152; spacing, 153
Modern Language Association standards. *See* MLA style
Monetary units, 148–49
Monograph, bibliography form for, 201, 207
Monthly Catalog of United States Government Publications, 26, 43, 47–48, 54
Ms, mss, 133
Music
  bibliography form for, 207; reference sources, 262
Mythology, reference sources, 257–58
Mythology of All Races, 21

N., nn., 133
Name and year system, 211–30
  agriculture, 224–25; anthropology and archaeology, 225–26; biological and earth sciences, 224–29; business, 229–30; disciplines using, 211; economics, 229–30; education, 222–23; geology, 228–29; home economics, 223; in-text citations, 211–13; linguistics, 223–24; physical education, 224; political science, 221–22; psychology, 220–21; reference form, 213–14; social sciences, 220–24; sociology, 221–22
Name of research writer
  as running head, 148, 152; on title or opening page, 128–29
Names of persons, in text of paper, 148

National Union Catalog, 36
N.d., 133
Newspaper articles
  bibliography card for, 27; bibliography form for, 202–203; footnote form for, 239; indexes to, 42–43; unsigned, 203
New York Times Guide to Reference Materials, 33
New York Times Index, 27, 42–43
No., nos., 133
Nonprint sources
  citation omitted for, 115; in the library, 23; reference for, 115, 183
Note cards
  paraphrase, 72–73; personal, 67–68; plot summary, 69–70; précis, 70–72; quotation, 74–76; reviewing, 89; summary, 68–69; technique of, 66
Notes in periodicals, bibliography form for, 201
Note-taking, 55–77
  with a computer, 76–77; methods of, 67–77; note cards, 66–76; using preliminary outline, 55–59; and thesis development, 18
Novel, reference sources, 258
N.p., 133
Ns, 133
Numbering footnotes, 238
Numbering pages. *See* Page numbers
Number system, 231–37
  applied sciences, 232–36; chemistry, 232–33; computer science, 233–34; disciplines using, 211, 231; mathematics, 234–35; medical sciences, 236–37; physics, 235–36
Numerals. *See* Arabic numerals; Roman numerals; Superscript numerals
Nursing. *See* Medical sciences

Objective writing, 90
Observation
  in empirical research, 3; as information source, 54; and terminology, 19
Official Index (to *The London Times*), 43
Op. cit., 133
Opening of the paper. *See* Introduction
Opening page, 128–30
Outline
  balanced and parallel form in, 85–86; decimal, 85; deductive ordering, 58; dynamic order in, 87, 103–104; inductive ordering, 58; final, 84–89, 130; headings and subheadings, 84–87; indentation, 84–85; page numbers, 130; paragraph, 89; preliminary, 55–59; reviewing, 90; revising, 58–59; Roman numerals for, 152; of sample paper, 162–64; sentence, 88–89; standard outline symbols, 84–85;

and thesis sentence, 87; topic, 87–88; and unity, 96

P., pp., 133
Page numbers
bibliography form for books, 189; bibliography form for periodicals, 198–99; in-text citations, 108–11, 113; for final paper, 131, 148; as running head, 152; Roman numerals for, 152
Pamphlets
bibliography form for, 207; indexes to, 43
Paper, bond or theme, 148–49
Paper, research. *See* Research paper
Paperbound Books in Print, 36
Paradigms, for papers in special fields, 91–94
for advancing theory, 91; for analysis of artistic works, 91–92; for analysis of historic events, 92–93; for comparative study, 93; to maintain order, 104; for position papers, 92
Paragraph outline, 89
Paragraphs
editing, 122–23; indentation, 147; introduction, 98–99; single aspect in, 96; topic sentences for, 94
Paraphrase
citation for, 108–10; and coherence, 96; in name and year system, 212–13; notes, 72–73; and plagiarism, 78–81
Parentheses, 151–52
and brackets, 121; and comma, 150; for first use of abbreviation, 152; for headings in a series, 152; for independent matter, 152; for in-text citations, 108–11, 135–36, 152–53; period with, 151
Passim, 133
Past tense, for writing, 97–98
Percentages, 148–49
Period, 151
with page citation, 110; with quotation marks, 111–13; in bibliography, 186
Periodicals
bibliography form for, 198–202; indexes to, 15, 40–42
Permuterm Subject Index, 54
Persona, writing, 17
Personal experience, for topic discovery, 3–4
Personal note cards, 67–68
Philosophy
footnote system, 240–44; paradigm for position papers in, 92; reference sources, 262–63
Photocopiers, 23

Photographs, bibliography form for, 208
Physical education
in-text citation form, 224; name and year system, 224; reference form, 224; reference sources, 253–54
Physics
in-text citation form, 235; number system, 235–36; reference form, 235–36; reference sources, 264
Physiology. *See* Biological sciences
Plagiarism, 77–81
and common knowledge, 81; defined, 78–81; and paraphrasing, 72
Plays, bibliography form for, 194–95
Plot summary cards, 69–70
Poems
bibliography form for, 195; incorporating into text, 116–17; reference sources, 258; writing strategy for, 104
Poetry Explication, 45
Political science
in-text citation form, 221; name and year system, 221–22; paradigm for analytical paper, 92–93; paradigm for position paper, 92; primary and secondary sources, 65; reference form, 221–22; reference sources, 263–64; writing strategy for, 104
Position papers, paradigm for, 92
Possessive, apostrophe in, 134
Postal abbreviations, 149
Précis note cards, 70–72
Preface
bibliography form for, 194; to evaluate sources, 60, 64; page numbers for, 152
Prefixes, hyphenation of, 151
Preliminary outline, 55–59, 66
Preliminary reading, 21
Preliminary thesis
developing, 17–18; and final thesis, 82
Present tense, for writing, 97–98
Prewriting, to discover audience, 16
Primary sources, 65–66
in argumentative papers, 2; quotation from, 74–76; in topic discovery, 6
Proc., 133
Process, in topic development, 6
Proofreading, 121, 124, 127
Pseud., 133
Pseudonymous author, 190
Psychological Abstracts, 44–45, 60
Psychology
indexes, 44–45; in-text citation form, 220; name and year system, 220–21; reference sources, 264–65
PSYCINFO, 44, 50–51
Pt., pts., 133
Public address
bibliography form for, 207; as information source, 54

Public Affairs Information Service Bulletin, 47

Publication information, in bibliography form for books, 188–89

Publication Manual of the American Psychological Association, 211

Publishers Weekly, 36

Punctuation, 150–52
of quotations, 111–13. *See also* individual punctuation marks

Purpose of research paper, 1–3; adapting language for, 95–96; analytical, 2; argumentative, 1–2; and audience, 16; explanatory, 2–3; and writing situation, 17

Queries, bibliography form for, 201

Question mark, 111–12

Questions
interview, 19; question outline for note-taking, 57; in revising outline, 59; for topic development, 6

Quotation marks, 151
and comma, 150; for definitions in text, 141, 151; enclosing direct quotations, 111–13; for English translations, 151; with page citations, 110; punctuation with, 111–13; single, 111–12, 141, 151; for titles, 155; for words discussed, 151

Quotations
in article title, 202; brackets inserted within, 120–21; changing initial capital in, 117–18; in-text citation, 108–11; and coherence, 96; in the conclusion, 105–106; direct, 111–13; ellipsis points in, 118–20; foreign language, 142; indented long, 110–11, 115–17, 147; in the introduction, 101; in name and year system, 212–13; note cards, 74–76; in paraphrase, 72; and plagiarism, 78–81; in précis notes, 70–71; of primary sources, 74–76; punctuation of, 111–13; from secondary sources, 74–75

Radio programs
bibliography form for, 209; as information source, 54

Readers' Guide, 15, 25, 40–41

Reading
preliminary, 21; and terminology, 19

Recording on record or tape, bibliography form for, 207–208

Reference form
agriculture, 225; anthropology and archaeology, 225–26; APA style sample, 219; biological sciences, 226–27; business, 229–30; chemistry, 232–33; computer science, 234; economics, 229–30; education, 222–23; fine arts, 242–43; footnote system, 238–44; geography, 221–22; geology, 228–29; humanities, 240–44; linguistics, 223–24; mathematics, 235; medical sciences, 236–37; MLA style (*see* Works Cited); name and year system, 211–30; number system, 231–37; physical education, 224; physics, 235–36; political science, 221–22; psychology, 220–21; sociology, 221–22

Reference room, 22

Reference sources. *See* individual disciplines

Reference works
bibliographies in, 33; general, 21

Religion
footnote system, 241; paradigm for position papers in, 92; reference sources, 265–66

Reports, bibliography form for, 201, 208

Reprint of a journal article, bibliography form for, 201

Republished book, bibliography form for, 195–96

Research
applied, 3; empirical, 3; market, 3; technical, 3

Research paper
analytical, 2; argumentative, 1–2; explanatory, 2–3; format, 128–32; length, 147; purpose of, 1–3; sample in APA style, 214–17; sample short essay with documentation, 155–60; sample with outline and content notes, 160–82; technicalities in the manuscript, 132–55; writing (*see* Writing the paper)

Reserve desk, 22

Results, in empirical study, 3, 16

Rev., 133

Review paper, 2–3

Reviews
bibliography form for, 201; footnote form for, 239; to narrow topic, 21

Revising the first draft, 104, 121–22, 126

Roman numerals, 152
list of, 152; in outline, 152; for pagination, 130, 148, 152; for titles of persons, 152

Rpt., 133

Running heads, 152

Russian, reference sources, 260

Sample bibliography entries
for books, 189–98; for periodicals, 199–202

Sample paper
in APA style, 214–17; formal paper with outline and content notes, 160–82; short essay with documentation, 155–60

Science Citation Index (SCI), 54
Sciences
    date citation, 210; decimal outline, 85;
    periodical indexes for, 42; primary and
    secondary sources, 65; underlining
    special words in, 155. *See also* individual
    disciplines
Sec., secs., 133
Secondary sources, 65–66
    in argumentative papers, 2; quotation
    from, 74–75; in topic discovery, 7
Selected bibliography, defined, 183
Semicolon, 150
    with quotation marks, 111–12; with
    several works in citation, 113
Sentence outline, 88–89
Ser., 133
Series, bibliography form for books, 187,
    196; periodicals, 202
Sess., 133
Setting, as writing strategy, 104
Shakespearean plays, documentation for,
    152–53
Shortened title, within citation, 113
Short story, reference sources, 258
Sic, 74, 120, 133
Significance, establishing in introduction,
    98–100
Single quotation marks, 111–12
Slang, 151, 153
Slash mark, 116, 121
Social sciences
    book reviews in, 61; name and year
    system, 220–24; primary and secondary
    sources, 65
Social Sciences and Humanities Index, 42
Social Sciences Citation Index (SSCI), 54
Social Sciences Index, 41
Social work, reference sources, 266
Sociological Abstracts, 21
Sociology
    in-text citation form, 221; name and year
    system, 221–22; reference form, 221–22;
    reference source, 266
Sourcebooks, bibliography form for, 196
Source Index, 54
Source materials
    blending into writing, 108–21;
    documentation on note cards, 66;
    evaluation of, 59–66; gathering data in
    the library, 21–23; and narrowing the
    topic, 19; nonprint, 23, 54; and
    plagiarism, 77–81; preliminary reading
    for, 21; primary, 65–66; recent, 59;
    relevance of, 60–61; reliability of, 59–60;
    secondary, 65–66; for topic discovery,
    6–15
Sources cited, defined, 183
Spacing, 153
    footnotes, 238; on Works Cited page, 184

Spanish
    reference sources, 260; titles, 143
Speech, reference sources, 266–67
Spelling, 153
    of foreign cities, 142
St., sts., 133
State names, abbreviations for, 149
Statistics, 153
    in content endnotes, 140; in the
    introduction, 102; underlining symbols,
    155
Stereotypes, avoiding, 123–24
Strategies of writing, 104
Structure, as writing strategy, 104
Subject. *See* Topic
Subject cards, 28–29
Subject Headings, Library of Congress, 15
Subject Guide to Books in Print, 35
Subject Index to Psychological Abstracts, 44
Subjective writing, 90
Subtitle, book
    to determine relevance, 60; separation
    from title, 186
Summary, in the introduction, 102
Summary note cards, 68–69
Sup., supra, 133
Superscript numerals, 154
    for acknowledgments, 133; with content
    endnotes, 131, 138; in footnote system,
    237–43; in number system, 231–33, 235
Suppl., 133
S.v., 133
Synthesis, in analytical paper, 2

Table of contents
    book, 7, 60; paper, 154
Tables, 143–47, 183
    bibliography form for, 208
Technical research, 3, 16
Technology, periodical indexes for, 42
Television programs
    bibliography form for, 209; as
    information source, 54
Textual commentary, content endnote for,
    139–40
Tense, for writing, 97–98
Terminology
    adapting, 95–96; in disciplinary topics,
    19; explaining in the introduction, 103;
    in glossary, 61; key words, 5, 84, 96, 103
Test results, discussed in conclusion, 107–
    108
Theater, reference sources, 257
Theology. *See* Religion
Theory
    in conclusion, 107; paradigm for
    advancing, 91
Thesis statement
    conventions of, 82–83; examples, 83;

final, 82–83; in the introduction, 99; limiting note-taking, 18, 55; and outline, 87; preliminary, 17–18; restatement in conclusion, 105; reviewing before writing, 90; and writing situation, 17
Third person voice, 96
Title card, 31
Title of research paper, 84
Title of sources
on bibliography cards, 24; bibliography form for articles, 198, 202; bibliography form for books, 186–87, 196–97; capitalization, 136–37; to determine relevance, 60; foreign, 142–43, 196–97, 202; journal abbreviation in CBE style, 214; omitted, in article, 202; quotation marks for, 155; quotation within, 202; shortened, 113, 153; subtitle, 186–87; title within, 202; underlining, 154–55, 186–87
Title page, 128–29
in APA style, 215; of sample paper, 161
Titles of persons
Roman numerals for, 152; in text of paper, 148
Topic, 1–19
and audience, 16; comparison topics, 18–19; disciplinary topics, 19; discovery, 3–15; in the introduction, 98; narrowing, 3–4, 7, 10, 12, 16–19, 21, 90; source materials for topic discovery, 6–15
Topic outline, 87–88
Topic sentence, for a paragraph, 94
Trade bibliographies, 34–36
Trans., tr., 133
Translator, in bibliography form for books, 187, 197
Transparency, bibliography form for, 209
Twentieth Century Short Story Explicator, 45
Typescripts, bibliography form for, 206
Typing the paper, 154

Ulrich's International Periodicals Directory, 36
Underlining
for emphasis, 155; for italics, 147; foreign words, 142–43; of linguistic forms, 151; special words and symbols, 155; titles, 154–55, 186–87
Union List of Serials in Libraries of the United States and Canada, 36
Unity, in writing, 96
University Microfilms, Ins., 40
Unpublished interview, bibliography form for, 206
Unpublished paper, bibliography form for, 209

Vertical File Index, 43
Video Source Book, 54
Videotape, bibliography form for, 209
Virgule, 116
Viz., 133
Voice, in writing, 96
Vol., vols., 133
Volume number
in bibliography form for books, 189, 197; in citation, 113; periodical, 198–99
Volumes, number of, in bibliography form for books, 188, 197–98
Vs., v., 133

Wall Street Journal Index, 43
Webster's Biographical Dictionary, 21
Where to Find What, 33
Who's Who in American Art, 60
Women's studies, reference sources, 267
Word division, 155
Word processor
for note-taking, 76–77; pagination and accuracy with, 154; writing the paper with, 125–127
Works Cited, 183–209
alphabetization, 184; author not listed, 110; bibliography cards for, 24, 108; with BIBLIO document, 76, 125; book form, 185–98; content endnote documentation, 138; double reference, 114; in final paper format, 131–32; format for, 184; government documents, 203–204; headings, 143, 183; illustration and table documentation, 145, 183; indentation of entries, 147; nonprint sources, 115, 204–209; numeral usage with, 135; periodical form, 198–202; sample, 184; of sample papers, 160, 180–82
World Bibliography of Bibliographies, 33
World literature, reference sources, 258
Writing
free write, 5; persona, 17; prewriting, 16; situation, 17, 56; strategies, 104
Writing the paper, 82–127
blending in reference material, 108–21; body, 103–104; conclusion, 105–108; continuous paragraphing, 131; drafting, 94–98; editing, 121–24, 126; final outline, 84–89; introduction, 98–103; preparation for, 89–94; proofreading, 121, 124, 127; revising, 121–22, 126; title, 84; with word processors, 125–27

Year, in name and year system, 212–14

Zoology. *See* Biological sciences

ACKNOWLEDGMENTS (cont.)

M. Thompson, and Alberta Cognata, "Stability of the California Short Form Test of Mental Maturity: Grades 3, 5, and 7," *California Journal of Educational Research,* 17 (September, 1966), 165. Reprinted by permission of the *Educational Research Quarterly.* **P. 147** From "Toxigenicity of Clostridium Histolticum" by Shoki Nishida & Masaaki Imaizumi from *Journal of Bacteriology,* Vol. 91, 1966. Copyright © 1966 by American Society for Microbiology. Reprinted by permission. **P. 167** From "Physical and Sexual Abuse of Children: Causes and Treatment" by David R. Walters, 1975. Copyright © 1975 Indiana University Press. Reprinted by permission. **P. 172** From "Economic Antecedents of Child Abuse & Neglect" by Laurence D. Steinberg, R. Catalano and D. Dooley from *Child Development,* Vol. 52. Copyright © 1981 by Society For Research in Child Development. Reprinted by permission. **P. 173** From "Child Abuse and Violence Against the Family" by Peter C. Kratcoski in *Child Welfare,* September/October 1982. Copyright © 1982 by the Child Welfare League of America, Inc. Reprinted by permission. **P. 175** From "Self-Injurious Behavior in Incest Victims: A Research Note" by Mary de Young in *Child Welfare,* November/December 1982. Copyright © 1982 by the Child Welfare League of America, Inc. Reprinted by permission.